Podcasting Between Entertainment and Education

I0875937

Podcasting Between Entertainment and Education explores the critical and conceptual foundations that make podcasting an increasingly valuable and appealing tool for teaching, learning and assessment and suggests how it can be effectively integrated into different educational settings.

This book introduces key concepts for embedding audio into curricula, unpacks debates shaping the use of podcasting in education and examines case studies from a range of disciplines. Bringing together theory and practical insights, this book bridges the gap between entertainment and learning using real-life examples from academics and practitioners from across the world. Supported by a dedicated podcast series that showcases best-practice examples as well as interviews that extend the discussion beyond the page, *Podcasting Between Entertainment and Education* is an essential read for those interested in the evolving relationship between podcasting and learning, whether they are an educator looking to introduce podcasting into the classroom, a researcher exploring its impact or a media professional interested in its educational potential.

This book is ideal for educators seeking to incorporate podcasting into their teaching, researchers investigating its impact and media professionals interested in its educational applications.

Camilo Salazar is a sound engineer, radio and podcast producer and educator. He is the Morley Radio and Studios Manager at Morley College London, where he also lectures in Sound Engineering and Radio Production.

Lindsay Persohn is Assistant Professor of Literacies Studies in the College of Education at the University of South Florida.

Joanna Duchesne is a sessional lecturer at Morley College London, where she is a regular contributor to Morley Radio. She also works in multimedia content production.

Carl Hartley is Lecturer in Journalism Practice at the University of Leeds, drawing on more than 25 years of experience in the broadcast industry.

Carola Boehm is Professor of Creative and Cultural Industries at the University of Staffordshire, working across arts, technology and cultural policy. She is also active in podcasting as part of her creative practice.

Education Through Podcasting

Series Editor: Carola Boehm, Camilo Salazar, Joanna Duchesne, Carl Hartley & Lindsay Persohn

Education Through Podcasting investigates the modern intersection between podcasting and various forms of education at all levels. Linked to an annual conference, each volume encourages chapter proposals from those involved in education and podcasting across disciplines to discuss audio-related aspects of using podcast technologies in learning environments.

The series offers both scholarly and professionally informed contributions, providing theoretical frameworks as well as practical advice on how to apply a specific podcasting practices. In so doing it provides a solid grounding in both theoretical and practical considerations when adopting podcasting for learners. Each volume features concepts and frameworks, discourse, controversies and debates, and case studies.

Books in the series will be of interest to academics and industry professionals interested in how podcasting can be used in an educational context.

Podcasting and Education
Concepts, Communities and Case Studies
Edited by Carola Boehm, Tim Canfer, Camilo Salazar

Podcasting Between Entertainment and Education
Balancing Media Industry Expectations within Educational Contexts
Edited by Camilo Salazar, Lindsay Persohn, Joanna Duchesne, Carl Hartley and Carola Boehm

For more information about this series, please visit: https://www.routledge.com/education-through-podcasting/book-series/ETP

Podcasting Between Entertainment and Education

Balancing Media Industry Expectations within Educational Contexts

Edited by
Camilo Salazar, Lindsay Persohn,
Joanna Duchesne, Carl Hartley
and Carola Boehm

Routledge
Taylor & Francis Group
LONDON AND NEW YORK

Designed cover image: Camilo Salazar

First published 2027
by Routledge
4 Park Square, Milton Park, Abingdon, Oxon OX14 4RN

and by Routledge
605 Third Avenue, New York, NY 10158

Routledge is an imprint of the Taylor & Francis Group, an informa business

British Library Cataloguing-in-Publication Data
A catalogue record for this book is available from the British Library

ISBN: 9781041150169 (hbk)
ISBN: 9781041150152 (pbk)
ISBN: 9781003677253 (ebk)

DOI: 10.4324/9781003677253

Typeset in Sabon
by codeMantra

Contents

About the Editors

Lead Editors

Camilo Salazar is a sound engineer, radio and podcast producer and educator. He is the Morley Radio and Studios Manager at Morley College London, where he also lectures in Sound Engineering and Radio Production. He has produced numerous podcast series and radio shows and collaborates regularly with renowned musicians. He is also the founder and lead curator of The Engine Room International Sound Art Exhibition and Competition. He is a co-founder, editor and organiser of the Education through Podcasting Conference and book series.

Lindsay Persohn is Assistant Professor of Literacies Studies in the College of Education at the University of South Florida. Her research and teaching focus on stories – those we tell, those we don't and how we understand ourselves and the world around us through stories of all kinds.

Co-editors

Joanna Duchesne is a sessional lecturer at Morley College London. She also works in multimedia content production and is a regular contributor to Morley Radio. She is the producer of the student-led podcast series *Try Making This* and *Getting to Know You*. She is an author, editor and organiser of the Education through Podcasting Conference and book series.

Carl Hartley is a lecturer in Journalism Practice at the University of Leeds, drawing on more than 25 years of experience in the broadcast industry. He continues to work as a broadcaster and journalist for the BBC and other media organisations. Carl has produced several podcast series, including *The Sound of Politics* hosted by Professor Stephen Coleman, and contributes to research in the field of podcasting.

Carola Boehm holds degrees in Computer Science and Music and is Professor of Creative and Cultural Industries at the University of Staffordshire. She is the author of more than 60 publications and a few podcasts. She is the co-chair of Stoke Creates, a cultural compact and a member of the College of Experts of DCMS, advising the government on creative industry policy.

Contributors

Joel Agius is a researcher and podcast co-creator whose work explores identity, culture and equity in professional and educational contexts. Their research-led pilot podcast, produced as part of a Warwick Institute of Engagement module redevelopment project, focused on amplifying marginalised voices through accessible dialogue. Joel holds an MSc in Intercultural Communication for Business and the Professions from the University of Warwick.

Simon Barber is Associate Professor of Songwriting in the School of Arts at Birmingham City University. He was co-lead on the AHRC/DFG-funded project Songwriting Camps in the 21st Century (SC21) and is the producer and co-presenter of the popular Sodajerker podcast, which features interviews with some of the world's most successful songwriters.

Stephanie Branson is Assistant Professor of Literacy Studies in the College of Education at Northern Arizona University, Flagstaff Mountain campus. Her research examines teacher learning across the lifespan and early literacy development within inquiry-based contexts, with particular attention to multimodal pedagogies.

Leah Burger is a doctoral candidate at the University of South Florida pursuing her PhD in Literacy Studies at the College of Education. Her research aims to elevate children's literacy practices on/with digital platforms, focusing specifically on youth's writing processes with generative AI through the lenses of raciolinguistics and digital composition.

Joe Cain is Professor of History and Philosophy of Biology in the UCL Department of Science and Technology Studies (STS). He hosted the podcast WeAreSTS. He is an expert in the history of evolutionary biology, especially Darwinism and evolutionary studies in the twentieth century. Recent projects have focused on the legacies of eugenics at UCL and the famous dinosaur statues in Crystal Palace Park.

Sam Coley is Course Director for the MA Media Production at Birmingham City University. He is a member of the Birmingham Centre for Media and Cultural Research and has written several chapters and articles about popular music, podcasting and radio production. Coley is a Grand Jury member of the New York Festivals Radio Awards and is a Trustee of the Charles Parker Archive Trust.

John D'Arcy is an artist-researcher based at the Sonic Arts Research Centre at Queen's University Belfast. John directs vocal ensemble HIVE Choir and curates sound art events and exhibitions at Sonorities Festival Belfast. He is a board member of Digital Arts Studios Belfast, the Belfast Region Music Board and was a member of the Steering Group for Belfast's successful bid for UNESCO City of Music status.

Nathan Dodzo is a Senior Lecturer in Media and Journalism at the University of Northampton. Bringing decades of industry experience to his teaching practice, he developed a Visual Podcasting module to bridge academic learning with professional standards. His approach mirrors real-world production workflows, utilising iterative cycles to foster technical and ethical excellence. Dodzo also researches emerging technologies like AI and VR.

Adam Gratton, journalist and community engagement practitioner, is the founder of The Community Cast, an initiative empowering community to raise their voices, addressing matters that impact them. With a career spanning print, digital, broadcast media and charity sector, Adam has cultivated expertise in storytelling and social action. The Community Cast works with diverse communities, aiming to amplify stories and lived experiences of individuals, leveraging their collective strengths for meaningful change.

Nicola Gratton is an independent co-production specialist, researcher, evaluator and trainer. She has extensive experience of youth work, community development practice, higher education and participatory action research. Nicola launched Nicola Gratton Consulting in 2025. She uses her platform to support communities to have a voice and create systems change by influencing people in positions of power to listen and act on those voices.

Alex Hough is a lecturer at the University of Staffordshire teaching on the Music Production & Sound Design degree programmes. He specialises in recording studio fundamentals, advanced recording techniques, mixing, mastering, sampling and synthesis, as well as audio for multimedia post-production.

Duncan Lees is Assistant Professor in Applied Linguistics at the University of Warwick, where he teaches on undergraduate and postgraduate programmes, including the MSc in Intercultural Communication for Business and the Professions. His growing interest in educational podcasting is informed by his research on intercultural communication, language education, and Ethnomethodology/Conversation Analysis.

Marianna Patrick is a research fellow at the School of Education, Learning and Communication Sciences (SELCS) at the University of Warwick. She has taught on the School's Globalisation, Diversity and Public Engagement module and was involved in the co-creation of a podcast episode as a member of the Warwick Institute of Engagement-funded team that redeveloped this module to focus on public engagement.

Stephanie Schnurr is Professor in Sociolinguistics at the University of Warwick. Her main research interests are professional and medical communication with a particular focus on leadership discourse, gender, humour and culture. She has widely published on those topics, including several monographs, edited volumes and journal articles. She has a keen interest in podcasting and has introduced this as the main assessment component on the Globalisation, Diversity and Public Engagement module that she teaches.

Patrice Seuwou is Associate Professor in Learning and Teaching with expertise spanning digital media education, business analytics and computer science. He holds two PhDs, in Computer Science and in the Sociology of Education, and his research bridges technology, pedagogy and equity in higher education. His work focuses on industry-aligned learning, digital innovation and the experiences of ethnically diverse students in contemporary educational contexts.

Connor Thompson-Poole is a Senior Lecturer and Specialist Pharmacist Prescriber at the University of Brighton with over ten years of clinical experience. He teaches across pharmacy and prescribing programmes, with a particular focus on experiential learning, professional practice and prescribing education. He also co-hosts The Mug-Hub, a university podcast running since 2021.

Matthew W. Turner is a lecturer at the Tokyo University of Science's Institute of Arts and Sciences. His research interests include podcast studies, language teacher development, reflective practice and science communication. He is a co-founder and co-presenter of The TEFLology Podcast – a podcast about language teaching and applied linguistics.

Diana Wang recently completed an MSc in Intercultural Communication for Business and the Professions at the University of Warwick. She was introduced to podcasting as an educational tool through her involvement in a collaborative project to redevelop an existing MSc module, which saw her co-create a podcast episode and then co-present her experiences of doing this at the EPOD Conference in London in 2025.

Sian Williams is Senior Lecturer in Medicines Use at the University of Brighton, where she has worked for 18 years. With a background in psychology and over 20 years' experience in academia, she teaches psychology of medicines use, statistics and research methods. Her research focuses on adherence to medicines and pharmacy education. She also co-hosts The Mug-Hub, a university podcast running since 2021.

Yvette Yitong Wang is a researcher and educator specialising in intercultural language education and teacher education. Advocating for a hermeneutic and dialogic approach, her work explores how to support teachers and learners to transform their understandings of self, other and the world through explicit engagement with interpretation and critical reflection.

Genesis Zabrzenski is a doctoral student in Curriculum and Instruction with a focus on literacy studies at the University of South Florida. Their research centres on queer pedagogy, multimodal literacy and research-to-practice initiatives, with particular attention to belonging, inclusion and knowledge translation in educational spaces.

VC Zhang recently graduated with an MSc in Intercultural Communication for Business and the Professions from the University of Warwick. During her postgraduate studies in the UK, she became a member of the University of Warwick's Ultimate Frisbee team. This led to experiences and contacts that she later called upon when co-producing a podcast on inclusion and exclusion in sports as part of a collaborative project to introduce podcasting to an MSc module on Globalisation, Diversity and Public Engagement.

Foreword

The Airiness of the In Between

Professor Stephen Coleman, Emeritus Professor of Political Communication, University of Leeds

Not all categories are, or should be, stable. Neat distinctions between education and entertainment; didacticism and distraction; intellectual edification, replete with evidential veracity, and perfunctory dissipation, offering little more than the froth of fun, speak to a world in which everything is in its own place, manifest and uncomplicated. Every now and then categories are productively disrupted. For example, each new form of communication that has emerged over the past three centuries, from the eighteenth-century novel to the twenty-first-century podcast, has been met with attempts to characterise it as one thing or another: edifying or timewasting; cerebral or sensuous; masculine or feminine. It is time, perhaps, to embrace porosity and nuance; to recognise that human creativity and intersubjectivity thrive best when they are beyond categorisation; when, indeed, they move us because of what they have to tell rather than where they belong within some spurious hierarchy of cultural identities.

The inception of the novel as an innovative form of storytelling in the eighteenth century triggered a wave of contempt from cultural critics who widely dismissed novel-reading as little more than frivolous amusement, only suitable for women, whom they saw as being 'creatures of the imagination, of limited intellectual capacity, both frivolous and emotional' (Lyons, 1999). As one contemporary writer commented, aghast at the spread of this new literary diversion, 'My sight is every-where offended by these foolish, yet dangerous, books. I find them on the toilette of fashion, and in the work-bag of the sempstress; in the hands of the lady, who lounges on the sofa, and of the lady, who sits at the counter' (Sylph, 1796). This sense of the novel as 'mere entertainment' was regurgitated in the twentieth century by critics who regarded broadcasting in the most condescending terms as a medium 'you can listen to ... virtually everywhere' in a state of 'psychological state of distraction' (Benjamin, 2008/1936). When television first appeared, it was condemned as a 'children's medium' on which 'the young have become the acknowledged resident experts'. At its core, this repeated refrain against the vapidity of popular entertainment emanated from a much older suspicion that most people are simply too stupid to sup from the font of pure knowledge, preferring to be amused to distraction by ephemeral thrills. As Leo Rosten put it, 'The deficiencies of mass media are a function, in part at least, of the deficiencies of the masses'.

Podcasting has unleashed a new generation of sniffy cultural detractors, eager to point out that these upstart broadcasters are taking up communicative space that should be reserved for authorised experts. The snobbery and erroneousness of such a perspective ought to embarrass its proponents, but far from doing so, it leads them to shout louder in their insistence that podcasters are little more than garrulous impostors, daring to invade the hallowed halls of legitimate public communication. For example, writing in *The Spectator* magazine, Sam Kriss (2023) opined that

> Across the world, thousands of people are doing the same thing: plonking themselves down in front of mics, setting up a camera and talking in a genial, conversational style to absolutely no one. They give business tips or wellness advice or share embarrassing details about their lives in 20-second fragments, that they pluck from a long, loose, free-form chat that didn't actually take place. It's a mass sustained illusion of conversation.

Note that podcasters *plonk themselves* in front of microphones while, we must suppose, legitimate broadcasters gracefully ease themselves into their anointed studio seats. When podcasters talk to their guests, it is merely an *illusion of conversation*, while broadcasters do the same thing; they are engaged in the art of the well-constructed interview. What is at stake here? What is it about podcasting that affronts the cultural proprieties of those who would have us gathered quietly before our wireless sets waiting for members of the *Brains Trust* to scatter their pearls of highbrow wisdom?

As ever in such cases, it is the bitter taste of democracy that is the cause of offence. The image of 'ordinary people' sitting before microphones and speaking their own truths disrupts the notion that epistemic sovereignty is reserved for a handpicked cultural elite. Those who find it unpalatable for everyone to possess an equal right to occupy space in the public sphere, sharing their experiences and perspectives regardless of the mediation of gatekeepers, are bound to regard podcasting as a cultural threat. For, by its nature, its content is unauthorised. It is a mode of thinking aloud that marks a truly reflective democratic society. Such epistemic inclusivity does not crudely separate the intellect from the senses; the educational from the recreational; or the established from the emergent.

In this sense, podcasting occupies an ambivalent space, neither *just* education, in its old monological form of the exercise of pedagogical authority at the expense of the fearful silence of knowledge recipients (think Gradgrind's positivist fetishism of facts), nor *just* entertainment, in the sense characterised by the Frankfurt School as a vast machinery for the generation of alienating diversion. Podcasting, I would argue, in accordance with the title of this volume, lies somewhere *between* education and entertainment; neither one nor the other, but a hybrid product of impulses to know and enjoy the world in which we happen to co-exist.

Podcasting at its best invites us to think beyond the clichés of ingrained categories. Or, to put that another way, podcasts are at their most creative when they transcend and combine genres. This is not an entirely new phenomenon. Writing in 1998, the Dutch media theorist Kees Brants (1998:327) observed that, in order to reach citizens who showed little interest in the conventional forms of political discourse, Western parties and politicians were increasingly presenting themselves in contexts traditionally associated with entertainment:

> Infotainment is situated between the two poles and mixes political informative elements in entertainment programmes or entertainment characteristics in traditionally informative programmes.

While broadcast infotainment constituted a bold experiment in genre-mixing, podcasting has taken such hybridity as its natural form. This has important implications for the social circulation of ideas, as it calls into question the assumption that educative content should be confined to the domain of the 'serious', its sobriety well insulated from the blithe realm of entertainment. This coincides with a number of other changes in pedagogical practice: from the authority of monological authority to an acknowledgement that the best ideas emerge from noisy dialogue; from learning as the absorption of definitive answers to education as an endeavour to ask better questions; and from the classroom as a site of disciplinary control to the school as a base camp for experiential discovery. Of course, there are still pressures to squeeze education back into its categorical silo, just as there are efforts to co-opt podcasts into the realm of professional broadcasting. But the best of podcasting will resist such incorporation by continuing to work with ideas in ways that defy the borders of obsolete categories. As the chapters of this book seek to demonstrate, it is within the amorphous 'in between' that new footings are most likely to be found.

Stephen Coleman is Emeritus Professor of Political Communication at the University of Leeds and presenter of *The Sound of Politics* podcast.

References

Benjamin, W. 2008. (originally 1936) 'The Work of Art in the Age of Its Technological Reproducibility', in Michael W. Jennings et al. (eds.), *The Work of Art in the Age of Its Technological Reproducibility and Other Writings on Media*, Cambridge, MA: Harvard University Press, pp.21–22.

Brants, K., 1998. Who's afraid of infotainment? *European Journal of Communication*, *13*(3), pp.315–335.

Kriss, M. 2023. The problem with podcasts: Most of them are overrated. *The Spectator*, 15 July.

Lyons, M. 1999. New readers in the nineteenth century: Women, children, workers. *A History of Reading in the West*, pp. 313–344.

Rosten, L. in Jacobs, N. (ed.). *Culture for the millions? mass media in modern society*. No. 184. Van Nostrand, 1961, p.72.

Anonymous. *The Sylph* no. 5, October 6, 1796, pp. 36–37.

Part A

Consuming Podcasts as a Tool for Teaching and Learning

Chapter 1

On the Record

Music Podcasts as Aural Pedagogies

Sam Coley and Simon Barber

Introduction

At their best, music podcasts combine the immediacy of radio with the depth of academic discourse, and the accessibility of popular media with the rigour of scholarly investigation. Edutainment – a portmanteau of education and entertainment – describes media designed to educate through entertainment. In the context of music podcasting, edutainment operates through the integration of scholarly research, critical analysis, and engaging presentation styles that prioritise listener enjoyment alongside knowledge transmission. McDaniel defines the music podcast as being one that uses 'music as a primary subject matter' and often features a combination of 'banter between hosts and music recordings'.[1] They employ a range of production styles, such as artist interviews and songwriter discussions, explorations of music theory and movements, episodic documentary-style productions, and fan discussions, to name just a few. As Liz Giuffrè notes, music podcasts can employ storytelling techniques, pedagogical strategies, and accessible formats to convey complex musical concepts.[2] The use of emotive music, presenters who can connect with listeners, and engaging production values can convey complex themes and principles in accessible, thought-provoking ways, helping music podcasts become one of the fastest-growing areas of music explanation.[3] Music podcasts can be a powerful way to share music knowledge, allowing scholars to communicate research findings in engaging, accessible formats to diverse audiences.[4]

This chapter begins by considering the relationship between music podcasts and radio. The authors locate the origins of music-based podcasts in radio's pedagogical traditions, from the spontaneous presenter links of knowledgeable announcers and live discussion panels to the more structured format of pre-produced radio documentaries and features dedicated to musical subjects. This chapter then examines how music podcasts function as dual-purpose tools – simultaneously serving as popular entertainment and as vehicles for practice-based research. It argues that music podcasts function as 'aural pedagogies', creating spaces in which teaching and learning occur through dialogue, reflection, and listening. In this process, podcast makers refine their educational practices through production and audience engagement, while listeners develop musical knowledge through active participation.[5] Through case studies including *Sodajerker on Songwriting* and the *Frontiers* podcast, the authors demonstrate the key identifiers and attributes of the genre, exploring how narrative-based production techniques engage listeners and facilitate informal learning. Finally, this chapter examines the role of music podcasts within the wider framework of academic research, including empirical analysis of listener engagement and

DOI: 10.4324/9781003677253-2

motivations. As Allen notes, music podcasts are ideal tools for public musicology, as they enable scholars to 'communicate ideas and findings to a multitude of listeners'.[6] The relative ease of production and listener access in a range of languages are also major benefits. Although music podcasts are a useful way to disseminate research, scholars are increasingly using podcasting as a form of practice-based research, employing sonic analysis and creative storytelling to explore musical topics in innovative ways.

The relationship between music podcasts and music documentaries for television/film/radio is also important here. While there are similarities between the two forms, there are also marked differences. By assessing these distinguishing features, we can better understand and more clearly define what makes the music podcast distinct. Although the music documentary has been a significant strand of broadcasting since the 1960s, it has often been neglected in academic analysis. Chanan describes the form as paradoxical, 'both pervasive and under-analysed', arguing that music documentaries frequently view musicians 'with the eyes of the fan', which has led to their dismissal as little more than promotional tools.[7] This perception began to shift with the publication of *The Music Documentary: Acid Rock to Electropop*, which helped to legitimise the field and map its varied practices.[8] Yet, while this collection addressed cinema and television, audio-based music documentaries and their podcasting successors have remained largely unexplored, despite their importance in shaping music discourse.

The biggest challenge for music podcasts has always been copyright. Radio broadcasts are covered by blanket licensing agreements (e.g. PPL/PRS in the UK), allowing for extensive use of music in documentaries etc. Podcasts, by contrast, often struggle with copyright restrictions, limiting the ability to incorporate full musical works into discussions.[9] As a result, many music podcasts resort to talk-driven formats, which Morris describes as 'chat-casts' or 'chum-casts', characterised by informal, long-form conversations.[10] Despite these challenges, the democratisation of music criticism and discourse through podcasting represents a fundamental shift in media consumption. Previously, music journalism was dominated by a select group of critics, radio producers, and publishing houses who acted as gatekeepers of musical knowledge. Podcasting has disrupted this hierarchy, allowing independent creators to share insights and expertise outside traditional media institutions.[11] However, this unregulated media environment also raises concerns about the de-professionalisation of music journalism, as many podcast producers lack formal training and receive little to no financial compensation for their work.

It can be argued that music-based podcasts have supplanted music documentaries on the radio and have subsequently emerged as the dominant medium for discussing popular music, connecting with huge global audiences. Nevertheless, the music podcast did not completely obliterate the radio music documentary. As Markman suggests, podcasting's ultimate success might not be its 'status as a radio disruptor' but instead its revitalisation of traditional forms of radio.[12] Instead of replacing the music documentary, music podcasts have, in fact, found new audiences and gained greater prominence.

One of the most popular music podcasts is *Switched on Pop*, hosted by musicologist Nate Sloan and songwriter Charlie Harding, which discusses music history and analysis for listeners with or without musical backgrounds. According to Skjerseth, *Switched on Pop* has two key strengths that help listeners' understanding of popular music. Firstly, the podcast is able to play and discuss specific audio examples to help clarify certain topics. The podcast's conversational format is seen as another benefit. The hosts' easy relationship and relaxed discussions with occasional guest musicians help to provide 'inclusive ways of dissecting the medium and the message of pop music'.[13]

The *Song Exploder* music podcast, which went on to become a Netflix series, is a further example of this kind of aural pedagogy. Each episode, presented by the host Hrishikesh Hirway, dissects individual tracks and often features interviews with artists who discuss their creative processes. Liz Giuffrè identifies the pedagogical attributes of *Song Exploder*, such as the 'clean production and careful editing', which help to make the podcast an 'ideal teaching tool for aspiring podcasting and music students'.[14] The relatively short duration of each episode, averaging between 15 and 20 minutes, is considered another strength, as this makes it easier for students to listen repeatedly in order to fully absorb the content. The podcast has an accompanying website, which provides listeners with transcriptions for each episode and helps to mitigate any music licensing issues by directing visitors to purchase related music tracks. Giuffrè sees *Song Exploder* as an example of how musical exploration, examination, and education can come together in podcast form. She argues that these types of music podcasts have created entirely new methodologies for musical understanding, combining intimate audio storytelling, serial structure, and accessible analysis to democratise musical knowledge production.

Another notable example of pedagogical music podcasting is *Popcast*, a weekly series produced by the *New York Times*, hosted primarily by music critic Jon Caramanica. *Popcast* provides regular, accessible insights into pop music alongside music news and criticism. Boston claims the series offers outstanding pop scholarship as 'the topics are always fresh and deal not just in the content of the music, but the mediums where it appears, the models that produce it, and the methods that we consume and track it'.[15]

The examples presented here support Allen's claim that podcasts can provide useful platforms for academic discourse, offering 'a multitude of listening experiences between dialogue, music, and other sounds', while also encouraging engagement with traditional publishing formats.[16] Yet recognising podcasts' potential as educational tools raises important questions about their function as research. If music podcasts exemplify aural pedagogies in action – facilitating informal learning through accessible formats – how do podcast producers themselves navigate the dual imperatives of entertainment and scholarly rigour? The following section examines this tension through practice-based research, exploring how podcasting can function simultaneously as popular media and as a legitimate tool for academic inquiry.

From Practice to Research

When co-author Simon Barber launched the *Sodajerker on Songwriting* podcast in 2011 along with his colleague Brian O'Connor, his motivation was twofold. As a music fan and practitioner, he sought to understand the art and craft of songwriting more deeply. As an academic researcher, he recognised an opportunity to gather insights about creative practice that would be hard to capture through conventional means. What emerged was a project with a dual-purpose: popular entertainment designed for general audiences that simultaneously acts as a tool for data gathering and research inquiry.

This approach fits with contemporary theories of aural pedagogy that recognise sound's unique capacity to convey knowledge through embodied, relational engagement rather than abstract analysis. Steven Feld's concept of acoustemology – 'knowing-with and knowing-through the audible' – provides theoretical grounding for understanding how podcast conversations enable forms of knowledge exchange that transcend traditional academic boundaries.[17] The intimate, conversational nature of long-form audio interviews allows understanding to emerge through ongoing interaction rather than simple acquisition of information.

The long-form interview format fundamental to *Sodajerker* creates pedagogical space for nuanced discussion, which is rare within traditional media formats. When guests explain their songwriting processes over the course of an hour, they reveal insights about creativity, collaboration, and artistic decision-making that brief radio segments or written interviews struggle to capture. The emotional dimensions conveyed through vocal tone, hesitation, enthusiasm, and spontaneous laughter create information that exists only in this realm and are absent when translated into other forms such as text. When Paul McCartney describes his creative breakthrough moments on the *Sodajerker on Songwriting* podcast, the excitement and wonder still audible in his voice captures something absent from written scholarship about songwriting practice.

The podcast's teaching and learning pedagogy also emerges from what the presenters provide beyond the conversations themselves. Detailed episode introductions function as contextualising frameworks, offering historical background, technical explanations, and context that can transform mainstream entertainment into a structured learning experience while maintaining the accessibility and engagement that characterise successful popular media.

However, it is important to point out that researchers employing podcasting as a dual-purpose methodology must acknowledge significant complexities. Professional musicians participating in promotional cycles present themselves strategically, and access to voices is invariably shaped by a range of factors, including genre preferences, economic considerations, business agendas, and systemic inequalities related to gender, race, and class. Writing in the *Journal of Popular Music Studies*, Morgan Bimm offers a relevant critique of popular music analysis podcasts:

> Popular music analysis podcasts, on their surface, are a project of taking pop music seriously. When we scratch this surface, however, what we find is a mixed bag of tactics that seek to affirm the majority white, majority male creators as uniquely positioned to analyze, evaluate, and respond to music, much of which they are encountering considerably after it has already achieved the success that codes these songs as "popular" in the first place.[18]

Bimm urges us to consider whose voices gain legitimacy through podcast platforms and whose perspectives remain marginalised. If producers and platforms privilege familiar voices and established canons, existing hierarchies could be continually reinforced and reproduced. As a result, it is always necessary to approach the aural contributions of practitioners with appropriate critical distance while recognising the significance of insights that may only be accessible through sustained engagement in this format. This can help entertainment-focused podcasts to generate rigorous scholarly contributions that go beyond what either pure entertainment or traditional academic research might achieve independently.

The productive relationship between entertainment and research in music podcasts, where scholarly rigour is maintained alongside accessible presentation, proves particularly valuable in developing scholarly networks and establishing emerging academic fields.

Unlike content that prioritises entertainment at the expense of accuracy, these podcasts demonstrate how engaging formats can serve rather than undermine academic integrity. The access provided by creating mainstream audio content has facilitated research collaborations, academic conferences, and peer-reviewed publications that might not otherwise exist. For example, the body of practitioner knowledge about songwriting generated through the *Sodajerker* podcast has become foundational to establishing Songwriting Studies as a legitimate academic discipline.[19] This model distinguishes itself from entertainment-driven misinformation by maintaining the researcher-led, evidence-based foundations of academic discourse while adopting more accessible formats.

The dual-purpose approach embodies what Göran Folkestad calls the formal-informal continuum of musical learning.[20] Drawing on Folkestad's framework distinguishing formal/informal learning situations (the contexts in which learning occurs) and formal/informal ways of learning (the methods and approaches to learning), the term 'aural pedagogies' denotes the listening-centred teaching and learning practices embedded in music podcasting. While podcasts may constitute formal learning situations (intentionally structured for educational purposes), they primarily facilitate informal ways of learning, knowledge transmission through conversation, demonstration, and repeated listening rather than notation or systematic instruction. Aural pedagogies encompass both the tacit learning undertaken by listeners as they develop critical listening skills and conceptual frameworks, and the pedagogical development of podcast makers as they learn to teach through editorial choices, interview techniques, and presentational strategies. Folkestad's continuum model is particularly apt here: podcasting exists neither entirely in the formal nor informal realm but occupies a shifting position between these poles, depending on the specific contexts and approaches employed.

Sodajerker has now accumulated over 10 million downloads across more than 300 episodes, demonstrating the potential of approaches that refuse to view entertainment and education as separate categories. However, the effectiveness of aural pedagogies depends not only on production strategies but also on how podcast makers employ specific narrative and sonic techniques to engage listeners. The formal characteristics of edutainment – the deliberate fusion of entertainment with educational content – manifest through concrete production choices. The following section examines how narrative techniques, temporal framing, and sound design function as pedagogical tools, transforming music podcasts into 'portals' that connect listeners across time and musical experience.

Podcasts as Portals

Regardless of their production style, effective podcasts need to engage listeners and hold their attention. This section examines how narrative techniques function as pedagogical tools within music podcasts, demonstrating the practical application of edutainment principles. By exploring how podcasts create temporal links to the past through archival material, ambient sound, and storytelling, we observe aural pedagogies in practice: informal learning facilitated through absorbed, narrative-driven listening experiences that make scholarly discourse both accessible and engaging.

The authors draw on a podcast project previously carried out by Coley, which adopted a different approach from the *Sodajerker on Songwriting* interview format. The *Frontiers* podcast, devised and presented by Dr Ed McKeon, employed a documentary style of production, incorporating on-location recordings, ambient sounds, and a strong emphasis on narrative. The series was designed to accompany and promote live concert events connected to McKeon's research on the Downtown New York music scene of the 1970s. The production was subsequently nominated as a finalist in the UK Radio Academy's Audio and Radio Industry Awards (ARIAS) in 2014. Reflecting on the project, McKeon observed:

> The podcasts are not simply evidence, witnesses to what happened, nor merely explanatory and supplementary, but more like portals that connect different times, that wire them so that they might inspire and spark something new in response from those who listen, both now and in the future.[21]

This notion of podcasts as portals to past events highlights their pedagogical value. Listening to a podcast that recounts – or was itself produced in relation to a past event – can be understood as a distinctive form of phenomenological time. Corner's study of documentary and temporality defines phenomenological time as the relationship between the 'time' represented in a production and the 'time' of the audience's engagement with it.[22] In this respect, a music podcast, even if it was recorded years earlier, is encountered in the immediacy of the present moment, while simultaneously pointing listeners towards histories, events, and voices beyond their current experience. The recording mediates a temporal layering: the listener hears a voice or musical performance from the past in the present, while also anticipating meanings and resonances projected into the future.

As McKeon suggests, the podcast functions as a portal to the past, particularly when it incorporates archival material or other historically embedded content. These types of elements do not merely represent the past but allow listeners to cross an experiential bridge between *then* and *now*. For instance, in one episode, McKeon travelled to Paris to meet the influential minimalist composer Tom Johnson. When Johnson passed away in 2024, McKeon noted how the podcasts had become 'important documents in their own right'; a form of oral history that preserved insights from the past, including his conversation with Johnson. He later reflected: 'The whole process has given me much pause to appreciate the value not only of documentation for creative work but also and especially of creative and reflexive storytelling around projects'.[23]

Sonically, these podcasts were very different from the earlier *Sodajerker* example, drawing instead on more of a radio-documentary style of podcast production, in which the listener quite literally follows the presenter on a journey. McKeon's reflections after the series concluded highlight the pedagogical value of this approach. The podcasts did more than introduce his research and its key figures; they became primary source material capturing hesitation, irony, humour, and other subtle vocal inflections often lost in transcription. McKeon emphasised the narrative power distinguishing complex music podcasts from simple recorded interviews, underlining their capacity to shape the listener's experience by building tension, providing humour, or defying expectation. These production choices exemplify the practical application of key theoretical concepts. In this way, edutainment serves as the operational mode through which aural pedagogies are enacted in music podcasting. Where aural pedagogies describe the bidirectional teaching and learning processes (podcast makers refining pedagogical approaches; listeners developing musical understanding), edutainment defines the specific methodology employed: the deliberate fusion of entertainment elements with educational content. In music podcasts, this manifests through dialogue-based formats rather than lecture-style monologues, the use of musical examples and demonstrations, personal anecdotes from practitioners, and careful audio production that maintains listener attention while conveying complex musicological concepts. The edutainment approach thus enables the informal ways of learning central to aural pedagogies by making scholarly discourse accessible beyond traditional academic gatekeeping structures.

Regardless of the technical or editorial approach a podcast producer may use, there is a need to recognise that effective music podcasting requires an understanding of audio as a distinct medium with its own expressive possibilities. One way to engage listeners is to employ narrative techniques that elicit an emotional response. McHugh draws attention to the work of US neuroscientist Antonio Damasio and his studies on the connections between feeling and cognition.[24] This pioneering work showed how sounds that trigger an emotional response have a higher probability of being noticed and retained. In this respect, podcasts, which use sound to craft emotive reactions, are more likely to connect with the listener in meaningful ways. Creating a sense of intimacy is an effective way to build a bond with audiences. As McDaniel observes, podcasts like *All Songs Considered* use an informal and conversational approach to build feelings of intimacy. The hosts often share personal reflections to create a more relatable listening experience. The editing style also comes into play, helping to create a 'collective listening experience, enhancing the sense of vulnerability and openness'.[25]

The use of music in music podcasts is also an important production element. Huber claims that music can be used to 'conjure up a time, era, or place, calling on a viewer's or listener's cultural knowledge to unlock these connotations'.[26] However, as Carter and Lunt note, copyright restrictions present a significant challenge for music-oriented podcasts, leading many to rely on spoken-word content rather than including extensive music excerpts.[27] Yet, for all this discussion about the use of narrative techniques, it would seem the most effective approach is to build a basic bond between the speaker and the listener. Hall's experience as an audio producer led him to believe that podcast listeners appear to desire a straightforward relationship with the 'presenter/host/storyteller', instead of 'highly textured mixes and sophisticated narratives'.[28]

While the case studies examined here demonstrate various approaches to aural pedagogies, from *Sodajerker's* long-form interviews to *Frontiers*' documentary-style narratives, understanding how these techniques actually function as learning tools demands empirical evidence of listener engagement. Aural pedagogies operate through bidirectional processes: podcast makers develop pedagogical strategies, but listeners actively construct meaning through their engagement practices. The following section examines empirical research into listener motivations and behaviours, providing evidence for how audiences themselves understand and experience music podcasts as sites of informal learning.

Understanding Audiences for Music Podcasts

In 2022, co-author Simon Barber collaborated with Dr Craig Hamilton to conduct an empirical analysis of listener responses to music podcasts. The study examined over 16,000 listener reviews from the top 50 music podcasts in the UK Apple charts, employing natural language processing algorithms to identify patterns in audience motivations and engagement behaviours. The findings provide empirical evidence for understanding how music podcasts function as edutainment and as aural pedagogies.[29]

In the research, computational analysis employing topic modelling techniques was used to organise the vast corpus of listener reviews into discrete thematic categories.

This enabled the researchers to identify patterns that would be difficult to detect solely through traditional close reading. These unprompted responses from listeners provided insights into how audiences themselves understand and articulate their podcast engagement. Through natural language processing analysis, Hamilton and Barber identified seven distinct motivational themes that drive listener engagement with music podcasts. Three themes related specifically to podcasting as a medium: listeners integrate podcasts into daily routines (commutes, exercise, domestic activities), value the long-form conversational structure, and derive pleasure from the intimate audio experience itself. However, the four remaining themes focused directly on musical content and learning:

Experiential Engagement and Cultural Connection revealed listeners' desire to understand music within broader cultural contexts, connecting songs to social movements, historical periods, and artistic communities. This theme demonstrates how podcasts generate understanding through the experience of sound, what Feld might call 'sound as a way of knowing', rather than abstract analysis.[30] Reviews frequently mention gaining new appreciation for musical genres, historical periods, or cultural contexts they had previously overlooked or misunderstood.

Learning and Knowledge Acquisition represented the most explicitly pedagogical theme, with listeners actively seeking information about creative processes, technical approaches, and industry practices. The computational analysis revealed this category leaned heavily towards knowledge-seeking vocabulary, indicating the conscious educational intentions of listeners rather than merely passive entertainment consumption. Typical review language included phrases like "learn so much", "fascinating insights", and "educational value".

Celebrity Access and Insider Knowledge reflected listeners' interest in gaining unprecedented access to established artists and industry figures, speaking to the idea of observational learning through exposure to expert practitioners.[31] The podcast format's conversational intimacy provides access to knowledge and perspectives typically unavailable through traditional media or academic sources.

Fan Relationships and Community Building demonstrated how podcast engagement extends beyond individual learning to community formation around shared musical interests. It showed how listeners develop shared vocabularies, references, and knowledge bases through sustained engagement with podcast content and related discussions.

Here is a representative listener review, cited in Hamilton and Barber, that exemplifies the pedagogical value that emerged across the dataset:[32]

> Great show, revealing the approaches, the ideas, the technique and the inner workings of some of the great classic songs... If you have any interest in the practice of songwriting, you need to be subscribed to this podcast.

This response demonstrates several key characteristics of effective aural pedagogy: recognition of systematic knowledge transmission ("revealing the approaches"), appreciation for insider access ("inner workings"), and active recommendation to others with shared interests ("you need to be subscribed"). The review's language indicates conscious educational engagement rather than passive consumption.

The data analysis also revealed changes in listener responses across different types of music podcasts. Shows featuring detailed analytical discussion (such as *Switched on Pop* or *Dissect*) generated higher proportions of learning-focused reviews, while celebrity interview formats produced more access-oriented responses. This variation suggests that pedagogical effectiveness does not just occur accidentally through entertainment programming but is closely connected to the style and format of the show.

There are, of course, potential issues with drawing conclusions from this one study. Most significantly, the absence of detailed demographic data from podcast platforms prevents analysis of how educational engagement varies across different social, economic, and cultural contexts. As Christine Hine argues, internet-based research often reflects the perspectives of digitally active participants while potentially marginalising voices with limited technological access or different participatory preferences.[33] This limitation is particularly relevant given ongoing concerns about representation within podcast production and consumption.

This analysis of podcast reviews also cannot address the temporal dimensions of learning. For example, initial educational engagement could lead to sustained knowledge acquisition, practical application, or deeper involvement with musical communities. Longitudinal questions like these require a different methodological approach that the published research did not incorporate.

Despite these limitations, the research reveals that music podcasts occupy a distinctive position within contemporary media ecology, functioning simultaneously as entertainment and education in ways that challenge traditional boundaries. Listeners actively seek substantial, informed content while valuing accessibility and conversational formats that make complex musical concepts approachable. Podcast listeners engage in self-directed educational activities that combine structured content consumption with community participation, peer discussion, and practical application. Indeed, the scale of engagement indicates significant untapped potential for audio-based pedagogical approaches. Rather than relying on traditional instructional design, educational institutions might benefit from understanding how podcast formats achieve educational effectiveness through conversational intimacy, narrative engagement, and community building.

Most significantly, the evidence demonstrates that entertainment and education need not function as opposing categories within contemporary media culture. Instead, the most effective music podcasts achieve pedagogical success precisely through their capacity to engage audiences emotionally and culturally while simultaneously transmitting substantial musical knowledge and encouraging critical thinking about creative practices.

Conclusions

This chapter has examined music podcasts as sites of aural pedagogies: listening-centred teaching and learning practices that operate through the edutainment model of combining entertainment formats with scholarly rigour. By analysing both production practices and audience engagement, we have demonstrated how music podcasts facilitate informal ways of learning that complement rather than displace traditional music education.

The concept of aural pedagogies, grounded in Folkestad's continuum between formal and informal learning, captures the distinctive pedagogical work accomplished through music podcasting. Podcasts like *Sodajerker on Songwriting* and *Frontiers* demonstrate how sustained audio engagement enables knowledge transmission through conversation, narrative, and repeated listening rather than notation or systematic instruction. These are not merely simplified versions of academic discourse but rather different modes of knowing that leverage sound's unique capacity for conveying embodied, relational understanding. As Feld's concept of acoustemology suggests, podcasts enable forms of musical understanding that emerge through sonic immersion rather than abstract analysis.

Edutainment serves as the operational methodology through which these aural pedagogies function effectively. The deliberate integration of entertainment values (conversational intimacy, narrative engagement, careful sound design, and emotional resonance) with substantive musical content creates what listeners themselves describe as simultaneously enjoyable and educational experiences. The empirical analysis of over 16,000 listener reviews confirms that audiences actively seek rigorous content while valuing accessibility, demonstrating that entertainment and education need not function as opposing categories. The most pedagogically effective music podcasts succeed precisely through their capacity to engage audiences emotionally and culturally while transmitting substantial musical knowledge and encouraging critical thinking about creative practices.

The practice-based research examined here also reveals how music podcasts function as bidirectional pedagogical spaces. Podcast makers themselves engage in informal learning as they develop interview techniques, editorial strategies, and production approaches. Simultaneously, they generate valuable research data and practitioner insights that contribute to emerging academic fields such as Songwriting Studies. This dual-purpose methodology challenges traditional distinctions between research and dissemination, between practice and scholarship, suggesting new possibilities for how academic knowledge can be produced and shared.

However, significant challenges and limitations persist. Copyright restrictions continue to constrain podcast producers' ability to incorporate extensive musical examples, leading to talk-heavy formats that may limit certain types of musical analysis. Access to prominent practitioners often depends on existing industry relationships and promotional cycles, potentially reinforcing familiar voices while marginalising others. The structural inequalities identified by Bimm regarding whose voices gain legitimacy through podcast platforms – particularly concerning race and gender – demand ongoing critical attention. Podcast audiences, while substantial, may not represent the full diversity of music learners, and the absence of demographic data from podcast platforms prevents comprehensive analysis of how educational engagement varies across different social and cultural contexts.

Despite these limitations, music podcasts have created new pathways for sharing musical expertise that bypass both academic journals and traditional media gatekeepers. They demonstrate how specialist knowledge can engage broader audiences without abandoning analytical depth, suggesting possibilities for scholarly communication that transcends institutional boundaries while maintaining intellectual integrity. They represent a fundamental shift in how musical knowledge is produced, validated, and disseminated – a shift that music educators, researchers, and institutions would be wise to embrace. The evidence presented here suggests that aural pedagogies enacted through music podcasts are not peripheral to contemporary music studies but increasingly central to how musical understanding is cultivated, shared, and developed in the twenty-first century.

Notes

1 Byrd McDaniel, "All Songs Considered: The Persuasive Listening of Music Podcasts," *Twentieth-Century Music* 19, no. 3 (2022): 411, https://doi.org/10.1017/S1478572222000275.
2 Liz Giuffrè, "Lessons on Popular Music Form, Creation and Reception Through the Song Exploder Podcast," *Radio Journal: International Studies in Broadcast & Audio Media* 20, no. 1 (2022): 49–64, https://doi.org/10.1386/rjao_00055_1.
3 McDaniel, "All Songs Considered: The Persuasive Listening of Music Podcasts", 411.
4 Emily R. Allen, "A Review of Podcasting: Time for a Musicology Podcasting Revolution?," *Journal of Musicological Research* 42, no. 3 (2023): 184–189, https://doi.org/10.1080/01411896.2023.2190298.
5 Göran Folkestad, "Formal and Informal Learning Situations or Practices vs Formal and Informal Ways of Learning," *British Journal of Music Education* 23, no. 2 (2006): 135–145, https://doi.org/10.1017/S0265051706006887.
6 Allen, "A Review of Podcasting: Time for a Musicology Podcasting Revolution?", 189.
7 Michael Chanan, "Music, Documentary, Music Documentary," in *The Documentary Film Book*, ed. Brian Winston (London: Palgrave Macmillan, 2013), 337.
8 Benjamin Halligan, Robert Edgar, and Kirsty Fairclough-Isaacs, eds., *The Music Documentary: Acid Rock to Electropop*, 1st ed. (London: Routledge, 2013), https://doi.org/10.4324/9780203118689.
9 Edward L. Carter and Scott Lunt, "Podcasting and Copyright: The Impact of Regulation on New Communication Technologies," *Santa Clara High Technology Law Journal* 22, no. 2 (2006): 189, https://digitalcommons.law.scu.edu/chtlj/vol22/iss2/1.
10 Jeremy Wade Morris, *Podcasting* (Cambridge: Polity Press, 2024).
11 Simon Warner, Andy Bennett, and Steve Waksman, "In Print and on Screen: The Changing Character of Popular Music Journalism," in *The Sage Handbook of Popular Music*, ed. Andy Bennett and Steve Waksman (London: Sage, 2015), 439–455.
12 Kris Markman, "Considerations – Reflections and Future Research. Everything Old Is New Again: Podcasting as Radio's Revival," *Journal of Radio & Audio Media* 22, no. 2 (2015): 241, https://doi.org/10.1080/19376529.2015.1083376.
13 Amy Skjerseth, "Ride-along Listening: Inclusive Modes of Musical Analysis in Switched on Pop," *Radio Journal: International Studies in Broadcast & Audio Media* 20, no. 1 (2022): 34, https://doi.org/10.1386/rjao_00054_1.
14 Giuffrè, "Lessons on Popular Music Form, Creation and Reception Through the Song Exploder Podcast", 50.
15 Arthur J. Boston, "Popcast: A Music Podcast with Unexpected Scholarly Angles. A Review and Highlighted Episode Selection," *The Journal of Academic Librarianship* 48, no. 2 (March 2022): 102438, https://doi.org/10.1016/j.acalib.2021.102438.
16 Allen, "A Review of Podcasting: Time for a Musicology Podcasting Revolution?" 189.
17 Steven Feld, "Acoustemology," in *Keywords in Sound*, ed. David Novak and Matt Sakakeeny (Durham, NC: Duke University Press, 2015), 12, https://doi.org/10.2307/j.ctv11sn6t9.4.
18 Morgan Bimm, "Affect, Reactivity, and the Middlebrow in Popular Music Podcasting," *Journal of Popular Music Studies* 35, no. 4 (2023): 18–33, https://doi.org/10.1525/jpms.2023.35.4.18.
19 Simon Barber, "From The Ivors to The Ivory Tower: The Case of Songwriting Studies," in *Podcast Studies: Practice into Theory*, ed. Lori Beckstead and Dario Llinares (Waterloo, ON: Wilfrid Laurier University Press, 2025), 87–100.
20 Folkestad, "Formal and Informal Learning Situations or Practices vs Formal and Informal Ways of Learning," 135–145.
21 Ed McKeon, personal email communication, June 11, 2025.
22 John Corner, "Temporality and Documentary," in *Time, Media and Modernity*, ed. Emily Keightley (Basingstoke: Palgrave Macmillan, 2012), 78–96, https://doi.org/10.1057/9781137020680_4.
23 Ed McKeon, personal email communication, June 11, 2025.
24 Siobhan McHugh, "Audio Storytelling: Unlocking the Power of Audio to Inform, Empower and Connect," *Asia Pacific Media Educator* 24, no. 2 (2015): 141–156, https://doi.org/10.1177/1326365X14555277.
25 McDaniel, "All Songs Considered: The Persuasive Listening of Music Podcasts", 411–426.

26 Alison Huber, "Remembering Popular Music, Documentary Style: Tony Palmer's History in *All You Need Is Love*," *Television & New Media* 12, no. 6 (2011): 519, https://doi.org/10.1177/1527476411400838.
27 Carter and Lunt, "Podcasting and Copyright: The Impact of Regulation on New Communication Technologies", 190.
28 Alan Hall, "Cigarettes and Dance Steps," in *Reality Radio: Telling True Stories in Sound*, ed. John Biewen and Alexa Dilworth (Chapel Hill: University of North Carolina Press, 2010), 100.
29 Craig Hamilton and Simon Barber, "Rate and Review: Exploring Listener Motivations for Engagement with Music Podcasts," *Radio Journal: International Studies in Broadcast & Audio Media* 20, no. 1 (2022): 17–32, https://doi.org/10.1386/rjao_00053_1.
30 Feld, "Acoustemology", 12.
31 Albert Bandura, *Social Learning Theory* (Englewood Cliffs, NJ: Prentice Hall, 1977).
32 Hamilton and Barber, "Rate and Review: Exploring Listener Motivations for Engagement with Music Podcasts", 25.
33 Christine Hine, "Internet Research and Unobtrusive Methods," *Social Research Update* 61 (2011): 1–4.

References

Allen, Emily R. "A Review of Podcasting: Time for a Musicology Podcasting Revolution?" *Journal of Musicological Research* 42, no. 3 (2023): 184–189. https://doi.org/10.1080/01411896.2023.2190298.

Bandura, Albert. *Social Learning Theory*. Englewood Cliffs, NJ: Prentice Hall, 1977.

Barber, Simon. "From The Ivors to The Ivory Tower: The Case of Songwriting Studies." In *Podcast Studies: Practice into Theory*, edited by Lori Beckstead and Dario Llinares, 87–100. Waterloo, ON: Wilfrid Laurier University Press, 2025.

Bimm, Morgan. "Affect, Reactivity, and the Middlebrow in Popular Music Podcasting." *Journal of Popular Music Studies* 35, no. 4 (2023): 18–33. https://doi.org/10.1525/jpms.2023.35.4.18.

Boston, Arthur J. "Popcast: A Music Podcast with Unexpected Scholarly Angles. A Review and Highlighted Episode Selection." *The Journal of Academic Librarianship* 48, no. 2 (March 2022): 102438. https://doi.org/10.1016/j.acalib.2021.102438.

Carter, Edward L., and Scott Lunt. "Podcasting and Copyright: The Impact of Regulation on New Communication Technologies." *Santa Clara High Technology Law Journal* 22, no. 2 (2006): 187–203. https://digitalcommons.law.scu.edu/chtlj/vol22/iss2/1.

Chanan, Michael. "Music, Documentary, Music Documentary." In *The Documentary Film Book*, edited by Brian Winston, 337–354. London: Palgrave Macmillan, 2013.

Corner, John. "Temporality and Documentary." In *Time, Media and Modernity*, edited by Emily Keightley, 78–96. Basingstoke: Palgrave Macmillan, 2012. https://doi.org/10.1057/9781137020680_4.

Feld, Steven. "Acoustemology." In *Keywords in Sound*, edited by David Novak and Matt Sakakeeny, 12–21. Durham, NC: Duke University Press, 2015. https://doi.org/10.2307/j.ctv11sn6t9.4.

Folkestad, Göran. "Formal and Informal Learning Situations or Practices vs Formal and Informal Ways of Learning." *British Journal of Music Education* 23, no. 2 (2006): 135–145. https://doi.org/10.1017/S0265051706006887.

Giuffrè, Liz. "Lessons on Popular Music Form, Creation and Reception Through the Song Exploder Podcast." *Radio Journal: International Studies in Broadcast & Audio Media* 20, no. 1 (2022): 49–64. https://doi.org/10.1386/rjao_00055_1.

Hall, Alan. "Cigarettes and Dance Steps." In *Reality Radio: Telling True Stories in Sound*, edited by John Biewen and Alexa Dilworth, 96–107. Chapel Hill: University of North Carolina Press, 2010.

Halligan, Benjamin, Robert Edgar, and Kirsty Fairclough-Isaacs, eds. *The Music Documentary: Acid Rock to Electropop*. 1st ed. London: Routledge, 2013. https://doi.org/10.4324/9780203118689.

Hamilton, Craig, and Simon Barber. "Rate and Review: Exploring Listener Motivations for Engagement with Music Podcasts." *Radio Journal: International Studies in Broadcast & Audio Media* 20, no. 1 (2022): 17–32. https://doi.org/10.1386/rjao_00053_1.

Hine, Christine. "Internet Research and Unobtrusive Methods." *Social Research Update* 61 (2011): 1–4.

Huber, Alison. "Remembering Popular Music, Documentary Style: Tony Palmer's History in *All You Need Is Love*." *Television & New Media* 12, no. 6 (2011): 513–530. https://doi.org/10.1177/1527476411400838.

Markman, Kris. "Considerations – Reflections and Future Research. Everything Old Is New Again: Podcasting as Radio's Revival." *Journal of Radio & Audio Media* 22, no. 2 (2015): 240–243. https://doi.org/10.1080/19376529.2015.1083376.

McDaniel, Byrd. "All Songs Considered: The Persuasive Listening of Music Podcasts." *Twentieth-Century Music* 19, no. 3 (2022): 411–426. https://doi.org/10.1017/S1478572222000275.

McHugh, Siobhan. "Audio Storytelling: Unlocking the Power of Audio to Inform, Empower and Connect." *Asia Pacific Media Educator* 24, no. 2 (2015): 141–156. https://doi.org/10.1177/1326365X14555277.

Morris, Jeremy Wade. *Podcasting*. Cambridge: Polity Press, 2024.

Skjerseth, Amy. "Ride-along Listening: Inclusive Modes of Musical Analysis in Switched on Pop." *Radio Journal: International Studies in Broadcast & Audio Media* 20, no. 1 (2022): 33–48. https://doi.org/10.1386/rjao_00054_1.

Warner, Simon, Andy Bennett, and Steve Waksman. "In Print and on Screen: The Changing Character of Popular Music Journalism." In *The Sage Handbook of Popular Music*, edited by Andy Bennett and Steve Waksman, 439–455. London: Sage, 2015.

Chapter 2

Instructor Decision-Making around Podcasts as Course Materials in Higher Education

Lindsay Persohn, Stephanie Branson, Genesis Zabrzenski and Leah Burger

Introduction

Scholarly podcasts are increasingly becoming a feature of teaching and learning in higher education. We define scholarly podcasting[1] as the production of podcasts to facilitate the dissemination of knowledge, often created by scholars and experts within academic institutions. This innovative medium offers learning opportunities through knowledge translation with potential to generate practical connections for learners.[2]

Podcasts can offer a way for instructors in higher education to provide current information as well as meet the needs of students' diverse learning styles and schedules. The author team (as a group of podcast producers) has heard anecdotal reports of colleagues embedding episodes of podcasts into course materials, citing the relevance, accessibility, and multimodal appeal of the content. We wondered how instructors' integration of scholarly podcasts in higher education course materials might contribute to broader conversations about podcasting as a form of knowledge translation more generally. In addition to supporting instructors who may be leveraging scholarly podcasts as course materials, this study offers podcasters insight into practices, structures, and resources that facilitate the integration of podcasts into course content.

Despite anecdotal evidence from our colleagues, there is a notable lack of current empirical research examining how and why higher education instructors adopt podcasts as curricular tools. While earlier studies[3,4] explored podcasts primarily as supplementary teaching aids or lecture replacements, the landscape has since shifted to include research-informed podcasts that blend expert interviews, narrative storytelling, and disciplinary scholarship for a broader audience to enhance the learning environment. These evolving forms of podcasts and the act of podcasting invite a new examination of the role of podcasts in relation to instructors' curricular decision-making and epistemological commitments.

Accordingly, our research team sought to better understand how scholarly podcasts support teaching and learning in higher education contexts. We wanted to examine the ways in which instructors leverage podcasts that convey research-based content and how such content is used in learning contexts to frame inquiry, foster critical engagement, and connect theory to practice. Therefore, the purpose of this study is to investigate how

DOI: 10.4324/9781003677253-3

higher education instructors integrate scholarly podcasts into their instructional decisions. We ask:

1 How do instructors identify and evaluate podcasts that feature research-based content?
2 In what ways do podcasts influence instructors' design of assignments, discussions, and assessments?
3 How do instructors perceive student learning through podcasts?

By investigating how podcasts are taken up in university-level teaching, this study contributes to growing conversations about the role of open-access, multimodal scholarship in shaping research-to-practice pipelines. It addresses a gap in understanding how higher education instructors curate and mobilise digital knowledge sources and how podcasting may support more relational, accessible, and context-responsive forms of research engagement in the university classroom.

Review of the Literature

Transmitting Traditional Lectures

Research on podcasts in education initially emerged in the mid-2000s, at a moment when portable digital audio technologies were gaining traction. The rise of MP3 players, iPods, and early smartphones created new opportunities for students to access course content outside of the classroom. Much of the early work on educational podcasts reflected this technological affordance. For instance, Hew (2009) reported that students often considered podcasts useful for reviewing lectures or addressing gaps from absences, while McGarr (2009) highlighted their potential as review tools. Instructors, meanwhile, reported seeing podcasts as convenient supplements but not transformative to their teaching practice.

The assumptions embedded in this early research framed podcasts as neutral media for transmitting course lectures more flexibly. Rather than shifting specific instructional practices, podcasts were positioned as efficient "add-ons" to traditional teaching rather than catalysts for rethinking how learning might occur. In this way, early scholarship on educational podcasts mirrored broader trends in educational technology at the time, where new tools were celebrated primarily for their convenience, portability, and efficiency, rather than for their potential to reshape pedagogy.[5]

Toward Scholarly Podcasts as Multimodal Instructional Resources

In the 15 years since these early studies, however, both the podcast medium and higher education have evolved. Now, podcasts are a resonant and pervasive cultural form. This widespread cultural adoption has created fertile ground for higher education to reimagine podcasts as more than just supplementary tools, positioning them instead as rich, multimodal platforms for scholarly communication and learning. Current scholars of digital media define podcasts not only by their portability and accessibility, but also by their aesthetic qualities, such as narrative immersion, authentic voice, and broad reach.[6,7,8]

In higher education, the evolution of scholarly podcasts has shifted from lecture capture toward research-informed, story-driven episodes that blend disciplinary expertise with accessible communication.[9] Scholarly podcasts may be produced by institutions and organisations to highlight research, or by scholars and researchers seeking grassroots methods for sharing their ideas. Such podcasts do not replicate a lecture but instead reconfigure scholarship as affective, dialogic, and multimodal. It is not about using digital tools for efficiency but about asking how technology reconfigures and enhances learning relationships. This is a shift aligned with broader moves associated with higher education, moves aligned with goals of open scholarship and knowledge mobilisation,[10] leveraging digital technologies to support these moves.

With continuously evolving changes in teaching within higher education, scholarly podcasts offer the potential for deepening scholarly engagement, transforming teaching and learning, expanding research impact, and fostering public discourse. They can blur the boundaries between the classroom and public spheres, between formal and informal learning, and between scholarly authority and the often left-out lived narratives or human experience. When used as multimedia curricular texts, podcasts open opportunities for students to analyse voice, perspective, and storytelling as scholarly practices, helping them see research not only as static knowledge but also as dynamic, situated discourses.

Data Sources

Research Context

The research team hosts and produces a podcast designed to support the translation of literacy education research into practice. The *Classroom Caffeine* podcast launched in November 2020, and since then, the team has released over 100 episodes. We utilise a guest/host format, featuring new and experienced scholars and educators. Podcast guests are Teachers of the Year, Professors of all ranks, Endowed Chairs, and Center Directors. Many guests on the show are highly cited and well-recognised. They have served as leaders of national and international education organisations. They are members of the Reading Hall of Fame, Research Fellows for the National Academy of Education, and the like. They are award winners, and there are awards named in their honour. They are journal editors and reviewers. They teach and lead literacy and education initiatives locally and globally. As of January 2026, episodes of the show have collectively garnered over 38,000 downloads in 125 countries, indicating the series has a broad and diverse listenership.

While participants in this study utilise episodes of our show, they also integrate other education podcast resources into their course materials. We asked them about their use of podcasts in general during our interviews.

Participants

All study participants expressed that they have included episodes of *Classroom Caffeine* in their course materials. Five participants were drawn from a purposive sample of volunteers, all of whom were known to the research team and had previously reported their use of podcasts as course materials in professional or casual conversation. All participants teach undergraduate and/or graduate courses in a College of Education at a University in the United States. All participants hold an advanced graduate degree (Ph.D. or Ed.D.) in their field and possess a wide range of experience in teaching in K-12 and higher education settings (±5 years to ±35 years).

We chose semi-structured interviews to elicit how instructors used podcasts in coursework, why they do so, how they curate and vet episodes, how podcasts interact with readings and assignments, and what evidence they use to judge engagement and learning. A sample of questions from these conversations included the following:

- What motivated you to include podcasts in your course design? How do podcasts align with or differ from your overall teaching philosophy?
- How do you choose which podcasts or episodes to assign? What criteria do you use to evaluate credibility or scholarly rigor in podcast content?
- Do you pair podcasts with readings, discussions, or assignments? How do they interact? How do you assess student engagement and learning with podcasts?

The study received approval from our Institutional Review Board, and all participants provided verbal consent to participate in the study. Interviews typically lasted 30–40 minutes, and the primary source of data in this study included anonymised interview transcripts.

Methods

A qualitative case study approach[11] guided data collection and analysis. We bound the case by focusing on instructors in Colleges of Education who integrate podcasts into coursework. With an ongoing data collection plan, this report focuses on interviews with five instructors from three institutions who have participated so far. We conducted semi-structured interviews focused on podcast use, research integration, and instructional decision-making. Audio was transcribed and manually prepared to improve readability and interpretability by removing filler words, false starts, and idiomatic expressions that could confound algorithmic parsing while still preserving semantic integrity. All files were retained to maintain an audit trail. The edited transcripts were then imported into Microsoft Copilot to generate preliminary thematic clusters using built-in natural language processing capabilities.

We treated the machine outputs solely as sensitising prompts, not findings. *Sensitising prompts* are targeted analytic questions that oriented, but did not determine, our coding. Prompts were treated as provisional notions, systematically checked against transcripts for confirming and disconfirming evidence.

Human-led analysis proceeded through iterative coding aligned to our research questions. To further structure the analysis, we employed ChatGPT as an additional thought partner for assistance in grouping and refining the codes into thematic categories while maintaining reflexive oversight throughout the process. We leaned on a constant comparative method[12] as we reviewed AI-generated themes to ensure consistency with the data and to safeguard against semantic misclassification. Early support of generative AI as a thought partner pushed us to consider the data differently than we may have with only human-driven methods. Generative AI technologies encouraged the research team to consider and reconsider ways in which research participants talked about how they integrate podcasts into their courses. As we drafted this report, we ultimately rewrote and reorganised our themes and supporting evidence in a way that we felt was aligned with the flow of instructional planning, delivery, and assessment. Quotes from participant interviews were selected by the research team to explicate and enrich the themes.

This hybrid approach of AI-assisted and human-led thematic analysis aligns with recommendations for maintaining analytic rigor in tech-enhanced qualitative inquiry.[13,14] This chapter reports on our interview-based themes. Participants are recruited on an ongoing basis, and additional data sources will be integrated in subsequent analyses and reports.

Results

Instructors' responses can be clustered around three key topics: perceived value of podcasts, instructional design and implementation, and outcomes of student learning through podcasts as instructional tools.

Perceived Value of Podcasts

Analysis of interview conversations revealed that instructors actively sought podcasts featuring scholars who share research summaries and details to complement, supplement, or supplant readings. They cited perceived or possible benefits such as narrative explanations of complex theories, up-to-date perspectives, and accessibility for students with varied learning preferences. In these responses, instructors often cited their own learning experiences as podcast listeners as a driving force behind the decision to include podcasts as course materials. Instructors also perceived podcasts as a format for course materials that allows students to learn while multitasking (e.g., during commutes or chores), supporting auditory learners and busy schedules.

We heard from instructors that they believed the storytelling nature of podcasts and the personal narratives often shared within podcast episodes were effective resources to complement or replace traditional readings, especially when text-based materials for a particular topic were overly dense or confusing for students in the past. Additionally, they chose scholarly podcasts to provide explanations of theories in a dynamic and personal way. Instructors had the collective view of podcasts as useful tools for research mobilisation, effectively conveying complex ideas and fostering multimodal learning.

One participant stated, "I was enjoying the podcast myself and the way that I was hearing the information being shared,... it was something that was digestible for preservice teachers". Beyond the scope of higher education instruction, this instructor also noted that when graduates of her program enter the professional field, they typically lose access to print journal articles. She went on to explain that her other motivations included exposing her students to a freely available scholarly podcast as a way for her students to keep up with research in the field after they lose access to journal articles once they graduate from the university system. She was conceptualising the content of her course as a way to encourage lifelong professional learning.

Comments from other participants also highlighted the ways in which scholarly podcasts may support continued professional growth for both students and instructors. One instructor described leveraging podcast episodes "like a guest lecture". She has utilised podcast episodes to support delivery of information related to topics she does not feel are her specific area of expertise within her field. She said, "it's about showing [my students] like, look, there are these other people who've been doing this even longer than I have,... and so for me, it was about letting them hear it from somewhere else". She went on to explain how podcasts have also helped her reshape her instructional language around course concepts: "[Podcasts] make me think differently about how I talk about concepts that are not in my wheelhouse. It's been a really amazing tool for me personally and for me to pass on to my students."

We observed patterns in how instructors adapted research evidence: translating theoretical constructs into practical examples, encouraging student engagement by connecting them to original sources, and modelling critical engagement with media. Furthermore, several participants noted a shift in their own pedagogical reasoning, stating that podcasts inspired them to update readings or embed new instructional strategies into their courses.

Instructional Design and Implementation

For the instructors we spoke with, choosing podcasts as course content was often a part of a broader pedagogical commitment to using diverse media types. Several participants reported ways the format of podcasts specifically supported their instruction. One instructor remarked,

> I use a podcast just like any other text, because one of the things in disciplinary literacies is the multimodality of text. So, it allows me to use podcasts as my example of what I mean by multimodality in text.

Multimodal text is a central concept in the course described by this instructor and a concept that has been challenging for students to understand and integrate into their assignments. Sharing the big ideas of the course through a multimodal text appears to support the content of the course in at least two ways—as a source of information related to the topic of the course and as a strong example of textual multimodality.

When selecting episodes to integrate into their course content, instructors said that they did not question the credibility of guests on the podcast program that the authors produce. Many guests on the show that the authors produce are well-known in the field of literacy studies and education. The credibility of the research-based information relayed in each podcast episode was enhanced when episodes featured respected scholars or practitioners, which reinforced trust in the content. Study participants often knew the work of the scholars featured in the podcast episodes of their choice through the professional reputation these scholars have developed through traditional print publication venues, professional conference proceedings, and work in professional organisations in the field. Instructors indicated that featured guests who may not yet have name recognition in the field were deemed credible by association with the well-known scholars through the podcast series.

One instructor who incorporates other podcast programs in her courses other than *Classroom Caffeine* told us that she evaluates the quality of the information in a podcast based on her own expertise by listening to episodes in their entirety to ensure the content is research-based, in alignment with course content, that the episode does not "go off the rails" at any point, and that the selected episodes are not attempting to sell anything to listeners.

Like with any other instructional content, instructors sought podcast episodes that specifically aligned with the content of their course, often reporting that selected podcasts reinforced key themes in a timely, scaffolded manner. The episodes they selected were intentionally aligned with weekly topics or module objectives, often replacing dense readings with accessible audio.

Student Learning Outcomes

Additionally, through interview conversations, each instructor discussed student-reported learning outcomes and their own observations of student learning. In particular, podcasts seem to help students understand complex or theoretical ideas, encourage participation in class discussions and follow-up activities, and offer multimodal ways for students to respond to or convey their understanding of course content.

One instructor emphasised the way in which a podcast supported students' comprehension of theory. Her students told her,

> This is the first time I understand theory. I loved that we had these videos and these podcasts because it made [the content] more accessible. And now I understand what they're talking about. It's not just some theory I'm reading out of a book.

Her students had not understood a foundational education theory until they heard it explained by the theorists themselves in an assigned podcast episode.

Instructors also described increased student engagement in courses during weeks when podcasts were leveraged, evidenced by higher recall of content and greater participation. Learning assessment approaches included discussion boards, informal reflections, and/or short quizzes. Instructors noted more robust initial responses and continued engagement in discussion board posting when podcasts were part of the learning module material. One instructor provides "Read and React" prompts, which encourage students to make connections to what they read, listen to, and view for the week. She shared, "In their Read and Reacts... it's interesting how they talk about it... Most of them spent some time discussing this [episode], so I knew that it was a really good one". As another way to assess learning outcomes from podcasts, several instructors pose quiz questions related to podcast content, treating questions about podcast content and the content of traditional readings in the same way.

Some instructors encouraged their students to create their own podcasts as a way to demonstrate learning, promoting creativity, synthesis, and equity. One instructor reported that she asked her students to produce a podcast of approximately ten minutes in length to share their learning. Most podcasts submitted for the assignment were two to three times the required length, and the instructor conveyed that the quality of the work exceeded her expectations.

Another instructor promoted the use of podcasting as a response to course material, particularly for students with disabilities or diverse learning preferences. She noted,

> I have a student right now... who does his assignments as podcasts. He has a disability. Has trouble typing things out... He has a great radio voice, and he likes to do a podcast instead of a discussion board written assignment.

Instructors indicated that providing podcasting as one way to evidence learning resulted in high-quality submissions that offered helpful options for students and evidence of robust learning.

Two instructors expressed difficulty in formally assessing learning and engagement from podcasts, noting that they were not sure how to assess learning from an artefact that was not a traditional text and whether conventional forms of assessment (e.g., written summaries, reflections, quizzes) would reinscribe text-based expectations. In other words, they perceived podcasts as offering intellectual traction but lacking established pathways to capture that learning in summative tasks. This raises a question about what types of assessments would be most effective and how assessment practices may inadvertently privilege written modes even when course materials diversify. These instructors suggested it would be helpful to create a publicly available instructional resource guide to support the integration of podcasts into course materials.

Discussion

The results from this study highlight widespread recognition of scholarly podcasts as valuable components of higher education curricula. This aligns with broader research showing podcasts' pedagogical benefits, including flexibility, inclusivity, and multimodal engagement. Notably, participants expressed strong interest in continuing podcast integration and recognised their applicability across diverse learner groups and were seen as valuable for both undergraduate (i.e., pre-service teacher) and graduate (i.e., in-service teacher) learning. The strong endorsement by instructors suggests an increasing institutional and individual awareness of the potential of podcasts to enrich learning. The perception of scholarly podcasts as adaptable tools capable of integrating research-based content into coursework demonstrates a move beyond mere convenience toward meaningful and intentional pedagogical innovation. This resonates with scholarship emphasising podcasts' capacity to foster critical thinking, deeper comprehension, and affective learning connections through rich storytelling and multimodal engagement.[15,16] This move exceeds prior conceptions of podcasts as simple lecture supplements, positioning them as dynamic, dialogic learning spaces.[17]

However, some instructors expressed a desire for institutional support to find, integrate, and evaluate podcast content as course materials, highlighting challenges in operationalising widespread adoption. This indicates a gap between enthusiasm for using multimedia sources and the potential barriers to practical implementation. Prior research has shown that faculty may value media-rich learning materials but struggle to implement them within systems built around text-dominant norms.[18] According to Podcast-Statistics.com, more than four and a half million podcasts exist.[19] Therefore, identifying focused podcast content that supports learning in specific courses can pose time and effort challenges for instructors. Thus, the concerns raised by participants are not merely individual hesitations but may reflect a broader pattern. Effective use of scholarly podcasts in coursework requires dedicated resources, training, and infrastructure.

Overall, the results of this ongoing study highlight podcasts as adaptable tools that enable instructors to integrate research-based content into teaching while supporting inclusive and multimodal learning environments, while underscoring the importance of institutional supports.

Study Limitations

We acknowledge several study limitations. First, the study involved a small sample of five instructors within Colleges of Education, which limits transferability of the results. The reliance on self-report data also raises the possibility of bias, potentially compounded by the fact that all participants were previously known to the research team. However, we noted in our conversations that familiarity with participants seemed to work in our favour, offering a way to quickly get to the heart of participants' experiences and observations. Also, as participants and members of the research team teach in the same or similar fields, shared knowledge around specialised terms and course content already existed. However, in light of the small sample and the research team's familiarity with participants, the results presented here are preliminary and should be viewed as an early step in exploring this topic.

Methodologically, the use of AI tools to generate initial themes introduced both opportunities and constraints; while efficient, this approach may have encouraged surface-level pattern recognition and overlooked deeper nuance. However, our choice to utilise Microsoft Copilot as a first step in analysing transcripts offers security over other platforms like ChatGPT, because Microsoft Copilot does not retain data or use it to train large language models. Copilot utilises input data and organisational data in its analyses, ensuring data is private and secure. Our use of ChatGPT-4 to fine-tune key phrasing does not change this layer of data protection because we only input secondary data (i.e., ideas generated by Microsoft and not the original data sources) in ChatGPT. Therefore, limitations of the AI tools themselves, as well as broader questions of ethical and interpretive oversight, shape how the results should be understood.

Future Research

Future research should explore scalable integration practices, assessment, and student perspectives on how podcasts impact learning. Scalable integration practices should involve strategies (e.g., infrastructures, curated content, faculty development) that allow institutions and instructors to embed podcasts meaningfully while supporting sustained use without overwhelming resources or personnel.

Assessing learning from podcasts remains challenging for instructors, leading us to wonder how these challenges mirror or diverge from the assessment of learning from other media (e.g., videos, oral histories, live discussions). Key questions for future research include: What forms of knowledge do podcasts make visible or invisible to current assessment structures? How do instructors conceptualise critical engagement when the primary mode is auditory rather than written? Studies examining how instructors evaluate knowledge gained from podcasts versus written texts of videos could help identify which assessment barriers are structural and which are medium-specific.

Additionally, while this study has focused on instructors' choices and experiences, it is equally important to understand how students encounter podcasts as part of their learning. Questions might address how often students see podcasts included in course content, and whether these appear more so in in-person or online courses. It would also be useful to know if podcasts are framed as required texts or offered as optional enrichment, as well as how often or enthusiastically students take up the course directive to listen to a podcast. Results of this study also point to new questions about what type of content may be best suited for learning through podcasts. As one participant shared, her students successfully understood complex theories by listening to them explained through a podcast episode. This is a promising finding in support of higher-order and critical thinking for students.

Relatedly, future work might explore the level of student attention and engagement with podcasts, perceived accessibility to podcasts as a multimedia learning tool, the types of assignments that accompany them, and how these shape learning experiences. A student's perspective may differ significantly from an instructor's, and capturing those differences could deepen our understanding of podcasts as a viable pedagogical tool.

Conclusions

In conclusion, preliminary results from this study indicate that podcasts may offer an effective way for instructors in higher education to convey topics and ideas to their students. Podcasts may support an inclusive, multimedia learning environment that provides a path to learning opportunities for diverse learners. Podcasts can help to bridge research and practical application of ideas, convey complex concepts and details in a narrativised format, while enhancing student engagement. In the selection of podcast series and episodes to include in course materials, credibility of sources and curation of content matter. Participants in this study indicated that the use of podcasts as course materials is purposeful and evolving, and that the practice of integrating multimedia resources as course materials is a lasting phenomenon. With continued support and development, podcasts may function as an essential component of teaching and learning in higher education. While our small pool of participants all teach in a College of Education, we believe these results are not isolated to the field of Education. We believe podcasts hold great potential value as a tool for communicating knowledge in higher education settings and beyond.

Notes

1. Cook, Ian M. *Scholarly Podcasting: Why, What, How?* London: Taylor & Francis, 2023.
2. Persohn, Lindsay, and Stephanie Branson. "Broadening Legitimacy of Scholarly Podcasting as Knowledge Dissemination: Metrics, Opportunities and Considerations." *Publishing Research Quarterly* 40, no. 3 (2024): 269–286. https://doi.org/10.1007/s12109-024-10005-5.
3. Hew, Khe Foon. "Use of Audio Podcast in K-12 and Higher Education: A Review of Research Topics and Methodologies." *Educational Technology Research and Development* 57, no. 3 (2009): 333–357. https://doi.org/10.1007/s11423-008-9108-3.
4. McGarr, Oliver. "A Review of Podcasting in Higher Education: Its Influence on the Traditional Lecture." *Australasian Journal of Educational Technology* 25, no. 3 (2009): 309–321. https://doi.org/10.14742/ajet.1136. https://ajet.org.au/index.php/AJET/article/view/1136.
5. Reiman, Richard A. "Podcasting for Teaching and Research in History: A Case Study." Paper presented at the International Society for Technology, Education, and Science, New York, NY, 2021.
6. Cook, Ian M. *Scholarly Podcasting: Why, What, How?* Taylor & Francis, 2023.
7. Cox, Michael, Hannah L. Harrison, Stefan Partelow, Steven Curtis, Stephen R. Elser, Courtney Hammond Wagner, Robert Hobbins, et al. "How Academic Podcasting Can Change Academia and Its Relationship with Society: A Conversation and Guide." *Frontiers in Communication* 8 (2023): 1–9. https://doi.org/10.3389/fcomm.2023.1090112.
8. Symulevich, Allison, Matt Torrence, Jason Boczar, and Jessica Szempruch. "Podcasting as Open Access: A Review and Discussion of Potential Impact on Scholarly Communication and Promotion." *Journal of Librarianship and Scholarly Communication* 13, no. 1 (2025): 0_1–19. https://doi.org/10.31274/jlsc.18241.

9 Cox, Michael, Hannah L. Harrison, Stefan Partelow, Steven Curtis, Stephen R. Elser, Courtney Hammond Wagner, Robert Hobbins, et al. "How Academic Podcasting Can Change Academia and Its Relationship with Society: A Conversation and Guide." *Frontiers in Communication* 8 (2023): 1–9. https://doi.org/10.3389/fcomm.2023.1090112.

10 Cox, Michael, Hannah L. Harrison, Stefan Partelow, Steven Curtis, Stephen R. Elser, Courtney Hammond Wagner, Robert Hobbins, et al. "How Academic Podcasting Can Change Academia and Its Relationship with Society: A Conversation and Guide." *Frontiers in Communication* 8 (2023): 1–9. https://doi.org/10.3389/fcomm.2023.1090112.

11 Merriam, Sharan B., and Sharan B. Merriam. *Qualitative Research: A Guide to Design and Implementation.* The Jossey-Bass Higher and Adult Education Series Qualitative Research. 3rd ed. San Francisco, CA: Jossey-Bass, 2009.

12 Miles, Matthew B., A. Michael Huberman, and Johnny Saldaña. *Qualitative Data Analysis: A Methods Sourcebook.* 4th ed. Los Angeles, CA: Sage, 2020.

13 Saldaña, Johnny. *The Coding Manual for Qualitative Researchers.* 4th ed. London: Sage, 2021.

14 Miles, Matthew B., A. Michael Huberman, and Johnny Saldaña. *Qualitative Data Analysis: A Methods Sourcebook.* 4th ed. Los Angeles, CA: Sage, 2020.

15 Besser, Erin D., Lauren E. Blackwell, and Matthew Saenz. "Engaging Students through Educational Podcasting: Three Stories of Implementation." *Technology, Knowledge and Learning* 27, no. 3 (2022): 749–764. https://doi.org/10.1007/s10758-021-09503-8.

16 Engzell, Jeanette, Charlotte Norrman, Annelie Norberg, and Cia Lundvall. "Soundwaves of Knowledge: Using Podcasts to Facilitate Learning in Higher Education." *Educational Media International* 62, no. 3 (2025): 361–379. London: Routledge.

17 Engzell, Jeanette, Charlotte Norrman, Annelie Norberg, and Cia Lundvall. "Soundwaves of Knowledge: Using Podcasts to Facilitate Learning in Higher Education." *Educational Media International* 62, no. 3 (2025): 361–379. London: Routledge.

18 Shi, Youwen. "Multimodal Teaching in Digital Media Arts Education: Insights and Challenges from Teachers' Perspectives." *Cogent Education* 12, no. 1 (2025): 1–12. https://doi.org/10.1080/2331186X.2025.2590849.

19 "Podcastatistics.Com." 2025, accessed December 3, 2025, https://podcastatistics.com/.

References

Besser, Erin D., Lauren E. Blackwell, and Matthew Saenz. "Engaging Students Through Educational Podcasting: Three Stories of Implementation." *Technology, Knowledge and Learning* 27, no. 3 (2022): 749–764. https://doi.org/10.1007/s10758-021-09503-8.

Cook, Ian M. *Scholarly Podcasting: Why, What, How?* London: Routledge, 2023. https://doi.org/10.1332/174426413X662806.

Cox, Michael, Hannah L. Harrison, Stefan Partelow, Steven Curtis, Stephen R. Elser, Courtney Hammond Wagner, Robert Hobbins et al. "How Academic Podcasting Can Change Academia and Its Relationship with Society: A Conversation and Guide." *Frontiers in Communication* 8 (2023): 1090112.

Engzell, Jeanette, Charlotte Norrman, Annelie Norberg, and Cia Lundvall. "Soundwaves of Knowledge: Using Podcasts to Facilitate Learning in Higher Education." *Educational Media International* 62, no. 3 (2025), 1–19. https://doi.org/10.1080/09523987.2025.2533120.

Hew, Khe Foon. "Use of Audio Podcast in K-12 and Higher Education: A Review of Research Topics and Methodologies." *Educational Technology Research and Development* 57, no. 3 (2009): 333–357. https://doi.org/10.1007/s11423-008-9108-3.

McGarr, Oliver. "A Review of Podcasting in Higher Education: Its Influence on the Traditional Lecture." *Australasian Journal of Educational Technology* 25, no. 3 (2009): 309–321. https://doi.org/10.14742/ajet.1136.

Merriam, Sharon B. *Qualitative Research: A Guide to Design and Implementation.* 3rd ed. San Francisco, CA: Jossey-Bass, 2009.

Miles, Matthew B., A. Michael Huberman, and Johnny Saldaña. *Qualitative Data Analysis: A Methods Sourcebook*. 4th ed. Los Angeles, CA: Sage, 2020.

Persohn, Lindsay, and Stephanie Marie Branson. "Broadening Legitimacy of Scholarly Podcasting as Knowledge Dissemination: Metrics, Opportunities and Considerations." *Publishing Research Quarterly* 40, no. 3 (2024): 269–286. https://doi.org/10.1007/s12109-024-10005-5.

Podcastatistics.com. "Podcastatistics.com." Accessed December 3, 2025. https://podcastatistics.com/.

Reiman, Richard A. "Podcasting for Teaching and Research in History: A Case Study." *International Society for Technology, Education, and Science* (2021): 1–10.

Saldaña, Johnny. *The Coding Manual for Qualitative Researchers*. 4th ed. London: Sage, 2021.

Shi, Youwen. "Multimodal Teaching in Digital Media Arts Education: Insights and Challenges from Teachers' Perspectives." *Cogent Education* 12, no. 1 (2025): 2590849.

Symulevich, Allison, Matt Torrence, Jason Boczar, and Jessica Szempruch. "Podcasting as Open Access: A Review and Discussion of Potential Impact on Scholarly Communication and Promotion." *Journal of Librarianship and Scholarly Communication* 13, no. 1 (2025): 1–19. https://doi.org/10.31274/jlsc.18241.

Chapter 3

Using Podcasts to Grow Your Skills Garden into an Orchard

Alex Hough

The traditional role of the university lecturer has been that of a subject specialist, an authority, and a gatekeeper of knowledge. However, continuing financial pressure across UK higher education (HE) increasingly leads to lecturers being required to teach beyond their core specialisms. This chapter draws from the author's experiences as a music production lecturer tasked with delivering sound design content, an area where his professional experience is comparatively limited.

Through engagement with specialist sound design podcasts such as *AMPS* and *Tonebenders*, the author accessed practice-led insights from industry experts, leading to significant pedagogical and curricular innovations that would have been difficult to achieve using traditional academic sources alone. Podcasts offer immediacy, authenticity, and access to contemporary creative practices that books and journal articles often cannot match at pace. This chapter argues that curated podcast listening can operate as an informal but impactful mode of continuing professional development (CPD). By enabling educators to bridge knowledge gaps and extend their disciplinary reach, podcasts support the cultivation of an expanded 'skills orchard', enriching both teaching practice and student experience.

Introduction

Podcasts have become widely recognised as powerful, open-access instruments for learning within HE. They offer many opportunities to support learners in addressing knowledge gaps and reinforce their understanding of key concepts, regardless of the discipline.[1] While research has focused on podcasting as a tool for enhancing learning and engagement for students, the aim of this chapter is to explore the use of podcasting as a resource for personal and professional development for university lecturers. This will be undertaken through the lens of a series of autoethnographic reflections.

The Role of the Lecturer

The traditional role of the university lecturer has been that of a subject specialist, an authority, and a gatekeeper of knowledge. A large part of this traditional role is to distil information, knowledge, skills, and expertise, and to infuse them into a coherent curriculum.[2] There is still a strong expectation that lecturers act as authorities and subject specialists, but there is an increasing demand that lecturers cover areas where they may only have limited or peripheral experience.

DOI: 10.4324/9781003677253-4

Due to the shifting sands within UK HE, there is an increased need for efficiencies across the sector.[3] Downward financial pressure inevitably means that the role of the lecturer is changing and will likely continue to do so. Lecturers are now required to take on even more responsibilities, be more adaptable, more flexible, and teach and devise entire modules outside of their immediate specialism; the goal being to make degree programs more financially viable for the institutions at large.

The author has experienced this firsthand and, as a result, teaches a mixture of music production and sound design undergraduates within the same core recording studio modules and classes. There is obvious potential for tensions for a lecturer who does not know enough about a subject that they are supposed to teach, then needing to create an entire set of classes or curriculum around that subject. So where does this leave the modern university lecturer who has such a skills, knowledge, or experience gap?

Time vs Money vs Opportunity

CPD is something lecturers are encouraged to engage with. This comes in many guises, from short courses to conferences to accredited qualifications. However, given that the necessity to teach additional classes that are adjacent to a lecturer's specialism stems from financial pressures, it seems unlikely that institutions are going to be able to afford to equip lecturers adequately in this regard. The additional knock-on effect of having to *do more with less* is that you may also find yourself with less time to do more CPD.

Even in a blue-sky world where your institution affords staff the luxury of additional funding and time to reduce your knowledge gap, there may not be an appropriate or sufficient opportunity to capitalise on it. In the author's case, he is trying to gain knowledge and experience of how professional audio is recorded, edited, and created for a wide range of multimedia outputs. However, due to the commercial nature of such projects, it is relatively fanciful to believe that a 'Steven Spielberg' would entertain the idea of a lecturer joining the sound team on set for CPD purposes during the production of a multi-million-pound Hollywood blockbuster. However, listening to sound design podcasts where industry experts discuss their experiences while working on such projects can help do just that.

Using Dead Time for Passive Learning

Engaging with subject-specific textbooks can be a richly rewarding activity, but it is one that requires dedicated time to reap any meaningful benefits. It is an active process that requires full attention. In the current cash-poor, time-poor world of HE, podcasts offer a partial solution to growing your skills garden by facilitating passive learning. The ability to gain insights from leading professionals and connect to a community of elite practitioners while commuting to work, doing the school run, or working your way through the mundane chores of day-to-day life is an unbelievable educational opportunity.

Utilising this ordinarily 'dead time' with a few simple clicks of a smartphone or computer can unlock the doors to a gated community that would not normally be accessible to most lecturers. To date, the author has listened to over 200 podcast episodes about sound design. The run time of each podcast episode is variable, but most come in somewhere between 30 and 90 minutes. This has equated to at least 150 hours of passive learning. This has endowed the author with a whole new tome of knowledge that can now be passed on to students and has subsequently been integrated into the curriculum. The author argues that this process is entirely replicable across academic disciplines once curation of suitable specialist podcasts has been undertaken.

Discovering Audio Gold

The 'Tonebenders',[4] 'Beards, Cats And Indie Game Audio',[5] and 'AMPS'[6] podcasts were used with the specific purpose of educating the author about the different worlds of sound design.

Tonebenders is primarily hosted by Timothy Muirhead, who works as a professional sound designer on animated TV series for children. His credits include Paw Patrol, W5, and Bakugan Battle Brawlers.[7] At the time of writing, the podcast has amassed over three hundred episodes where the host interviews prominent audio professionals and talks to them about their specific audio job roles on the TV shows, films, and video games that they have recently worked on. The calibre of guests they have had on the show is simply staggering, with multiple award winners from some of the most critically acclaimed entertainment projects on the planet.

Listening to the combined wisdom and experience of such guests has obvious benefits for anyone trying to upskill. Many podcast episodes cover TV shows and films that have either recently been released, are currently in the cinema, or are scheduled for imminent release on the various streaming platforms. The contemporary nature of these podcasts is something that textbooks simply cannot compete with due to the lead time and rigor of the editorial process. Podcasts can therefore help educate lecturers about current industry trends in a much more up-to-date way.

The focus of most Tonebenders podcast episodes is linear media, with only occasional episodes centred around non-linear video games. Therefore, the author turned to Beards, Cats and Indie Game Audio podcast to learn more about the processes of sound design within professional video games. The podcast started in 2014 and currently has a library of over 60 episodes.

This podcast differs from Tonebenders not only in content but also in style. The hosts Matthew Marteinsson and Gordon McGladdery talk about their experience working both as freelance and in-house sound designers for AAA and independent (indie) games studios. The difference between AAA and indie game studios is broadly centred around scale, budget, creative control, and the overall production values of the video games.

The duo are clearly friends who conversationally recount tales from their past, present, and future projects. This is interspersed between their commentary on current technological issues and stylistic trends within their specific corner of the video game industry. One of the standout themes within this podcast is the duo's commitment to building up community. They discuss the value community brings to their professional practice and the positive influence it has had on their careers to date. During the episodes, they often talk about what they recently learned at the local 'meet up' and 'hang out' groups they founded or are helping to nurture.

The Association of Motion Picture Sound (AMPS) itself is a well-respected guild for UK-based sound professionals working within TV, film, and game audio. It has nearly six hundred members, was founded in 1989, and presents an annual award for *excellence in sound* for TV, films, and the manufacturers of professional audio software and hardware used within the industry. The AMPS podcast is very similar in nature and form to that of Tonebenders, but with a slight emphasis toward the UK TV and film industries.

Curating a solid collection of discipline-specific podcasts is key to using them for CPD. Vetting the credentials of the hosts, guests, and topics discussed makes the content much more viable in relation to using podcasts as a CPD tool. The curation process should therefore be considered the first step in effective utilisation of podcasts to enhance your own knowledge base.

Multiple Perspectives, Putting a Nail in the Coffin of Misguided Dogma

Using podcasts as an educational CPD tool can offer a wide range of perspectives on a wide range of issues. Even within a niche field like sound design there are some recurring topics. It is interesting to hear how the guests and hosts alike have tackled various technical and creative challenges in a variety of different ways. While there are certain workflows, tools, and principles that are commonly practiced, it is not unusual to hear how the different practitioners occasionally stray from the norm to serve the greater purpose of enhancing the final sonic results. This can be extremely helpful to cite when fighting any mistaken dogmas around there being only one *right way* to achieve a specific result or undertake a specific task.

It can be comforting to learn that even award-winning professionals come unstuck on their journey toward the finished product. Many of the podcast guests talk about the struggles and failures encountered within the specific projects they are working on. This humanises the creative process in a much more accessible way. Passing on anecdotal evidence of professionals struggling can reduce dejected looks upon student faces, motivating them to pick themselves back up from a creative slump and carry on persevering toward their goals.

The multiperspectivity from the podcasts endows listeners with a rich cumulative overview of the different specialisms in a way that would be difficult to replicate within a single career. These perspectives are often candid and unfiltered, which only adds to the sense of realism, lending even more credibility to the guest's words.

Listen Now, Google Later

Part of not having a deep knowledge of an adjacent niche specialism means that information listeners encounter within the podcasts may be completely new to them. There may be terms, technologies, and workflows that crop up which are either not known to listeners or known in an adjacent context. Passive learning via podcasts will therefore likely create branches of inquiry for the listener to investigate later. When encountering a term, tool, or workflow that is alien to the listener, it is relatively easy to perform a quick Google search to clarify what is being spoken about within the podcast. If the subject matter is too deep a rabbit hole to engage with at the time, an open tab within your browser can always be returned to later.

As a direct result of listening to podcasts, the author has often found himself retrospectively acquiring new knowledge, or knowledge that was new to him. This is an important distinction to make and one which has had a positive impact on the author's subsequent teaching of the discipline. Each lesson learned from listening to specialist podcasts can make any lecturer more knowledgeable about their own discipline. Their skill garden will continue to grow and, over time, they will become even better equipped to advise budding students about contemporary issues as a result.

A Suggested Framework for Turning Passive Learning into Concrete Actions

The author suggests the following simple framework for using podcasts as a tool for CPD. Once suitable podcasts have been curated, the framework revolves around three key areas... *listen and learn, reflect and research, design and adapt.*

The first area is centred around listening to the specialist podcasts. Use the information within them to build up a knowledge base around specific topics previously unknown to the listener. This will help build an awareness of key issues within the field and keep the listener connected to current thinking, practices, or trends within the industry. This foundational stage is relatively basic in nature, but of the highest importance in relation to actioning subsequent curriculum improvements for the students. This stage relies heavily on the concept of 'communities of practice',[8] whereby the individual can infiltrate specific communities that they are not members of via the podcasts.

This second area of the suggested framework integrates elements of Kolb's 'experiential learning cycle',[9] placing specific importance on the themes of abstract conceptualisation and reflective observations. Individual reflection and further independent research into the specific topics are encouraged. Digest the information over time and think about its impact or relevance in relation to your own practice. Reflect on how the information broadly aligns or clashes with your own teaching methodologies. Ask yourself if there are emerging trends that you don't currently include within the curriculum that are worthy of further exploration. This will likely lead to further questions, new research areas, and new branches of inquiry that the individual can explore based on the information contained within the podcasts.

The final area focuses on transforming the passive learning into concrete actions and aligns with Schon's 'reflection for action' model.[10] Using knowledge acquired from the podcasts alongside any additional research undertaken can then inform the design of new learning materials and schemes of work used within classes and the wider curriculum. Where appropriate, new insights and information learned through the podcasts can lead to retrospective adaptation of existing materials. This can potentially enrich current content even further with the inclusion of new perspectives, innovative practices, or provide resources that form the basis of extension opportunities to challenge students further.

Educated (No Longer) Guessing

Due to the overlapping nature of two adjacent disciplines, it is easy to attempt to fill in the blanks by offering an educated guess as to how a specific element was likely achieved. A great deal of value is placed on developing 'active listening' skills within the field of music production education. This skill is the ability to break down what can be heard and reverse-engineer the various sonic components in your mind's ear. The very nature of analysing how recorded sound of any kind was created inevitably leads to a certain degree of speculation.

This is because it is very rare to be able to hear all the elements of a piece of recorded music soloed in isolation. After all, this is not how the original creator of the music intended for it to be consumed, nor is it likely that you have access to the artists, producers, or engineers that worked on the piece. Naturally, this is similar for sound design-based artefacts, both linear (such as TV shows and films) and non-linear (such as video games). One caveat for TV and film is that they can include 'extra features' sections that go behind the scenes in a documentary fashion to educate the viewers, lifting the curtain on how specific elements were created.

Not having a direct firsthand experience of working as a sound designer on TV shows, feature films, or video games left the author to fill in the blanks when students inevitably ask him *how do they make 'X' sound?*. This is not unique to sound design, and similarly themed questions arise from music students. In both cases, the author makes educated guesses to the best of his ability and advises them honestly and accordingly.

Prior to engaging with sound design-based podcasts, the author's internal levels of certainty were vastly different when venturing potential answers for sound design-related questions compared to music production questions. This gap continues to narrow with the lessons learned from each episode consumed. The author has found this to be an important and surprising benefit from using podcasts for CPD, which has had positive manifestations in several unexpected ways.

Connecting the Curriculum to Industry

Undergraduate students, by definition, are in your company to learn new skills, knowledge, perspectives, and to hone their ability to think critically about the subject area they are studying. Even the most talented students do not have all the answers already. Occasionally, undergraduates have a hard time accepting that they should learn about 'X' within the wider curriculum of a degree program.

For example, a minority of sound design students don't see the value in learning about music theory when they aspire to work as professional sound designers. On the surface, it is not completely unreasonable to ask, *why do I need to know about 'X'? It does not directly relate to what I want to do for a living.* However, the wider curriculum team knows the relationship between sound design and music is an important one to understand at a deeper level. Having a working knowledge (at least) of how melody, harmony, dissonance, tonality, scales, rhythms, and timbre all function is an extremely useful skill for a sound designer. However, the word of a lecturer does not always cut it when it comes to credibility within a student's mind.

Being able to link skills and expertise from the curriculum to working professionals from various podcasts can secure much more buy-in from the students. An example of this that the author now cites comes from episode 173 of the Tonebenders podcast, where the host talks with Emmy-nominated supervising sound editor Brent Findley about his work on the TV show Ted Lasso.[11] Findley talks about working closely with the music team to ensure their sound design does not clash harmonically or tonally with the score on the TV show. On the rare occasions that it did, Findley's team adjusted the sound design, placing utmost importance on making sure the combined soundtrack of dialogue, sound effects, background ambiences, Foley, and music all work with the emotional direction of the narrative at all times.

During the Beards, Cats and Indie Game Audio podcast, Marteinsson talks about his initiative 'reel talk', where aspiring sound designers wanting to break into the video game industry send him their showreel (*which can be thought of as the professional audio industry's digital equivalent of a* CV). He proceeds to critique their showreels and gives advice on areas for improvement. This initiative comes up across multiple episodes, and both Marteinsson and McGladdery recount the common pitfalls and weaknesses of recent graduate showreels. They discuss that it isn't the more glamorous, large, bombastic sound effects that are lacking within the work, but rather the smaller sounds, the background ambiences, and the general attention shown to more delicate details that stick out as the biggest weaknesses of the showreels.

Sound design students are inevitably drawn toward creating sounds that are more sonically exciting, such as explosions, weaponry, intergalactic spaceships, monsters, and underwater alien creatures. But what ties these 'sexier' sounds together on screen are the more 'mundane' sounds of cloth tracks simulating movement as the protagonist tries to escape the action, or the subtle sounds of the wind, streams, and the quieting of the wildlife within the forest just before a dragon emerges to unleash its fiery carnage. When giving feedback to help students improve their practice, the author can now point out these 'sonic blind spots' while citing the importance that industry professionals place on such issues.

There are some common music production workflows that would be negligent to omit within the shared classes. Historically, the author found teaching MIDI sequencing and editing workflows to sound design students difficult to make fully relevant. When music production students load up virtual instrument tracks to explore the rich palette of sounds available to them via their MIDI-based keyboards, the benefits are self-evident. Invariably, these classes can appear significantly less relevant to the purist sound designer who does not have a musical background.

However, in one episode of the Beards, Cats and Indie Game Audio podcast, the hosts discuss their love of using MIDI to trigger virtual synthesisers to create 'heads up display' (HUD) sound effects within video games. HUD sounds are often short 'bleep and bloop' type sounds used when playable characters interact with anything technological within a video game. This could be as simple as a menu system to navigate the basic controls of the game, through to the complex interactive hacking of a computer terminal within an action thriller game such as Cyberpunk 2077.[12] As a result, the author has subsequently included some gameplay footage of HUDs in action as material for sound design practice within MIDI sequencing classes, leading to greater engagement from sound design students.

Using podcasts as a passive learning tool for CPD has enabled the author to better demonstrate the concrete links between the job roles that the students aspire to do and the taught curriculum. Using this aggregated knowledge from the podcasts has helped facilitate a change in attitude toward the content, often now invigorating rather than frustrating students. Additionally, it can be reassuring to confirm that the curriculum teaches the right types of skills and concepts to students aspiring to work at the level of the guests within the podcasts.

Connecting Industry to the Curriculum

Being able to link the curriculum to the wider industry is incredibly valuable. So too is linking industrial practice to the curriculum itself. Using the podcasts for inspiration, the author has been able to devise a series of sound design-specific workshops and activities for several classes that run in parallel to the music production activities.

An example of this is a class on recording using stereo microphone techniques. The theory for most of the techniques covered within the class can be applied just as easily to a sound design context as a music production one. The author separated the sound design students into their own group and used a scene from the Bourne Ultimatum[13] to devise a 'loop group' workshop. The task the students had to complete was to record the background crowd ambiences of a busy King's Cross station. By extracting and isolating just the dialogue within the digital audio workstation (DAW) session, the scene feels incomplete and sparse to the viewer.

Using the stereo microphone techniques discussed within the lecture, the students had to set up multiple microphone arrays and record themselves walking around each quadrant of the large live room space, saying the words 'rhubarb' and 'walla'. They repeated this process multiple times to cover each quadrant of the live room and to create an artificial sense of scale. The layering up of these random speech recordings reduces the intelligibility of the words and blurs them into an unrecognisable ambience on aggregate. This process is known as a 'loop group' recording, and the session was inspired by a loop group roundtable discussion in episode 197 of the Tonebenders podcast.

Once completed, the students came back into the studio control room to evaluate the recordings against the different stereo microphone techniques. This gave the students more relevant material to discuss when evaluating the spatial nuances between the different recording techniques. Not only was the class more enjoyable for the students, but hearing these techniques implemented in a discipline-specific and professional context added greater educational value to the session (Figure 3.1).

In an episode of the Beards, Cats and Indie Game Audio podcast, the hosts discuss the process of prototyping sounds for characters and environments within a video game.

Figure 3.1 Stereo microphone techniques 'loop group' workshop.

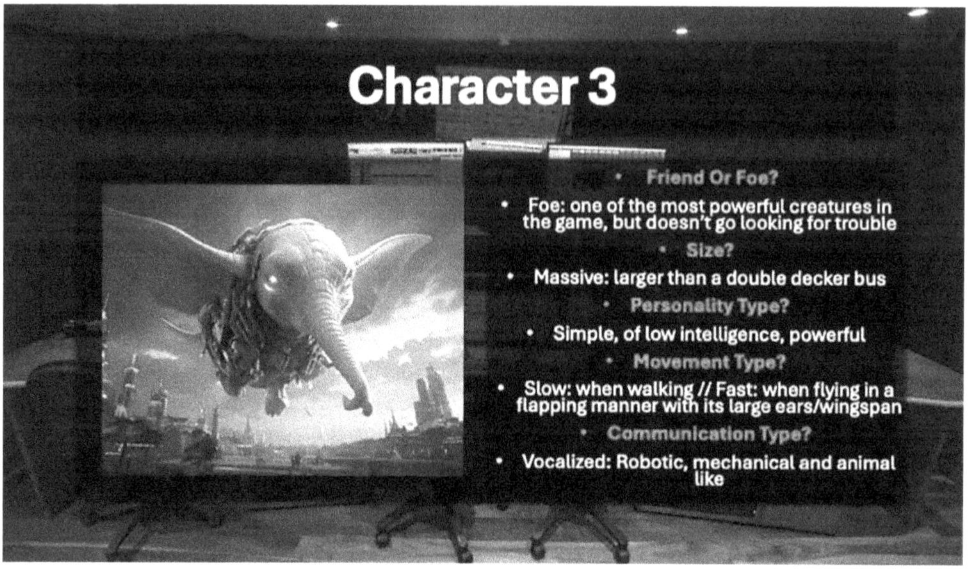

Figure 3.2 An example from the character prototyping workshop.

They talk about the trial-and-error nature of coming up with signature sounds, as well as the iterative process of working with other stakeholders to get feedback on the direction of their designs before they are signed off as complete.

This inspired the author to create a parallel sound design workshop where students were tasked with prototyping the signature sounds of fictitious cyberpunk sci-fi video game characters based on the concept art. The images were accompanied by other descriptors (e.g., size, gait, friend or foe, etc.) to inform the student's 'sonic thinking'. They then had the morning to create their first draft of the sounds before presenting them to the author (acting as the 'client') for feedback. The workshop mirrored the scaled-down industrial practices learnt from the podcast and proved extremely popular with the students, who have asked for the workshop to be repeated next academic year (Figure 3.2).

Listening to various sound design podcasts inspired the author to undertake additional research into the discipline. This has inevitably led toward different discoveries and other areas of the discipline that link to the podcast episodes but are not strictly covered within them. In turn, these have inspired the creation of additional classes and extra workshops for students.

One example of this is the 'Universal Category System' (UCS), which is an initiative to standardise metadata within professional sound library recordings.[14] Many professional sound library companies, such as Pro Sound Effects[15] and Soundly,[16] have adopted the UCS protocol. This is quickly becoming an industry standard and is therefore worthy of coverage within the curriculum for sound design students.

The author subsequently created a two-part workshop around the UCS. The first part consisted of a visit to the woodwork and metalwork facilities at the university, where the wonderful technicians kindly allowed the students to record the industrial machines in action. During the second part, the recordings were used to explore the concept of the UCS, including how to render a bespoke sample library with the correct metadata for professional and commercial use (Figure 3.3).

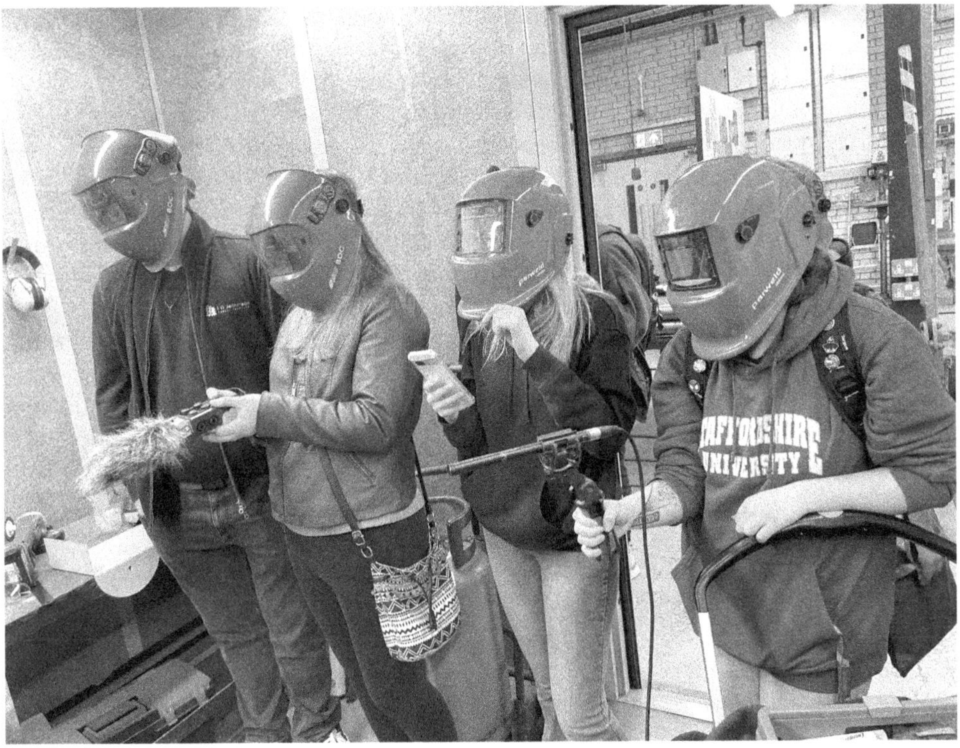

Figure 3.3 Student recording the sounds of the metalwork machinery to use with the UCS in the creation of professional sound libraries. UCS, Universal Category System.

Conclusions on Using Podcasting as a CPD Tool

The author's experiences to date of passive learning through podcasts have been nothing short of transformational. They have helped him grow his knowledge, skills, experience, confidence, and self-belief when teaching the adjacent discipline of sound design. The author has managed to devise more interesting learning materials for the students. Selective areas of the curriculum have been revised and informed by up-to-date industry practices, with students more actively participating as a result. Department funds have been invested in specific sound design equipment such as hydrophones (underwater microphones) that were discussed within the podcasts. Valuable online learning resources that were discovered through the podcast are now shared with students and added to relevant virtual learning environments. This was all facilitated by positive engagement with sound design podcasts.

While this chapter has been written through an autoethnographic lens and centres around the subject of sound design, it can be argued that the author's experiences are entirely replicable within other disciplines. The author's proposed framework aligns with other key theories around informal and incidental learning proposed by Marsick et al.[17] and takes advantage of infiltrating existing communities of practice to gain knowledge and understanding as part of the CPD process. The suggested framework also borrows from well-established ideas such as Kolb's experiential learning cycle and elements of Schon's reflective practitioner model, which are all applicable beyond the author's specific areas of expertise.

Turning passive learning gained from podcasts into active learning through reflection and further research can help shape the design of more engaging and relevant learning materials. The ability to adapt and extend existing materials into adjacent areas of specialism can also be potentially transferable across disciplines. The author feels that this methodology would be particularly beneficial for academics who have not been active within their industry recently, or who are required to branch out beyond their immediate specialism. The author therefore encourages any reader to think about how they could positively utilise podcasts as a powerful CPD tool within their own area of specialism. He sincerely hopes that your future podcast experiences allow you to grow your own skills garden into an orchard of knowledge and wisdom.

Notes

1 Cox, J. (2024) *How Podcasts in the Classroom Can Power Up Learning* Available at: https://www.teachhub.com/teaching-strategies/2024/06/how-podcasts-in-the-classroom-can-power-up-learning/ (Accessed: 25/05/2025).
2 Bohem, C. (2022) *Arts and Academia: The Role of the Arts in Civic Universities (Great Debates in Higher Education)*. Emerald Publishing Limited.
3 Universities UK (2025) *Universities Grip Financial Crisis – But at What Cost to the Nation?* Available at: https://www.universitiesuk.ac.uk/what-we-do/creating-voice-our-members/media-releases/universities-grip-financial-crisis-what (Accessed: 20/07/2025).
4 Muirhead, T., Coronado, R., Morrow, T. (2025) *Tonebenders Podcast* [Podcast]. Available at: https://tonebenderspodcast.com/ (Accessed: 22/04/2025).
5 Marteinsson, M., McGladdery, G. (2025) *Beards, Cats and Indie Game Audio* [Podcast]. Available at: https://indiegameaudio.podbean.com/ (Accessed: 22/04/2025).
6 Peters, O., Shirley, O. (2020) *The Association Of Motion Picture Sound* [Podcast]. Available at: https://www.amps.net/podcasts (Accessed: 22/04/2025).
7 IMDB (2025) *Timothy Muirhead.* Available at: https://www.imdb.com/name/nm1131452/?ref_=tt_ov_st_1 (Accessed: 23/04/2025).
8 Wenger-Trayner, E., Wenger-Trayner, B. (2015) *Introduction to Communities of Practice, Wenger-Trayner.* Available at: https://www.wenger-trayner.com/introduction-to-communities-of-practice/.
9 Kolb, D. A. (1984) *Experiential Learning: Experience as the Source of Learning and Development.* Prentice-Hall.
10 Schon, D. (1983) *The Reflective Practitioner: How Professionals Think in Action.*
11 Apple TV+ (2025) *Ted Lasso.* Available at: https://tv.apple.com/gb/show/ted-lasso/umc.cmc.vtoh0mn0xn7t3c643xqonfzy (Accessed: 31/08/2025).
12 CD Projekt Red (2025) *Cyberpunk 2077* [video game]. Available at: https://www.cyberpunk.net/dk/en/ (Accessed: 31/08/2025).
13 Bourne Ultimatum (2007) [film]. *Directed by Paul Greengrass.* Universal Pictures.
14 Nielsen, T., Drury, J., Paquin, K. (2025) *Universal Category System.* Available at: https://universalcategorysystem.com/ (Accessed: 25/04/2025).
15 Pro Sound Effects (2025) *Pro Sound Effects* [blog]. Available at: https://blog.prosoundeffects.com/ (Accessed: 26/04/2025).
16 Soundly (2025) *Soundly.* Available at: https://getsoundly.com/ (Accessed: 26/04/2025).
17 Marsick, V. J., Watkins, K. (1990). *Informal and Incidental Learning in the Workplace.* Routledge.

Bibliography

A Shell in the Pit (2025) *A Shell in the Pit.* Available at: https://ashellinthepit.com/ (Accessed: 23/04/2025).

A Sound Effect (2025) *A Sound Effect* [blog]. Available at: https://www.asoundeffect.com/blog/ (Accessed: 25/04/2025).

Amberscript (2025) *Dubbing: What Is It, and How Does It Work?* Available at: https://www.amberscript.com/en/blog/what-is-dubbing-and-how-does-it-work/#understanding-dubbing (Accessed: 22/04/2025).

Amnet, V. (2021) *The Foley Grail: The Art of Performing Sound for Film, Games, and Animation.* 3rd Ed. Routledge.

AMPS (2025) *History Of Amps Awards.* Available at: https://www.amps.net/awards/about-awards (Accessed: 25/04/2025).

Apple TV+ (2025) *Ted Lasso.* Available at: https://tv.apple.com/gb/show/ted-lasso/umc.cmc.vtoh0mn0xn7t3c643xqonfzy (Accessed: 31/08/2025).

Articulated Sounds (2021) *Mosasaurus Sound Design - Behind the Scene II [Extinct Animals] - Tibo Csuko [Bruits Studio].* Available at: https://www.youtube.com/watch?v=Df4tks94sOM (Accessed: 26/04/2025).

Audio Field (2024) *Electromagnetic Field Microphone Equipment.* Available at: https://audio-field.com/electromagnetic-field-microphone-equipment/ (Accessed: 25/04/2025).

Audiokinetic (2025) *WWise.* Available at: https://www.audiokinetic.com/en/wwise/overview/ (Accessed: 25/04/2025).

AVID (2025) *Avid Certified Expert: Pro Tools | Post.* Available at: https://www.avid.com/certifications/pro-tools-expert-post (Accessed: 31/08/2025).

Bohem, C. (2022) *Arts and Academia: The Role of the Arts in Civic Universities (Great Debates in Higher Education).* Emerald Publishing Limited.

Bourne Ultimatum (2007) [film]. *Directed by Paul Greengrass.* Universal Pictures.

CD Projekt Red (2025) *Cyberpunk 2077* [video game]. Available at: https://www.cyberpunk.net/dk/en/ (Accessed: 31/08/2025).

Cox, J. (2024) *How Podcasts in the Classroom Can Power Up Learning.* Available at: https://www.teachhub.com/teaching-strategies/2024/06/how-podcasts-in-the-classroom-can-power-up-learning/ (Accessed: 25/05/2025).

Creative Field Recording (2025) *Creative Field Recording* [blog]. Available at: https://www.creativefieldrecording.com/ (Accessed: 25/04/2025).

Dallas Audio Post (2025) *Dallas Audio Post.* Available at: https://dallasaudiopost.com/ (Accessed: 25/04/2025).

Designing Sound (2019) *Designing Sound.* Available at: https://designingsound.org/ (Accessed: 22/04/2025).

EA (2025) *Electronic Arts.* Available at: https://www.ea.com/ (Accessed: 31/08/2025).

Factory (2025) *Factory.* Available at: https://factory.uk.com/ (Accessed: 25/04/2025).

Fitzrovia Post (2025) *Fitzrovia Post.* Available at: https://www.fitzroviapost.com/ (Accessed: 22/04/2025).

FMOD (2025) *FMOD.* Available at: https://www.fmod.com/ (Accessed: 25/04/2025).

Games Developer Conference (2025) *GDC Vault* [archive]. Available at: https://gdcvault.com/ (Accessed: 26/04/2025).

Goldcrest (2025) *Goldcrest.* Available at: https://goldcrestfilms.com/ (Accessed: 25/04/2025).

Gray, C. (2025) *Podcast Statistics & Industry Trends 2025: Listens, Gear, & More.* Available at: https://www.thepodcasthost.com/listening/podcast-industry-stats/ (Accessed: 22/04/2025).

Harrison, T. (2021) *Sound Design for Film.* The Crowood Press Ltd.

IMDB (2025) *René Coronado.* Available at: https://www.imdb.com/name/nm2040879/bio/?ref_=nm_ov_bio_sm (Accessed: 23/04/2025).

IMDB (2025) *Timothy Muirhead.* Available at: https://www.imdb.com/name/nm1131452/?ref_=tt_ov_st_1 (Accessed: 23/04/2025).

iZotope (2025) *RX11 The Definitive Toolkit for Audio Repair.* Available at: https://www.izotope.com/en/products/rx.html (Accessed: 31/08/2025).

Jeffreys, B., Rhodes, H. (2024) *University Cash Crisis to Get Worse Despite Tuition Fee Rise.* Available at: https://www.bbc.co.uk/news/articles/c14lv7e61d3o (Accessed: 22/04/2025).

Jungle Studios (2025) *Jungle Studios.* Available at: https://www.junglestudios.co.uk/ (Accessed: 22/04/2025).

Klei Entertainment (2025) *Klei Entertainment.* Available at: https://www.klei.com/ (Accessed: 23/04/2025).

Kolb, D. A. (1984) *Experiential Learning: Experience as the Source of Learning and Development.* Prentice-Hall.

Lewis, J., Bolton, P., Wilson, S. (2024) *Tuition Fees in England: History, Debates, and International Comparisons.* Available at: https://commonslibrary.parliament.uk/research-briefings/cbp-10155/#:~:text=What%20is%20happening%20with%20tuition,the%202025%2D26%20academic%20year. (Accessed: 22/04/2025).

Marsick, V. J., Watkins, K. (1990). *Informal and Incidental Learning in the Workplace.* Routledge.

Marteinsson, M., McGladdery, G. (2025) *Beards, Cats and Indie Game Audio* [Podcast]. Available at: https://indiegameaudio.podbean.com/ (Accessed: 22/04/2025).

Motion Picture Sound Editors (2025) *Wavelength* [e-magazine]. Available at: https://www.mpse.org/Wavelength (Accessed: 26/04/2025).

Muirhead, T., Coronado, R., Morrow, T. (2025) *Tonebenders Podcast* [Podcast]. Available at: https://tonebenderspodcast.com/ (Accessed: 22/04/2025).

Nabeel, I. (2025) *Indie, AAA, and AA Games: A Comparison.* Available at: https://gameopedia.com/blogs/indie-aaa-and-aa-games-a-comparison (Accessed: 25/04/2025).

Nashville Film Institute (2025) *How Much Does it Cost to Make a Movie? Everything You Need to Know.* Available at: https://www.nfi.edu/how-much-does-it-cost-to-make-a-movie/ (Accessed: 22/04/2025).

Nielsen, T., Drury, J., Paquin, K. (2025) *Universal Category System.* Available at: https://universalcategorysystem.com/ (Accessed: 25/04/2025).

Of S (2024) *Bold and Transformative Action' Needed to Address Financial Sustainability.* Available at: https://www.officeforstudents.org.uk/news-blog-and-events/press-and-media/bold-and-transformative-action-needed-to-address-financial-sustainability-ofs/ (Accessed: 25/04/2025).

Ofcom (2024) *Top Podcast Listening Trends from Our Research.* Available at: https://www.ofcom.org.uk/media-use-and-attitudes/media-habits-adults/top-podcast-listening-trends-from-our-research (Accessed: 22/04/2025).

Perry, C. (2023) *Behind The Sound of The Mandalorian and Obi-Wan Kenobi.* Available at: https://www.skysound.com/c/latest/#behind-the-sound-of-mandalorian-and-obi-wan-kenobi (Accessed: 25/04/2025).

Peters, O., Shirley, O. (2020) *The Association Of Motion Picture Sound* [Podcast]. Available at: https://www.amps.net/podcasts (Accessed: 22/04/2025).

Practera (2025) *What Is the Experiential Learning Theory of David Kolb.* Available at: https://practera.com/what-is-the-experiential-learning-theory-of-david-kolb/ (Accessed: 25/11/2025).

Pro Sound Effects (2025) *Pro Sound Effects* [blog]. Available at: https://blog.prosoundeffects.com/ (Accessed: 26/04/2025).

Schon, D. (1983) *The Reflective Practitioner: How Professionals Think in Action.*

Soho Square Studios (2025) *Soho Square Studios.* Available at: https://sohosquarestudios.com/ (Accessed: 25/04/2025).

Sonnenschein, D. (2001) *Sound Design: The Expressive Power of Music, Voice and Sound Effects in Cinema.* Michael Wiese Productions.

Sound Disposition (2025) *Sound Disposition.* Available at: https://sounddisposition.com/ (Accessed: 25/04/2025).

Sound Ideas (2025) *The Sound Ideas Blog* [blog]. Available at: https://www.sound-ideas.com/blog (Accessed: 25/04/2025).

SOUNDCHICK SFX (2025) *SOUNDCHICK SFX.* Available at: https://www.soundchicksfx.com/about/ (Accessed: 26/04/2025).

Soundlister (2025) *Soundlister.* Available at: https://soundlister.com/ (Accessed: 27/04/2025).

Soundly (2025) *Soundly*. Available at: https://getsoundly.com/ (Accessed: 26/04/2025).
Soundminer Inc. (2023) *v6 On Boarding (Confidential Please)*. Available at: https://www.youtube.com/user/Soundminer/videos (Accessed: 26/04/2025).
The Time Preservation Society (2024) *LOM Elektrouši Electromagnetic Mic*. Available at: https://www.youtube.com/watch?v=rJ18aQY8bW0 (Accessed: 25/04/2025).
Thornton, M. (2024) *Why We Choose 44.1K And 48K? A Historical Look At Audio Sample Rates*. Available at: https://www.production-expert.com/production-expert-1/why-we-choose-441k-and-48k-a-historical-look-at-audio-sample-rates (Accessed: 25/04/2025).
Universities UK (2025) *Universities Grip Financial Crisis – But at What Cost to the Nation?* Available at: https://www.universitiesuk.ac.uk/what-we-do/creating-voice-our-members/media-releases/universities-grip-financial-crisis-what (Accessed: 20/07/2025).
Viers, R. (2008) *The Sound Effects Bible: How to Create and Record Hollywood Style Sound Effects*. Michael Wiese Productions.
Wenger-Trayner, E., Wenger-Trayner, B. (2015) *Introduction to Communities of Practice, Wenger-Trayner*. Available at: https://www.wenger-trayner.com/introduction-to-communities-of-practice/
Wong, B., Chiu, Y.-L. T. (2019) Let me entertain you: the ambivalent role of university lecturers as educators and performers. *Educational Review*, 71 (2). pp. 218–233. ISSN 1465–3397. https://doi.org/10.1080/00131911.2017.1363718 Available at: https://centaur.reading.ac.uk/72350/

Part B

Podcast Creation as a Tool for Teaching and Learning

Chapter 4

Podcasting Is a Versatile Tool for Assessment

Four Ways to Diversify Class Assignments

Joe Cain

Introduction

Podcasting offers versatile tools in higher education for those seeking to diversify assessment, amplify career relevance, and embed active learning.[1] It enjoys the appeal of currency in higher education. Uptake has become vastly simpler owing to rapidly changing technologies and collapsing start-up costs. Podcasting offers a valuable assessment tool for measuring integrated learning and academic reflection within both practice-focused and theory-focused curricula. Podcasting's appeal is bi-directional. Students are energised by its perceived relevance for career and entrepreneurial positioning. Tutors are drawn to the promise of active learning and the potential for embedding core theory and grounding experiences. Also tempting is the perceived snugness of fit between textbook and real-life application. The pedagogical value of podcasting rests in its ability to foster memorable and integrated learning experiences far beyond the final outputs students produce.

Constructive alignment is key for any strategy using podcasting. This student-centred approach emphasises coordination of learning outcomes, teaching activities, and assessment tasks. Consumption of podcasts is widely promoted to accelerate content ingestion and to encourage critical and interpretive analysis, especially when resistance to reading is high or when reading literacy is low.[2] Podcasts aren't simply substitutes for written texts. Fox and Singer propose a general pedagogy for exploiting the intimacy of podcasts to better embed new knowledge.[3] Podcast creation frequently is presented as a problem-based learning experience in which the problem is either the production of tangible outputs, the promotion of creativity, group work, or complex project design and development. Activities involving podcasts also serve simply as one additional set of techniques to practise a diverse range of basic professional skills.[4] Significantly, activities involving podcasts will contribute to oracy education and communicative justice.[5] In all these learning contexts, podcast-making is a means to pursue certain learning outcomes. Podcast making rarely is an educational end in itself. Constructive alignment reminds teaching professionals to keep learning objectives in the foreground when developing assessments: large, all-consuming projects may take a tutor off their instructional goals. Small component projects may deliver the same educational result at a fraction of the effort and time. Simply put, podcasting can easily be added to assessment without fully committing a class to making whole podcasts.

This paper reports on a series of assessment contexts in which elements of podcasting were used to deliver curriculum objectives. Contexts range from consumption of podcasts as texts to component creation to development of standalone major projects. The

DOI: 10.4324/9781003677253-6

ambition is to show a range of contexts in which podcasting as a concept can be used in higher education. The hope is to encourage wider experimentation with podcasting, in whole or part, as a route for many educational destinations.

Educational Context and Terminology

Examples presented in this paper derive from undergraduate teaching programmes in UCL's Department of Science and Technology Studies. These programmes deliver complete three-year BSc degrees as interdisciplinary offers in "history and philosophy of science" and "sociology and politics of science". They also deliver intercalated, or integrated, third-year programmes for MBBS medical degrees as well as service teaching for integrated science degrees (such as Human Sciences BSc, Natural Sciences BSc/MSci, and Arts and Sciences BASc). The department further delivers two MSc degrees in these general domains, plus one MSc degree specialising in science communication, for which podcasting is a component option. For historical reasons, science communication and public engagement are major elements of this department's undergraduate emphasis.

In this educational context, student module selection involves a high degree of disciplinary crossover, meaning tutors are likely to encounter students with training in a variety of science fields, science-adjacent subjects, and across the humanities. English proficiency in reading, speaking, and listening can range from outstanding to remedial.[6] These different ranges present opportunities, as well as challenges, when choosing podcasting for diversifying assessment.

Vague terminology in podcasting confuses expectations and ambitions. A proposal to "make a podcast" can sound both daunting and simplistic. One person will describe a short mp3 dictation of a story as a "mini podcast". Another will expect "podcasting" to involve enough work to deliver a large-scale audio serial supported by a dense promotional campaign. For the purposes of this paper, "podcasting" is treated as an overarching category of work combining components such as content design, content creation, and technical production. It also entails project planning, marketing, distribution, and review of series, their episodes, and component tracks. These activities may occur in the commercial, academic, or entrepreneurial sectors. To improve clarity, Figure 4.1 proposes vocabulary for use with podcasting products, with elaboration in Table 4.1.

Terminological clarity can seem tedious. The benefit of disassembly in this case is an increased clarity about work and deliverables. The lesson of constructive alignment is that not every type of work subsumed in "podcasting" needs to be undertaken for a tutor to develop assessments that take advantage of the medium or that seek a particular learning outcome. What does a tutor want to accomplish when assigning the task, "make a podcast"? The simple truth is that podcasting involves a diverse array of activities. Tutors risk distraction and dilution unless they have a clear understanding of that variety set against the learning objectives they have in the foreground. Conversely, a great many activities can be shed as superfluous by a tutor who judiciously aligns component activities with prioritised learning objectives. Simply put, a narrow focus on segments and tracks might deliver learning outcomes as effectively – possibly more so – compared with whole episodes or series. Likely too, delivery will come at a fraction of the time, cost, effort, and risk.

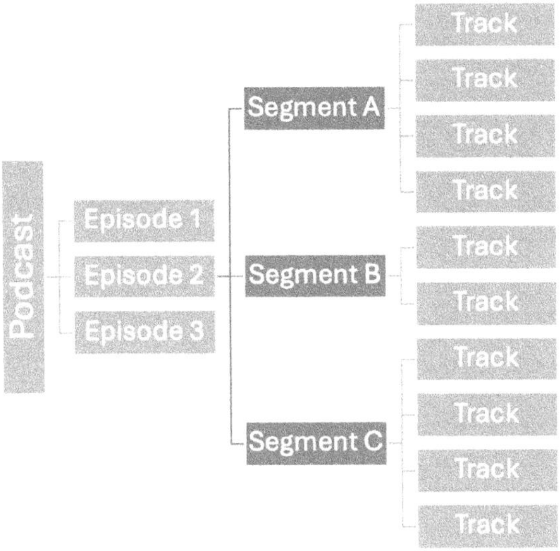

Figure 4.1 Hierarchy of elements in podcasting. **Podcasts** are series of coordinated episodes presented as packages within a unified brand and are frequently available through a common RSS (really simple syndication) feed. **Episodes** are individual, standalone instances of one podcast product, distributed in series, often in a sequence structured for cumulative consumption. Episodes frequently are assembled from **Segments**. **Tracks** are the component blocks of content brought together in multi-track mixing to compose an episode or segment. The purpose of this terminology is to disambiguate the term, "part", which is often used as a synonym for each of these elements.

Table 4.1 Hierarchy of elements in podcasting demonstrated for the podcast "WeAreSTS"

Term	*Definition*	*Example*
Podcast	A series of coordinated episodes presented as a package within a unified brand. One RSS feed normally distributes one podcast. Synonymous with "show" or "serial".	WeAreSTS
Episode	Individual standalone instances of one podcast, distributed in series, often in a sequence structured for cumulative consumption, one episode at a time.	#208 When Fieldwork Goes Wrong Go Public: Adventure in Venezuela #207 Can Generative AI Learn to Love Us? #206 Deaf Sentence – We May Be Losing Our Hearing
Segment	Subdivision of an episode, frequently produced as a modular or standalone product. Synonymous with "section" or "chapter"; comparable with "movement".	"Interview part 1" "Break" "Interview part 2"
Track	Blocks of content used to assemble an episode or segment. Synonymous with "component" or "element".	Narration Music Sound effect

Examples of Assignments Using Podcasting

As an overarching category of work, podcasting offers tutors a diverse range of activities to match specific learning objectives. This section presents a series of examples deployed at University College London (UCL), together with some pedagogical foundations. The purpose of presenting these exemplars is to demonstrate how constructive alignment can help with shedding superfluous work in assignments while also providing clear relationships with learning objectives.

Encourage Active Listening

Listening is an important skill. Oracy is sorely in demand. Assignments assessing listening skills can emphasise two types of activity. One type concentrates on the same analytical and interpretative capabilities expected of critical reading. In podcasting, assignments focusing on listening skills treat individual episodes or series as texts to be understood for their substance. A listener might be asked to focus on evidence, argument, and counter-argument. It might press a listener to identify perspective, assumptions, or narrative logic. It might ask questions about representation, voice, or communicative justice. Listening can result in assignments focusing on description (via synopsis) or analysis (via critique). It can also result in synthesis (via review or justification). Students could be assigned the role of an aggrieved listener submitting a complaint, or they might be assigned the role of a complaints office asked to reply. Generative AI services offer to summarise and encapsulate content. Listening projects can ask about the quality of those products judged against human experience: are those summaries and extracts balanced, fair, and trustworthy?

Listening also can replace reading, especially in a mixed economy of content ingestion that balances reading, listening, watching, and talking. Students consistently report listening to podcast episodes while multitasking, either in domestic work, while travelling, or during exercise. These reports are consistent with broad consumption data nationally and internationally. Module tutors who substitute audio episodes for printed texts open possibilities.[7] The supply of audio material also simplifies adjustments for students in some equity circumstances or with lower levels of reading comprehension. Listening to podcast episodes is not a panacea; it's simply one more tool in the educators' pedagogical box.

Another skill set grounded in listening focuses on the deconstruction and assembly skills of a composer or editor (what are the parts and how do they mix together?). Can a student produce an approximate multi-track diagram similar to Figure 4.2? This takes a step closer to the role of production manager (what is required to create each track, who contributes to the product, and how is "making" accomplished?). Production work can be extended to further listening role-playing in the form of an imagined series producer (who is understood to be the audience, how is genre manifested, how is the product packaged, and what work does the collateral perform?). This work is on paper. At the same time, it provokes imaginative play, and this can be used to extend learning, such as through producing similar content in original settings.

In a module at UCL, students used podcast episodes for an active listening exercise. It was timed to be due roughly 25% into the module timeline. It carried a non-trivial 20% weighting towards the final mark in the module. Students were required to select one episode from a prescribed list of podcast shows, and then produce a critical analysis of

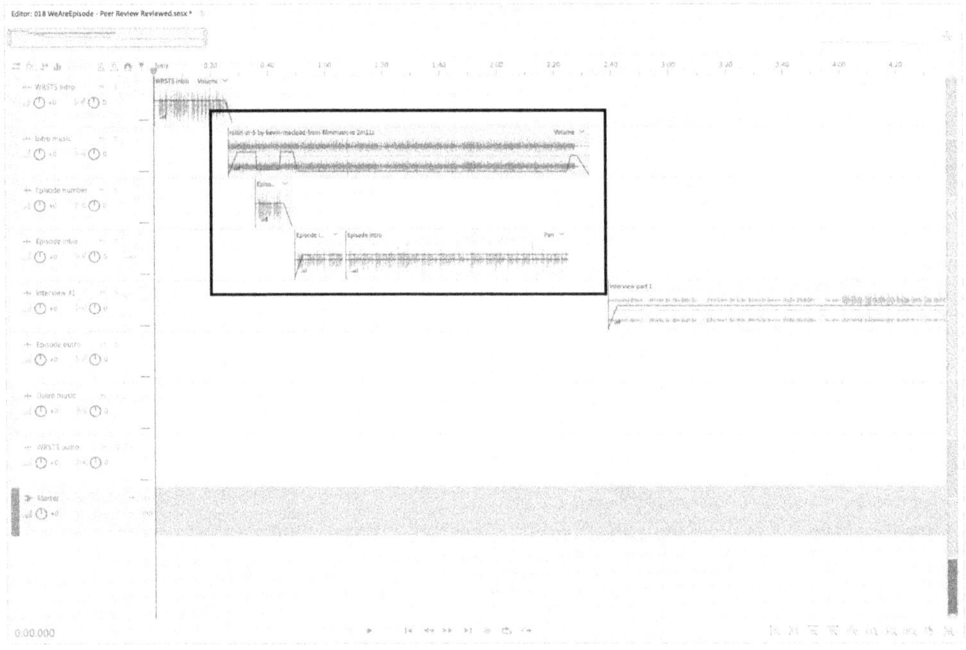

Figure 4.2 Multi-track display showing partial mix for an episode of WeAreSTS. Tracks 2–4 combine to form one Segment, in this case "Episode intro". This combines one track of music and two tracks of voice. The mixing interface is Adobe Audition.

that episode, prioritising thesis, argument, evidence, and editorial position. In addition, students were required to interpret the episode from the perspectives of a production manager and series producer as delineated above.

The assignment was aligned with learning objectives within the module (Table 4.2) as well as with those for their degrees as a whole. For the latter, it was a straightforward critical-reading-in-practice assignment. For the former, it sought to assess understanding of track creation, multi-track assembly, and story building within an overall focus on structure and composition. Subsidiary rationales for this listening assignment – deliberately set early in the module timeline – were (1) to encourage creative thinking about possibilities for upcoming project work, (2) to create a shared library for comparison later in the module, and (3) to introduce some content relevant to other degree-level learning objectives while embedding some EDI (equality, diversity, and inclusion) values through the curation of titles made available for study.

Make Components

No matter what their structure and scale, whole episodes require a considerable amount of work, much of which takes students beyond the needs of their programme in the moment or their available capacity for extra work in time budgets. One option is to abandon the idea of creating whole episodes and replace it with something else. This section considers options for "making" on different scales and for doing this without compromising learning objectives.

Table 4.2 Aims and objectives for the module, HPSC0161 Podcasting as Science Communication, offered in 2024–2025 academic session in UCL Department of Science and Technology Studies (STS). In this context, "aims" are defined as ambitions or aspirations for those attempting the module, and "objectives" are defined as demonstrable outcomes students should be able to accomplish at the completion of the module

Module aims
During the term, this module aims to: 1 Develop knowledge and critical thinking about podcasting as a medium for communication and engagement about science and technology, including STS 2 Develop skills and techniques required to create podcasts, such as interview techniques, basic storytelling and narration, and core production techniques, such as those appearing on the podcast show *WeAreSTS* 3 Integrate communication theory with practical projects, such as through projects that engage with critical debates around representation, voice, performance, authorship, narrative, post-truth, and topics of current interest 4 Develop skills to evaluate degrees of accessibility, inclusion, and accuracy, as well as production quality and suitability for broadcast 5 Identify and interpret industry trends 6 Identify paths for promoting social and commercial entrepreneurship 7 Identify career paths related to podcasting and other audio-dominant formats
Module objectives
By the end of the module, students should be able to: 1 Create podcast content to a high professional standard and that is suitable for publication 2 Demonstrate creativity and craftsmanship in science communication 3 Demonstrate skills and techniques required to create podcast elements 4 Relate theories of science communication to practical projects, and vice versa 5 Relate podcasting projects to themes in the industry, such as format, audience, voice, representation, structure, effectiveness, and social or commercial entrepreneurship 6 Demonstrate constructive peer dialogue and peer evaluation 7 Demonstrate time-management skills 8 Demonstrate self-reflection and self-improvement skills

Source: Module syllabus <https://profjoecain.net/0161>

One approach is to focus on making component pieces. A podcast episode typically has multiple segments (Figure 4.3). Each segment typically has multiple tracks (Figure 4.2). "Make a podcast" assignments can reduce workload and complexity by aligning their learning outcomes with the production of segments and tracks rather than whole episodes or series.

Focusing on segments and tracks offers options when working in tightly constrained timelines, limited resources, or within narrow learning objectives. For instance, interview skills are key to most podcasting formats, and developing good interview skills is a common learning objective in communication programmes and many social sciences degree programmes. An assignment to secure, record, and edit an interview – submitting the finished segment – can concentrate a student's attention and resources onto the essential learning project without additional loading into the work of distractions or superfluous content. This involves the student with the people and equipment management challenges expected of podcasting work without drawing them in too deeply in the first instance.

As a real-world example, for many years at UCL, science journalism students have been required to create three-minute single-interview pieces focusing on one recent press release or publication from within the institution. The conceit was to work as a serving

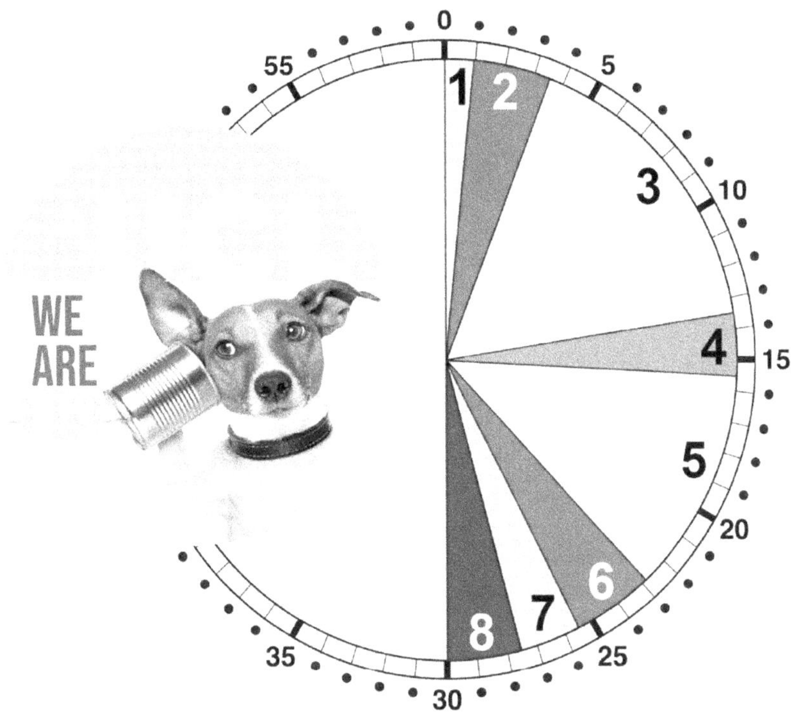

Figure 4.3 Broadcast clock for "WeAreSTS" episode showing sequence of segments within the 29-minute episode structure. This broadcast progresses from Series Intro to Episode Intro to three Segments. It closes by progressing from Episode Outro to Series Outro. One minute is reserved on the 30-minute broadcast clock for broadcaster continuity.

press officer to deliver a programme segment ready for insertion into a magazine-style news and current affairs broadcast.[8] This conceit gave clear structure to the assignment while prioritising specific interview skills with rapid turnaround: find the story, get the interview, edit for the prescribed format, and submit the result. In practice, many students added top and tail music tracks to their product. While these additions were invisible to the assignment's criteria for assessment, they allowed for creative licence and play.

Fractional approaches (create one track or segment) have value for some but not all learning objectives. Alternatives involve sharply reducing running time and curtailing complexity. These aim towards the notion of a "mini podcast" proposed by Cox.[9] As alternatives, consider the format of an advertisement, a trailer, or a public service announcement. In each case, tutors need to be clear on expectations with respect to upper limits of effort as well as minimum expectations. "Mini" projects tend to expand significantly in the hands of certain enthusiastic student personalities, losing the advantages hoped for with original project restraints.

Fractional approaches lend themselves to group projects and collective efforts. At a minimum, a set of students who do well individually but who fail as a group can submit a set of segments or tracks barely held together. With greater degrees of integration, groups can deliver fantastically integrated magazine-style formats or products that appeal to a multitude of audiences. Criteria for assessment can differentiate clearly between the contributions of individuals and those of the collective.

Imagine: Podcasting without Podcasts

Real-world content creation is not an inevitable choice when considering podcasting as a tool in assessment. Pitching and planning for imagined future work are options, just as hypothetical funding applications are common assessment tools in research methods modules. A pitch is a proposal for a product to be developed in the future. Pitching is a form of persuasive, speculative presentation delivered in short- or long-form writing, in-person, or via recorded formats. A pitch can serve as a single assessed item of coursework or as one component of a larger package.[10]

In a second-year module for a cohort of interdisciplinary science students with varied career trajectories, one assignment was to deliver a ten-minute in-person pitch either for a podcast series or for a single, standalone episode within an existing series. Students were presented with a small set of vague themes (e.g. "immersion" or "extreme" or "addiction"), and they were required to develop a concept for one theme in this set. The venue for delivering the pitch was a one-to-one interview setting in which the student spoke directly to the tutor in a conference room, speaking without a script but being allowed a single page of notes as an aid to memory. Visual aids were not allowed, save for a single piece of paper that could be left with the tutor. The student could expect an additional ten minutes of ad hoc questions from the tutor.[11]

The conceit was for students to role-play as a freelance content creator hoping to convince a commissioning editor that their project merited investment. No constraints were placed on budget, location, or personalities, provided decisions were justified in creative terms. No real-world content was created in this exercise, and all proposed involvement was hypothetical. For instance, a pitch for an episode about human travel to Mars might propose interviews with the UK chief science advisor and one or two astronauts, taikonauts, or cosmonauts currently in orbit. Provided the pitch showed knowledge of who those people were and what might be appropriate topics for discussion, those suggestions would be accepted as appropriate and researched, leaving room for more nuanced questions about diversity, dissent, and direction for the conversation. A well-considered project would show a densely structured synthesis of content based on research. A poorly considered proposal would show few connections to relevant knowledge, high levels of chronological description, unrealistic coverage, and weak connections with likely audience interests. Bloom et al.'s hierarchy of education objectives offers a template for differentiation when marking.[12]

Pitching delivers learning objectives associated with project development, design, and structure. It places a premium on audience-centred design and persuasive storytelling. It naturally places a premium on presentation skills, preparation, and project packaging. Students receive guidance on literature screening and sifting, triage, and listener engagement. The speculative nature of pitching also introduces elements of role-play, imaginative projection, and horizon scanning. Ambition and complexity can be rewarded without the need to devote superhuman and disproportionate levels of effort to the project. Practice and peer feedback are additional elements to stress in developmental stages of the pitching project. Moreover, it's hard to underestimate the value to some students of any assignment breaking the routine of examination and technical essay writing.

A supplemental learning objective in this pitching assignment was to develop research skills, especially knowledge collection through digital libraries, sourcing in academic literature, value appraisal and sifting, and annotation for literature review. To support this objective within the conceit of the pitch, students were required to submit at a later date an annotated bibliography offering briefing notes for the commissioning editor to use while promoting the pitch within their own review system. This secondary conceit highlighted the importance of briefing another person for questions about likely strengths and weaknesses in the evidence base for the subject, thus highlighting the importance of review, balance, and appraisal of literature over mere compilation. Undifferentiated lists, machine-generated generic compilations, and garbled light coverage were assessed as poor performances. Also in that secondary conceit, students were encouraged to highlight possible issues associated with sustainability, EDI, and social responsibility: better to alert the commissioning editor to potential flags than to let others do it around the decision table.

The single largest challenge of pitching was the time required to hear pitches, review assessments for consistency, and produce meaningful feedback. Student enthusiasm and world-building were contagious. Scheduling in-person interviews can be challenging when student numbers are large. In this case, online on-camera pitching was rejected as harder to monitor for scripts and inadequate for simulating the high-stakes environment of an in-person one-to-one setting similar to future job interviews. An in-person setting proved sufficiently familiar to all students that no additional support with technique from the tutor was required. Not only was that setting an appropriate challenge for second-year university students, but it also provided a protected space for those who showed low confidence, high anxiety, or relatively weak proficiency in spoken English.

Make Whole Episodes

The case study of whole-episode making derives from HPSC0161 Podcasting as Science Communication, a module designed to deliver learning objectives within science communication and adjacent subjects (Table 4.2). It is an undergraduate final-year module and serves as a supplemental option for students in adjacent interdisciplinary degrees and for students in subject-specific science degrees searching for a science communication option. The module requires no prerequisites.[13]

Module content was divided into four segments over an 11-week term: (1) producing, (2) on-mic, (3) in-studio, and (4) marketing and engagement. "Producing" focused on general principles of product design, including audience and purpose, structure, framing, and project management. The focus was on podcasts, or shows, as a complete product. "On-mic" focused on interview skills, interview formats, interviewee recruitment, best interview practice, and active listening to identify these features of individual episodes. It also demonstrated in-person hardware and online options for recording interactions. "In-studio" offered hands-on practice with production, such as single-track editing, multi-track mixing, and post-production techniques.[14] It also focused on copyright and legitimate sourcing as well as journalism ethics, consent, and documentation. Because skill development with software is time-consuming and highly specific, in-class attention focused on entry points and problem-solving; intermediate skill development was asynchronous through LinkedIn Learning modules. "Marketing and engagement" focused on audience targeting and engagement, discoverability and metadata, promotion, and evaluation.

This four-part content structure allowed a series of supervening threads to run through the module. First, basic themes in communication theory were introduced on demand, complemented by frequent touch points to material from other modules in the department's core programme. Second, EDI and sustainability themes were threaded across each section and reinforced in the criteria for assessment. The purpose was to normalise reflection on impact and consequence for both large and small decisions. Techniques for short-term and sustainable audience engagement were also considered as an entry point to workload management and well-being. Throughout, strategies (purpose, plan, execution, evaluation, reflection) were distinguished from activities (e.g. making a recording or using any one social media platform) to avoid becoming disproportionately bogged down in technical operations and to avoid detached theoretical idealisations.

Students submitted two items for summative assessment, plus a formative progress report. After the "producing" segment of instruction, students submitted a "listening" analysis of the type described above in "Encourage Active Listening" section. For the end-of-term assignment, students were required to submit one podcast episode suitable for inclusion in the department's external-facing series, WeAreSTS. The expectation was a substantial (>20-minute) standalone audio project for the student's own design within loose constraints of that show's genre and structure. As a minimum expectation, a straightforward one-to-one interview mimicking a model episode was offered as a perfectly acceptable project. Done to a high standard, that structure could result in first-class marks. Kept open were options for more complex, multi-interview investigations or an immersive journey of discovery. In addition to the audio product, students were required to submit metadata and production notes for their episode, ready for use by the hypothetical producer. That information was required via an in-real-life episode template from WeAreSTS. The pedagogical purpose of the additional text was to balance the skills of episode making with the skills of show making, especially applying the fourth segment of content in the module (marketing and engagement).[15]

Nudging students through project management was important. At the midpoint of the module, students submitted a five-minute filmed reflection on progress to date, highlighting concerns and asking for help where needed. This was formative. The primary pedagogical purposes of the work-in-progress report were (1) to force project work into student schedules, (2) encourage self-reflection, (3) identify projects that are wildly off track, overambitious, or severely underdeveloped, and (4) provide supporting guidance and problem-solving. A secondary pedagogical purpose was to further student experience with creating recorded messages in the context of work, as these are increasingly used to screen applicants for entry-level positions.

Career themes were introduced in each content section, including analysis of live job advertisements and the skills required to pursue those opportunities, creating touchpoints to local careers resources.[16] Most podcasting-specific advertisements offered freelance positions supporting industry projects or side-hustle enhancements within a portfolio career. Strategies to enhance institutional and corporate communications roles were discussed as well. The overall career philosophy was that podcasting was unlikely to offer a paid career in itself. But it, as well as associated content creation, could be part of a portfolio that improved employability, opportunity, and distinction. Inversely, podcasting was also presented as a means for demonstrating component skills in ways that stood out from competitors in a subject-specific job market.

Generative AI was treated as a positive set of resources in this project, within limits. Students were actively encouraged to experiment with AI-supported tools, acknowledging and reflecting on value as they proceeded. Surprisingly, in the experience of this project, some academically weak students proved highly competent with GenAI resources and nicely flipping relationships during group interactions as novices scrambled to catch up. Ultimately, individual students were held responsible for their final products regardless of the technology deployed, just as any content creator would be held responsible in a professional setting. Generative AI technologies proved especially helpful for students experimenting with idea generation, transcription-based audio editing, and metadata generation. It proved a hindrance for students attempting text-to-voice content and clipping for social media, as neither technology seemed sufficiently advanced in the moment (November 2024) to present an improvement over (even poor) human-driven work. Emerging technologies were demonstrated in the classroom within an overall strategy of experimentation and reflection.[17]

The largest concern arising in the episode-making project was authenticity, especially for interviews. Four routes dominated alternatives to doing the work as envisioned by the tutor: (1) hire a freelancer content creator to work as a ghost, (2) use automated voices to mimic an interview that did not take place, (3) use imposters to act the part of an interviewee, and (4) clip audio from pre-existing content. Each was observed, with clipping and imposters (in most cases, asking a friend to impersonate an "expert") dominant in the final products. Students sometimes requested the use of automated voices as a replacement for narration, citing their own lack of confidence in spoken English or citing fear of discrimination in marking for remedial skills. For voiceover tracks, this was allowed, but choices made when creating those tracks were interrogated. Tutors might consider how all students might benefit from experience with these technologies, as well as translation tools normally ignored by English-only students. These tools are now ubiquitous in multi-lingual environments, and English-only students do themselves no favours by ignoring their facilitating value.

As promised, several student projects met a standard sufficient for distribution as WeAreSTS episodes.[18] Others might have progressed to broadcast but were held back on minor grounds, such as withdrawn permission from interviewees, rights management issues, or failure to deliver revisions.

Conclusion: Where's the Theory?

Practical work in content creation frequently receives criticism for an overemphasis on making and an underemphasis on critical reflection and integration with theory. This criticism seems a little more than misplaced prioritisation of an academic self by the critic. Easily, project work can be designed to explicitly draw students into critical description, analysis, and synthesis, or to have them reflect upon a project's relevance to theory. For instance, programme notes can be written to develop relationships with specific clusters of content, methodological insights, and theoretical contentions. Proposals can be structured to express an intellectual niche. Reflective statements and self-assessment can assert justifications and rationales. In all, theory can be presented as the scaffolding for practice. Criteria for assessment are easily crafted so they reward whatever balance a tutor selects between theory and practice.

In the same way, marketing and promotion are little more than applied sociology, applied psychology, and applied behavioural science.[19] The practical work of marketing and evaluating podcast series can give focus to students working abstractly in those subjects as much as it can for those using hypothetical examples set within textbooks. There are no intrinsic tensions in podcasting work between theory and practice.

Podcasting has tremendous potential for student-centred learning and for tapping into the soaring ambitions of students to have a voice in a world seemingly uninterested in their future-building imaginations. Tutors can deploy podcasting in assessment without committing vast resources and without overly complicating the job of module delivery. The risks are few. The payoff is potentially considerable.

Notes

1 For discussions of diversifying pedagogy across a wide range of assessments, see Louise Jarvis and Joe Cain. "Diversifying Assessment 1: Essays and Examinations in Undergraduate History of Science." *PRS-LTSN Journal* 2, no. 1 (2002): 24–57. https://doi.org/10.5840/discourse2002219; Louise Jarvis and Joe Cain. "Diversifying Assessment 2: Posters and Oral Presentations in Undergraduate History of Science." *PRS-LTSN Journal* 2, no. 2 (2003): 50–72. https://doi.org/10.5840/discourse20032225; Louise Jarvis and Joe Cain. "Diversifying Assessment 3: Web Projects in Undergraduate History of Science." *Discourse: Learning and Teaching in Philosophical and Religious Studies* 3, no. 1 (2003): 27–40. https://doi.org/10.5840/discourse20033110. On students energised by perceived relevance for career and entrepreneurial positioning, see Michael Prosser and Keith Trigwell, *Understanding Learning and Teaching: The Experience in Higher Education*. London: McGraw-Hill Education, 1999.

2 On constructive alignment, see: John B. Biggs and Catherine So-kum Tang. *Teaching for Quality Learning at University: What the Student Does*. 4th ed. New York: McGraw-Hill Education, 2011. On podcasts encouraging various skills, see: Jennifer Woodward. "Podcasting as Pedagogy: Providing More Than Flexibility During Challenging Times." *Journal of Political Science Education* 18, no. 4 (2022): 614–623. https://doi.org/10.1080/15512169.2022.2102028. Also, Sheridan Center for Teaching and Learning. "Teaching with Podcasts." Brown University. Accessed August 28, 2025. https://sheridan.brown.edu/resources/classroom-practices/podcasts. For the value of surveillance within use and gratification theory, see Cynthia Vinney. "Uses and Gratifications Theory in Media Psychology: How and Why We Make Our Choices for Media Consumption." *Verywell Mind*. Last modified March 6, 2024. https://www.verywellmind.com/what-is-uses-and-gratifications-theory-in-media-psychology-5217572. For academic review of the theory, see Elihu Katz, Jay G. Blumler, and Michael Gurevitch. "Uses and Gratifications Research." *The Public Opinion Quarterly* 37, no. 4 (1973): 509–523. https://doi.org/10.1086/268109.

3 Fox and Singer propose a general pedagogy for exploiting the intimacy of podcasts to better embed new knowledge, in Mim Fox and Jonathan B. Singer, eds. *Podcasting in Social Work Education: A Way Forward for Educators*. London and New York: Routledge, 2024. Compare with Alyn Euritt. *Podcasting as an Intimate Medium*. New York: Routledge, 2023.

4 Presenting podcasting as a generic problem-based learning experience is in the sense of Maggi Savin-Baden and Claire Howell Major. *Foundations of Problem-Based Learning*. London: McGraw-Hill Education/Open University Press, 2004. Comparable advocacy is offered by the Educational Enhancement team at the University of Sussex, who offer podcasting for skill development: audio-visual skills, confidence in speaking and speaking effectively, researching, writing, solving problems, collaborative working, managing time and grabbing attention. See Educational-Enhancement. 2025, "How to Use Podcasts in Your Teaching." University of Sussex. 28 August 2025. https://staff.sussex.ac.uk/teaching/enhancement/support/tools/podcasting. Also see George Robinson. "Power up Your Pedagogy with Podcasts!"

University of Sussex (blog). November 12, 2019. https://blogs.sussex.ac.uk/tel/2019/11/12/power-up-your-pedagogy-with-podcasts/.

5 Commission on the Future of Oracy Education in England. *We Need to Talk: The Report of the Commission on the Future of Oracy Education in England*. London: Oracy Education Commission, 2024.

6 At UCL, enrolling students are required to show evidence of English language proficiency to an advanced standard. The author's direct experience is that, regardless of that requirement, practical English proficiency for any cohort can range from outstanding to remedial. This experience sits alongside often exceptional proficiencies in other subjects, especially when assessed in a home, or first, language. Such ranges of skill present teaching challenges; they also provide opportunities to stretch English-only students towards careers in a global community. Bilingual education works in both directions.

7 As one example of content creation to aid asynchronous ingestion of content, consider "The Sociology of Everything Podcast", hosted by Eric Hsu and Louis Everuss. https://www.sociologypodcast.com.

8 As an example, Professor Jean-Baptiste Gouyon used this technique in HPSC0107 Science Journalism, adapting a technique developed by his predecessor, Professor Steve Miller, and adopted by successors, such as Dr Scott Keir. Samples of single-interview segments are included in episodes of WeAreSTS <https://profjoecain.net/wearests-episodes>. See Episodes #17, #23, and #27.

9 Kirsten Cox. "Teaching with Podcasts: Designing a Podcast Assignment." Utah State University. Accessed August 28, 2025. https://libguides.usu.edu/teaching-with-podcasts/design.

10 Consider the examples promoted by The New York Times (NYT), "Project Audio: Teaching Students How to Produce Their Own Podcasts." April 19, 2018. https://www.nytimes.com/2018/04/19/learning/lesson-plans/project-audio-teaching-students-how-to-produce-their-own-podcasts.html and National Public Radio (NPR), "Teaching Podcasting: A Curriculum Guide for Educators." Accessed August 28, 2025. https://media.npr.org/assets/news/2018/11/teaching-podcasting_FULL-VERSION.pdf. Each includes large "storytelling," "planning," and "brainstorming" components.

11 The module was HPSC0019 Human Sciences and Society for both 2023–2024 and 2024–2025 academic sessions: https://profjoecain.net/0019. The pitch session was recorded as a confidential examination and made available only to other examiners and auditors. The student was offered a copy for their individual session as a personal aid for improving their interview skills.

12 The classic study is Benjamin Bloom, M. D. Engelhart, E. J. Furst, W. H. Hill, and D. R. Krathwohl. *Taxonomy of Educational Objectives: The Classification of Educational Goals. Handbook I: Cognitive Domain*. New York: David McKay Company, 1956, revised and extended in Lorin W. Anderson and Benjamin Samuel Bloom, eds. *A Taxonomy for Learning, Teaching, and Assessing: A Revision of Bloom's Taxonomy of Educational Objectives*. New York: Longman, 2001.

13 Module documentation, including syllabus and assignments, is provided online: https://profjoecain.net/0161. In practice, students received two hours' in-class tuition per week, and they were expected to undertake independent study and skills development for eight hours each week and to research an additional 50 hours over the term for project work.

14 Considerable effort was made to source options free to the user. For instance, Audacity was used to demonstrate editing and mixing. Demo and trial versions were encouraged, too, with appropriate accommodation for their limitations. Students could borrow industry-standard hardware from the department for in-person work. "Phone standard" was the expectation regarding voice quality, so personal smartphones and tablets were deemed acceptable. An important mitigation in assessment was the accommodation for work set against a baseline of resources deemed available to all students.

15 Criteria for assessment are shown in the blank feedback sheets appended to the module syllabus, https://profjoecain.net/0161. Assessment also could use criteria from academic peer review or from new models for interpreting academic standards in podcasting proposed by L. Persohn and S. Branson. "Broadening Legitimacy of Scholarly Podcasting as Knowledge Dissemination: Metrics, Opportunities and Considerations." *Publishing Research Quarterly* 40 (2024): 269–286. https://doi.org/10.1007/s12109-024-10005-5, or Robert O'Connor. "Towards a Framework for Scholarly Podcasting." Paper presented at the Education Through Podcasting Conference 2025 (EPOD), Morley College, London, 2025.

16 University College London (UCL). "Developing Your Employability Skills at UCL." UCL Careers. Accessed August 28, 2025. https://profjoecain.net/ucl-pillars-employability.

17 Such is the current educational reaction against generative AI that many tutors fail to consider its value for their own generation of ideas in the teaching space. Simple prompts can offer thought-provoking responses. For example, consider the prompt: "I want to teach history at university level, and I want to use 'make a podcast episode' as an assignment. Suggest a set of instructions to students AND a description of the underlying pedagogy that a university professor would appreciate to justify the assignment within typical learning objectives for a university degree in history." The result can be a useful starting point for project design.

18 Student projects from this module include WeAreSTS episodes #206, #207, #209 https://profjoecain.net/wearests-episodes.

19 For example, Kevin Mellet. *Marketing: A Sociological Approach*. Cambridge: Polity, 2025, and the impressive podcast, Phill Agnew, *Nudge*. Produced by HubSpot Podcast Network. Podcast, MP3 audio, 2025. https://www.nudgepodcast.com/podcast.

References

Agnew, Phill. *Nudge*. Produced by HubSpot Podcast Network. Podcast, MP3 audio, 2025. https://www.nudgepodcast.com/podcast.

Anderson, Lorin W., and Benjamin Samuel Bloom, eds. *A Taxonomy for Learning, Teaching, and Assessing: A Revision of Bloom's Taxonomy of Educational Objectives*. New York: Longman, 2001.

Biggs, John B., and Catherine So-kum Tang. *Teaching for Quality Learning at University: What the Student Does*. 4th ed. New York: McGraw-Hill Education, 2011.

Bloom, Benjamin S., Max D. Engelhart, Edward J. Furst, Walker H. Hill, and David R. Krathwohl. *Taxonomy of Educational Objectives: The Classification of Educational Goals. Handbook I: Cognitive Domain*. London: Longmans, Green, and Co., 1956.

Commission on the Future of Oracy Education in England. *We Need to Talk: The Report of the Commission on the Future of Oracy Education in England*. London: Oracy Education Commission, 2024.

Cox, Kirsten. "Teaching with Podcasts: Designing a Podcast Assignment." Utah State University. Accessed August 28, 2025. https://libguides.usu.edu/teaching-with-podcasts/design.

Educational-Enhancement. "How to Use Podcasts in Your Teaching." University of Sussex, 28 August 2025. https://staff.sussex.ac.uk/teaching/enhancement/support/tools/podcasting.

Euritt, Alyn. *Podcasting as an Intimate Medium*. New York: Routledge, 2023.

Fox, Mim, and Jonathan B. Singer, eds. *Podcasting in Social Work Education: A Way Forward for Educators*. London and New York: Routledge, 2024.

Jarvis, Louise, and Joe Cain. "Diversifying Assessment 1: Essays and Examinations in Undergraduate History of Science." *PRS-LTSN Journal* 2, no. 1 (2002): 24–57. https://doi.org/10.5840/discourse2002219.

Jarvis, Louise, and Joe Cain. "Diversifying Assessment 2: Posters and Oral Presentations in Undergraduate History of Science." *PRS-LTSN Journal* 2, no. 2 (2003): 50–72. https://doi.org/10.5840/discourse20032225.

Jarvis, Louise, and Joe Cain. "Diversifying Assessment 3: Web Projects in Undergraduate History of Science." *Discourse: Learning and Teaching in Philosophical and Religious Studies* 3, no. 1 (2003): 27–40. https://doi.org/10.5840/discourse20033110.

Katz, Elihu, Jay G. Blumler, and Michael Gurevitch. "Uses and Gratifications Research." *The Public Opinion Quarterly* 37, no. 4 (1973): 509–523. https://doi.org/10.1086/268109.

Mellet, Kevin. *Marketing: A Sociological Approach*. Cambridge: Polity, 2025.

National Public Radio (NPR). "Teaching Podcasting: A Curriculum Guide for Educators." Accessed August 28, 2025. https://media.npr.org/assets/news/2018/11/teaching-podcasting_FULL-VERSION.pdf.

The New York Times (NYT). "Project Audio: Teaching Students How to Produce Their Own Podcasts," April 19, 2018. https://www.nytimes.com/2018/04/19/learning/lesson-plans/project-audio-teaching-students-how-to-produce-their-own-podcasts.html.

O'Connor, Robert. "Towards a Framework for Scholarly Podcasting." Paper presented at the Education Through Podcasting Conference 2025 (EPOD), Morley College, London, 2025.

Persohn, Lindsay, and Stephanie Branson. "Broadening Legitimacy of Scholarly Podcasting as Knowledge Dissemination: Metrics, Opportunities and Considerations." *Publishing Research Quarterly* 40 (2024): 269–286. https://doi.org/10.1007/s12109-024-10005-5.

Prosser, Michael, and Keith Trigwell. *Understanding Learning and Teaching: The Experience in Higher Education*. London: McGraw-Hill Education, 1999.

Robinson, George. "Power up Your Pedagogy with Podcasts!" University of Sussex (blog). November 12, 2019. https://blogs.sussex.ac.uk/tel/2019/11/12/power-up-your-pedagogy-with-podcasts/.

Savin-Baden, Maggi, and Claire Howell Major. *Foundations of Problem-Based Learning*. London: McGraw-Hill Education/Open University Press, 2004.

Sheridan Center for Teaching and Learning. "Teaching with Podcasts." Brown University. Accessed August 28, 2025. https://sheridan.brown.edu/resources/classroom-practices/podcasts.

University College London (UCL). "Developing Your Employability Skills at UCL." UCL Careers. Accessed August 28, 2025. https://profjoecain.net/ucl-pillars-employability.

University of Sussex. "How to Use Podcasts in Your Teaching." Educational Enhancement. Accessed August 28, 2025. https://staff.sussex.ac.uk/teaching/enhancement/support/tools/podcasting.

Vinney, Cynthia. "Uses and Gratifications Theory in Media Psychology: How and Why We Make Our Choices for Media Consumption." Verywell Mind. Last modified March 6, 2024. https://www.verywellmind.com/what-is-uses-and-gratifications-theory-in-media-psychology-5217572.

Woodward, Jennifer. "Podcasting as Pedagogy: Providing More Than Flexibility During Challenging Times." *Journal of Political Science Education* 18, no. 4 (2022): 614–623. https://doi.org/10.1080/15512169.2022.2102028.

Chapter 5

Podcasting in Learning and Teaching

Professional Identity within Pharmacy Education

Connor Thompson-Poole and Sian Williams

Introduction

In the past decade, higher education has been shaped by rapid technological change, shifting student expectations, and the need for more flexible, authentic, and engaging learning practices. Among the digital tools that have gained significant traction, podcasting stands out as one of the most accessible and versatile. What began as a form of entertainment and independent media has become a legitimate pedagogical approach across disciplines, valued for its capacity to deliver content, support reflection, and extend learning beyond the classroom.[1]

The rise of podcasting in universities coincides with wider developments in pedagogy, such as flipped learning, blended learning environments, and the push for authentic assessment. Unlike traditional lecture capture or e-learning resources, podcasts offer an intimate and conversational form of communication, enabling educators and students alike to present ideas through storytelling and personal narrative.[2] This makes podcasting particularly well-suited to fostering engagement and cultivating communities of practice (CoPs), while also supporting innovative assessment strategies which, among other things, have the potential to develop students' digital and communication skills.

This chapter examines podcasting as a means of education and assessment, with a particular focus on student co-creation and the development of CoPs. After a review of the literature on podcasting in higher education, co-creation, and authentic assessment, we present a case study of the MUGHUB (Medicines Use Group Hub) podcast, a staff–student partnership project within pharmacy education at the University of Brighton. We argue that podcasting has the potential not only to enhance learning and teaching but also to embed a culture of shared practice, professional development, and community-building that aligns with the evolving demands of higher education.

Podcasting as an Educational Medium

Podcasts have become increasingly integrated into higher education as both supplementary resources and core components of teaching. A review of podcast use in medical education indicates that learners prefer podcasts to traditional learning methods due to their portability, efficiency, and the integration of educational content with entertainment.[3] Their main strength lies in their flexibility: learners can access episodes asynchronously, replay sections, and fit learning into daily routines such as commuting or exercising. This accessibility supports inclusive education, particularly for students with diverse learning preferences and needs.[4]

DOI: 10.4324/9781003677253-7

Studies demonstrate that podcasts encourage deeper engagement with content through conversational delivery and authentic voice.[5] Rather than passively receiving lecture material, students often perceive podcasts as dialogue, which can foster a stronger sense of connection to both content and presenter.[6] This perceived intimacy is particularly beneficial in large or distributed cohorts where direct staff contact is limited.

However, the effectiveness of podcasts depends on intentional integration into pedagogy. Simply uploading recorded lectures rarely maximises their educational value.[7] Instead, research highlights the need for carefully designed episodes, aligned with learning outcomes, and often accompanied by structured reflection or follow-up activities.[8]

Podcasting and Assessment

Beyond delivering content, podcasting is increasingly recognised as a medium for assessment. Students can create podcasts as part of formative or summative assignments, demonstrating knowledge, critical thinking, and communication skills in an authentic format.[9] Unlike traditional written essays, podcast assessments require students to consider audience, clarity, and engagement, aligning closely with professional competencies in many disciplines.

Podcasting as assessment also reflects the sector-wide move towards "authentic assessment", which emphasises real-world relevance and transferable skills.[10] Tasks such as producing interviews, panel discussions, or explanatory episodes mirror professional practices in communication, journalism, education, and healthcare. For disciplines like pharmacy, where practitioners must explain complex information to varied audiences, podcasting can serve as a practical rehearsal for professional communication.[11]

It is important to recognise that the final produced content may not automatically be authentic due to advances in generative artificial intelligence capabilities and the ability to hide weaknesses in understanding behind performance and editing. However, authenticity in podcasting assessment relies not solely on the finished recording, but on externally observable processes that underpin it – activities such as developing interview questions, scripting explanations, and engaging in feedback and adaptations provide evidence of student effort and understanding. These activities provide students with opportunities to think more about clear communication and enhanced audience engagement, which are key skills for pharmacy professionals.

Student Co-Creation

Student engagement is strengthened when learners are not merely consumers of educational content but active co-creators of knowledge. Bovill and Woolmer (2019) argue that co-creation supports student agency, enhances motivation, and fosters meaningful learning relationships. Podcasting naturally lends itself to co-creation, as episodes can be collaboratively planned, recorded, and edited by staff and students.[12]

Involving students in production encourages ownership of learning and provides valuable opportunities to develop skills in communication, media literacy, and teamwork.[13] Moreover, when students share their lived experiences through podcasting – such as transition challenges, placement preparation, or study strategies – the outputs often resonate more strongly with peers.[14] This authenticity enhances the relevance and relatability of the learning material.

Communities of Practice

The concept of CoPs describes groups who share a concern or passion and who deepen their knowledge through ongoing interaction.[15] Within higher education, CoPs provide a framework for collaborative professional learning, knowledge exchange, and the sustainable embedding of innovative practices.

Podcasting can play a dual role in CoPs: both as a topic of shared practice and as a medium for sustaining dialogue. For example, academics who experiment with podcasting in their teaching may join together to share strategies and troubleshoot challenges to develop solutions. At the same time, podcasts themselves can act as boundary objects that circulate knowledge within and beyond the CoP, extending the reach of practice-based insights.

At the University of Brighton, a Podcasting in Learning and Teaching CoP has been established to connect staff and students across disciplines. This provides a fertile context for the case study explored in this chapter, the MUGHUB podcast, which demonstrates how podcasting can be embedded within healthcare education to support both teaching and assessment.

Staff Engagement and Influence on Teaching Practice

The establishment of a Podcasting in Learning and Teaching CoP at the University of Brighton played a significant role in supporting and sustaining podcasting initiatives such as MUGHUB. Initial reactions from colleagues ranged from curiosity and enthusiasm to scepticism, particularly regarding workload, technical expertise, and assessment standards. These concerns were addressed through open discussion, shared exemplars, and practical workshops that demystified podcast production and assessment.

Over time, the CoP has become a space for sharing practice, troubleshooting challenges, and exchanging ideas across disciplines. Staff have reported that hearing about podcasting in different contexts has helped them reimagine how audio-based approaches might complement their own teaching. For some, this has led to small-scale experimentation, such as incorporating podcasts as supplementary resources; for others, it has informed assessment redesign or collaborative projects with students.

Importantly, participation in the CoP has influenced teaching practice beyond podcasting itself. Conversations about accessibility, student voice, and authentic assessment prompted wider reflection on curriculum design and learning outcomes. While feedback from the community has largely been informal, sustained attendance and continued engagement suggest that podcasting functions as a catalyst for pedagogical dialogue rather than a standalone innovation.

In this way, the CoP has supported both staff buy-in and pedagogical sustainability. By embedding podcasting within a shared culture of practice, the initiative has moved beyond individual enthusiasm and towards a more resilient, institutionally supported approach to innovation in learning and teaching.

Podcasting in Higher Education: Pedagogical Potential

Podcasting intersects with several pedagogical priorities in higher education: accessibility, inclusivity, engagement, and employability. For students who may struggle with dense academic texts or time-limited lectures, podcasts provide flexible entry points into subject material. For staff, they represent a means to humanise teaching, bringing in stories, lived experiences, and professional insights that are often absent from textbooks.

At the University of Brighton, podcasts such as *Changing Spaces* and *Talking about Teaching* illustrate this potential. *Changing Spaces* explored students' transition into, through, and out of university, co-created with students to reflect real experiences of adjustment and belonging. The *Talking about Teaching* podcast, produced through the Learning and Teaching Hub, complements a university-wide programme of seminars and workshops by amplifying academic voices and sharing innovative practice. These projects, while not the central focus of this chapter, provided a foundation for embedding podcasting as a recognised educational practice and for building a cross-disciplinary CoP.

Case Study: The MUGHUB Podcast

Origins and Development

The MUGHUB podcast emerged as part of the University of Brighton's funded Digital Learning Partnerships project between 2021 and 2023. Led by staff in the School of Applied Sciences and developed with student partners, MUGHUB aimed to create an accessible, on-demand resource exploring contemporary issues in pharmacy and medicines use. The project drew on the principles of co-creation, authentic assessment, and community-building.

Conceived and delivered as a supplementary resource, MUGHUB has evolved into a platform that supports both education and professional development. Episodes feature interviews with practising pharmacists across sectors, short educational segments on clinical topics, and peer-to-peer content co-created with students. This variety reflects the pedagogical intention to bridge theory and practice while fostering student engagement.

The MUGHUB podcast is situated within a broader initiative to foster a Podcasting in Learning and Teaching CoP at the University of Brighton. This community connects academics, professional services staff, and students who share an interest in podcasting as pedagogy.

Patrick, a student pharmacist, states that the podcast has

> sparked an interest very early on in my degree to understand what the plethora of different types of pharmacy that exist are and also initiated an interest in understanding more about the worldwide role of pharmacists and led me to do some of my own independent learning about the role of pharmacists in different countries.

Content Themes

The podcast is currently structured around three main strands:

- **Meet the Team:** interviews with pharmacy professionals from community, hospital, GP practice, and national leadership roles.
- **Bitesize Learning:** concise episodes covering placement preparation, research methods, clinical skills, and professional practice tips.
- **Peer2Peer:** student-led episodes focused on transition, revision strategies, and placement experiences.

This blended approach ensures the podcast appeals to a diverse audience of students, academics, and practitioners.

Co-creation was at the heart of the "Meet the Team" interview with the Chief Pharmaceutical Officer for England, Mr David Webb, who was interviewed by student pharmacists. This experience enabled students from different stages in their undergraduate studies to feel empowered in interviewing a senior healthcare leader. From question design and reform to final editing and publicity, students were involved – allowing dialogue around what it means to be a pharmacist and what is next. By asking the questions our student pharmacists want the answers to, this episode has become our most-watched episode and is regularly cited in academic and professional meetings and conferences.

In addition to this, the "Bitesize learning" segments have been tailored towards specific aspects of yearly study – for instance, a series of interviews with academic staff have been conducted to discuss research to support final-year student pharmacists through their research module. This allowed students to engage with material otherwise available in written format through spoken dialogue that can be digested at their own pace.

Student Co-Creation and Assessment

A distinctive feature of MUGHUB is its commitment to student partnership. Student interns were involved in all stages of production, from planning and research to interviewing and editing. This hands-on involvement provided opportunities to develop transferable skills in communication, media production, and teamwork.

When reflecting on the impact of co-creation on their learning – students have stated:

> through my podcast experiences, there is a whole spectrum of complex underlying and development and that for a lot of people their professional identity is intrinsically linked to their own self-image. From discussing different backgrounds and struggles, I have learned that acting as a professional is not just a technical feat but also an emotional endeavour and subsequently the fire has light inside me to want to help future MPharm students to simultaneously embark on their own pharmacist journeys and grow as human beings.

Moreover, the project explored podcasting as a form of assessment. Students created short podcast episodes as part of formative activities, encouraging them to articulate complex concepts in accessible language. For this activity, students worked in groups of two or three to create a public health message suitable for a lay audience. This aligns with authentic assessment principles, offering practice in real-world communication skills essential to pharmacy professionals.

Student feedback from the activity revealed that while some students found the prospect of the activity to be daunting, overwhelmingly students reported it to be an engaging and informative activity.

Challenges and Adaptations

Our approach was informed not only by developments in pharmacy education but also by practices emerging in other disciplines, including medical education, journalism, and education studies, where learner-generated podcasts have been used to assess communication, critical thinking, and professional judgement. These cross-disciplinary examples highlight the importance of assessing process alongside product, particularly when creative outputs are involved.

One key challenge is ensuring the assessment is focused on learning rather than performance alone. A polished podcast episode can obscure uneven contributions, superficial understanding, or the use of externally generated content. To address this, the assessment design was adapted to foreground externally observable stages of production. Students were required to submit preparatory materials, including episode outlines, interview questions, and brief reflective accounts of their individual contributions. In group settings, roles were explicitly discussed and documented, enabling staff to assess both collaborative and individual engagement and offer useful formative feedback on performance and engagement.

Another challenge is related to balancing creativity with academic and professional standards. Students initially expressed uncertainty about how "creative" they were permitted to be within an assessed task. This was addressed by providing clear assessment criteria that prioritised clarity of communication, appropriateness for the audience, and accuracy of content over production polish. In doing so, podcasting was framed not as a departure from academic rigour but as an alternative medium through which disciplinary understanding could be demonstrated.

Challenges, Tensions, and Learning

While student co-creation has been central to the pedagogical approach underpinning the MUGHUB project, it was not without challenges. Students entered the project with varying levels of comfort with public-facing work. For some, the idea of contributing to a podcast, particularly one involving senior professionals, was initially intimidating, raising concerns about authority and expertise.

These tensions were addressed through structured scaffolding. Early activities focused on low-stakes participation, such as collaborative question design and mock interviews, allowing students to rehearse professional dialogue before recording. Group roles were clarified to ensure that all students could contribute in ways aligned with their strengths, whether through research, interviewing, editing, or production support. This flexibility proved important in maintaining engagement and reducing anxiety, particularly for students less confident in spoken communication.

Student feedback indicated that while the process was demanding, it was also perceived as meaningful. Several students reported that their initial apprehension shifted towards a stronger sense of ownership and confidence as the project progressed. Importantly, engagement extended beyond the immediate task: students described seeking out additional information, exploring professional roles independently, and reflecting more deeply on their developing identities as future pharmacists.

These experiences highlight a central tension in co-creative pedagogy: it requires time, trust, and careful facilitation. However, when supported appropriately, co-creation can move students beyond surface engagement towards deeper investment in their learning and professional development.

Impact on Learning and Professional Development

The MUGHUB podcast has had multiple layers of impact. For students, it has enhanced access to contemporary professional perspectives, providing insights into varied career pathways. For staff, it has offered an innovative mode of teaching delivery that complements traditional lectures and workshops.

Key areas of impact include:

- **Accessible Learning:** content available anytime, anywhere, supporting flexible study habits. Where the goal is to create flexibility in learning opportunities for a student body, podcasts are a useful tool.
- **Professional Insights:** exposure to diverse pharmacy career trajectories and role models. The episodes provide students with a point of reference from which to imagine themselves being that kind of person or having a specific type of career.
- **Skill Development:** enhanced communication, digital literacy, and professional confidence for student co-creators.
- **Curriculum Enhancement:** integration of podcast content into teaching sessions and assessment tasks.

Since inception the podcast has gained traction, drawing in close to 2500 plays across episodes and amassing over 200 hours of listening. The PEER2PEER episodes, which represent our venture into YouTube and the addition of visuals into the episodes, have attracted over 300 YouTube views and 250 Spotify listens across the three short episodes. This represents a growing popularity and sustained growth and need for education in multimedia formats for students' varied learning needs.

Discussion

When students are invited to participate not only as consumers of knowledge but also as co-creators of educational content, their sense of ownership and engagement is significantly enhanced. Co-creation through podcasting allows students to shape the direction of learning activities, select topics of relevance, and bring their voices into the academic conversation. This shift from passive to active participation is particularly powerful in disciplines where professional identity formation is critical, as students see themselves not only as learners but as emerging professionals contributing to knowledge exchange.

Podcasting also promotes creativity, both as a valuable skill in its own right and as a catalyst for deeper learning. The openness of the medium invites students to experiment with narrative forms, interview styles, sound design, and ways of communicating complex ideas for real audiences. This creative freedom contributes to higher levels of motivation and investment in learning; indeed, our own project evidenced this, with students describing how the opportunity to design and shape audio content led them to explore topics more fully and take greater ownership of their developing professional identities.

Another opportunity lies in the realm of authentic assessment. Traditional written assignments often prioritise academic conventions over professional communication, yet many graduate roles – particularly in healthcare – demand the ability to explain complex concepts to diverse audiences. Podcasting provides an assessment format that mirrors this real-world requirement. Students who prepare, script, and record podcasts must demonstrate subject knowledge, but they must also consider clarity and accessibility of the information to reflect the communicative demands of practice. In doing so, podcasting encourages creativity and offers a move towards an authentic assessment vehicle that aligns with sector-wide calls for assessments that develop transferable skills. Being a successful pharmacist goes beyond passing the registration assessment and thus diversifying the assessment modalities can encourage better and more embedded learning.

Podcasting also carries particular professional relevance within healthcare disciplines such as pharmacy, where clear and accessible communication is central to effective practice. Within our project, we observed this most clearly with the student-led public health messages used for formative assessment. These tasks provided structured opportunities for students to rehearse key professional behaviours, such as breaking down complex information, anticipating audience needs, and speaking with clarity and confidence. Episodes such as *Meet the Team: Chief Pharmaceutical Officer David Webb* demonstrate how students developed interviewing skills, navigated professional dialogue, and practised responsive questioning. Likewise, the *Peer2Peer* series shows how students articulated placement experiences and clinical concepts for their peers, illustrating the gradual strengthening of their communication and digital literacy skills.

Rather than suggesting podcasting is universally transformative, our evidence indicates that, when structured and supported, podcast production can act as a meaningful rehearsal space for the kinds of communicative practices pharmacy students must eventually perform in clinical and public settings.

Finally, podcasting projects have the potential to contribute meaningfully to community-building within and across institutions. The development of CoPs around podcasting enables academics, students, and practitioners to share expertise, collaborate on innovative approaches, and sustain momentum. For students, these communities offer a sense of belonging and validation of their contributions. For staff, they provide a supportive network to troubleshoot challenges and share pedagogical insights. Cross-disciplinary collaboration further enriches the process, as practices from one field can inspire novel applications in another.

While the potential of podcasting in education is significant, several challenges must be acknowledged. A primary concern is scalability. Podcasting projects often require substantial time and resources, including technical equipment, editing expertise, and staff guidance. For example, preparing interview questions for the *Meet the Team: Chief Pharmaceutical Officer David Webb* involved two student-tutor meetings to prepare a list of suitable questions, which then had to be sent to the CPO's communication team for approval. This required significant planning and time commitments from staff and students alike that go beyond routine teaching tasks. The benefit of this is that it encourages wider student engagement and understanding of their profession and provides an important opportunity to network. However, without adequate support, projects risk becoming isolated exemplars rather than widely adopted practices. For podcasting to become a sustainable element of higher education, institutions must provide infrastructure and training that allow both staff and students to engage without disproportionate workload pressures.

An additional consideration in the use of podcasting for education and assessment relates to ethical and institutional responsibilities, particularly when content is publicly accessible. Podcasting blurs traditional boundaries between classroom activity and public scholarship, raising questions around consent, representation, and professional accountability. In projects such as MUGHUB, where students engage with senior healthcare professionals or discuss aspects of professional identity, careful attention was required to ensure that participants were appropriately prepared and supported. This included clarifying expectations around public dissemination, ensuring informed consent, and guiding students on professional conduct and digital professionalism.

Such considerations highlight that podcasting is not a neutral pedagogical tool; rather, it operates within institutional, professional, and ethical frameworks that must be made explicit. Addressing these dimensions openly not only safeguards students and contributors but also reinforces podcasting as a legitimate and responsible form of educational practice.

Another challenge relates to the digital divide. Although podcasts are typically accessible on-demand and across devices, not all students have equal access to the technology required to create or engage with them. Variations in internet connectivity, device ownership, and digital literacy can create inequities in both production and consumption. Institutions, therefore, need to ensure that podcasting initiatives are supported by inclusive policies and that alternative formats or access routes are available where possible.

The issue of quality assurance also demands consideration. Podcasting is, by its nature, an informal and conversational medium, which can create tension when integrated into academic contexts. Ensuring that podcasts retain academic rigour while also remaining engaging and accessible requires careful design and guidance. Students may need support in balancing creativity with scholarly expectations, such as accuracy of content, critical engagement with evidence, and appropriate referencing.

Finally, the question of sustainability is central. Many podcasting initiatives, including MUGHUB, originate through funded projects or through enthusiastic individuals. While these beginnings are valuable, they often face difficulties in maintaining continuity once funding cycles end or staff move on. For podcasting to realise its long-term potential, it must be embedded institutionally, with recognition in workload models, professional development frameworks, and curriculum design. Without such structural support, there is a risk that podcasting will remain a short-lived innovation rather than a transformative practice.

These reflections align with the wider literature on digital innovation in higher education, which emphasises both the promise of new approaches and the need for systemic embedding.[16]

While the MUGHUB case study demonstrates the value of podcasting within pharmacy education, it is important to acknowledge the contextual factors that shaped its success. Access to institutional support, staff expertise, and student partnership funding all influenced the scope and sustainability of the project. As such, this model may not be directly replicable in all contexts. However, several core principles, such as process-based assessment, student co-creation, and alignment with professional identity formation, are transferable across disciplines and institutional settings.

Educators considering similar approaches may choose to adapt podcasting at smaller scales, for example, by integrating short audio tasks, internal-facing podcasts, or group-based reflective episodes. Recognising these limits avoids positioning podcasting as a universal solution and instead frames it as a flexible pedagogical approach that benefits from thoughtful adaptation. In doing so, podcasting becomes less about technological novelty and more about intentional learning design.

Future work could explore more systematic evaluation of podcasting as assessment, including longitudinal impacts on professional identity development and employability.

There is also scope to investigate how podcasting might intersect with emerging forms of digital assessment governance, particularly in relation to generative AI and academic integrity. As higher education continues to negotiate public-facing scholarship and creative assessment, podcasting offers a valuable site for ongoing pedagogical inquiry.

Conclusion

Podcasting represents a powerful tool for learning, teaching, and assessment in higher education. Its unique strengths – accessibility, intimacy, and authenticity – make it well-suited to supporting student engagement, co-creation, and professional development. The case study of MUGHUB demonstrates how podcasting can be effectively implemented within healthcare education, providing both supplementary learning resources and opportunities for authentic assessment.

More broadly, podcasting gains sustainability and impact when embedded within CoPs. By fostering collaboration between staff, students, and professionals, universities can ensure that podcasting becomes more than a temporary innovation, instead becoming an integrated element of pedagogy and assessment.

As higher education continues to navigate the challenges of digital transformation, podcasting offers not just possibility but potential, and its pursuit requires commitment to co-creation, community, and authentic learning.

Notes

1 Catherine Sutton-Brady, Karen M. Scott, Laurel Taylor, Gerard Carabetta, and Sharon Clark. 2016. "The Value of Using Short-Format Podcasts to Enhance Learning and Teaching." *ALT-J* 17 (3): 219–232. https://doi.org/10.1080/09687760903247609.
2 Graham Stevenson. 2013. "Finding Their Voice: Podcasts for Teaching, Learning and Assessment." In *Improving Student Engagement and Development through Assessment: Theory and Practice in Higher Education*, edited by Lorraine Clouder, Carole Broughan, Steven Jewell, and Graham Stevenson, 223–235. London: Routledge.
3 Jessica M. Kelly, Andrea Perseghin, Alan Dow, Shreya P. W.Trivedi, Adam Rodman, and Justin Berk. July 2022. "Learning Through Listening: A Scoping Review of Podcast Use in Medical Education." *Academic Medicine* 97 (7): 1079–1085. https://doi.org/10.1097/ACM.0000000000004565.
4 Daniela Gachago, Candice Livingston, and Eunice Ivala 2016. "Podcasts: A Technology for All?" *British Journal of Educational Technology* 47: 859–872. https://doi.org/10.1111/bjet.12483.
5 Marco Lazzari. 2009. "Creative Use of Podcasting in Higher Education and Its Effect on Competitive Agency." *Computers & Education* 52: 27–34.
6 Oliver McGarr. 2009. "A Review of Podcasting in Higher Education: Its Influence on the Traditional Lecture." *Australasian Journal of Educational Technology* 25 (3): 309–321.
7 Robin H. Kay. 2012. "Exploring the Use of Video Podcasts in Education: A Comprehensive Review of the Literature." *Computers in Human Behavior* 28 (3): 820–831.
8 Andrew Middleton. 2016. *Reimagining Spaces for Learning in Higher Education*. London: Palgrave Macmillan.
9 Andy Wakefield, Rebecca Pike, and Sheila Amici-Dargan. (2022). "Learner-Generated Podcasts: An Authentic and Enjoyable Assessment for Students Working in Pairs." *Assessment & Evaluation in Higher Education* 48 (7): 1025–1037.
10 Kevin Ashford-Rowe, Jan Herrington, and Coralie Brown. 2013. "Establishing the Critical Elements That Determine Authentic Assessment." *Assessment & Evaluation in Higher Education* 39 (2): 205–222. https://doi.org/10.1080/02602938.2013.819566.

11 Isabella Vainieri, Lisa Thackeray, Saul Hillman, Alejandra Perez, Ruth Roberts, and Elena Panagiotopoulou. 2024. "Evaluating Podcasts as a Science Communication Assessment for Postgraduate Students." *Innovations in Education and Teaching International* 61 (6): 1446–1459.
12 Catherine Bovill, and Catherine Woolmer. 2019. "How Conceptualisations of Curriculum in Higher Education Influence Student–Staff Co-Creation in and of the Curriculum." *Higher Education* 78 (3): 407–422. https://doi.org/10.1007/s10734-018-0349-8.
13 John R. Savery, and Thomas M. Duffy. 1995. "Problem Based Learning: An Instructional Model and Its Constructivist Framework." *Educational Technology* 35 (5): 31–38.
14 Emily Girard, Amanda Punch, and Yobelli Jimenez. June 2024. "A Wellbeing Podcast for Diagnostic Radiography Students." *Journal of Medical Radiation Sciences* 71 (2): 203–213. https://doi.org/10.1002/jmrs.785. Epub 2024 Mar 25. PMID: 38525902; PMCID: PMC11177020.
15 Etienne Wenger. 1998. *Communities of Practice: Learning, Meaning, and Identity*. Cambridge: Cambridge University Press.
16 Diana Laurillard. 2012. *Teaching as a Design Science: Building Pedagogical Patterns for Learning and Technology*. London: Routledge.

References

Ashford-Rowe, Kevin, Jan Herrington, and Coralie Brown. 2013. "Establishing the Critical Elements That Determine Authentic Assessment." *Assessment & Evaluation in Higher Education* 39 (2): 205–222. https://doi.org/10.1080/02602938.2013.819566.

Bovill, Catherine, and Catherine Woolmer. 2019. "How Conceptualisations of Curriculum in Higher Education Influence Student–Staff Co-Creation in and of the Curriculum." *Higher Education* 78 (3): 407–422. https://doi.org/10.1007/s10734-018-0349-8.

Gachago, Daniela, Candice Livingston, and Eunice Ivala. 2016. "Podcasts: A Technology for All?" *British Journal of Educational Technology* 47: 859–872. https://doi.org/10.1111/bjet.12483.

Girard, Emily, Amanda Punch, and Yobelli Jimenez. June 2024. "A Wellbeing Podcast for Diagnostic Radiography Students." *Journal of Medical Radiation Sciences* 71 (2): 203–213. https://doi.org/10.1002/jmrs.785. Epub 2024 Mar 25. PMID: 38525902; PMCID: PMC11177020.

Kay, Robin H. 2012. "Exploring the Use of Video Podcasts in Education: A Comprehensive Review of the Literature." *Computers in Human Behavior* 28 (3): 820–831.

Kelly, Jessica M., Andrea Perseghin, Alan W. Dow, Shreya P. Trivedi, Adam Rodman, and Justin Berk. July 2022. "Learning Through Listening: A Scoping Review of Podcast Use in Medical Education." *Academic Medicine* 97 (7): 1079–1085. https://doi.org/10.1097/ACM.0000000000004565.

Laurillard, Diana. 2012. *Teaching as a Design Science: Building Pedagogical Patterns for Learning and Technology*. London: Routledge.

Lazzari, Marco 2009. "Creative Use of Podcasting in Higher Education and Its Effect on Competitive Agency." *Computers & Education*, 52: 27–34.

McGarr, Oliver. 2009. "A Review of Podcasting in Higher Education: Its Influence on the Traditional Lecture." *Australasian Journal of Educational Technology* 25 (3): 309–321.

Middleton, Andrew. 2016. *Reimagining Spaces for Learning in Higher Education*. London: Palgrave Macmillan.

Savery, John R., and Thomas M. Duffy. 1995. "Problem Based Learning: An Instructional Model and Its Constructivist Framework." *Educational Technology* 35 (5): 31–38.

Stevenson, Graham. 2013. "Finding Their Voice: Podcasts for Teaching, Learning and Assessment." In *Improving Student Engagement and Development through Assessment: Theory and Practice in Higher Education*, edited by Lorraine Clouder, Carole Broughan, Steven Jewell, and Graham Stevenson, 223–235. London: Routledge.

Sutton-Brady, Catherine, Karen M. Scott, Laurel Taylor, Gerard Carabetta, and Sharon Clark. 2016. "The Value of Using Short-Format Podcasts to Enhance Learning and Teaching." *ALT-J* 17 (3): 219–232. https://doi.org/10.1080/09687760903247609.

Vainieri, Isabella, Lisa Thackeray, Saul Hillman, Alejandra Perez, Ruth Roberts, and Elena Panagiotopoulou. 2024. "Evaluating Podcasts as a Science Communication Assessment for Postgraduate Students." *Innovations in Education and Teaching International* 61 (6): 1446–1459.

Wakefield, Andy, Rebecca Pike, and Sheila Amici-Dargan. 2022. "Learner-Generated Podcasts: An Authentic and Enjoyable Assessment for Students Working in Pairs." *Assessment & Evaluation in Higher Education* 48 (7), 1025–1037.

Wenger, Etienne. 1998. *Communities of Practice: Learning, Meaning, and Identity*. Cambridge: Cambridge University Press.

Chapter 6

Pitch, Practice, Podcast

Reflections on a Podcasting Curriculum with Broadcaster Approaches in a University Context

John D'Arcy

Introduction

The course explored in this chapter is a Radio & Podcast Production module, part of the BA Media & Broadcast Production degree at Queen's University Belfast. The course was developed in collaboration with BBC Northern Ireland, in particular BBC Radio Ulster, whose presenters and producers made regular visits to the classroom for guest Q&A sessions. The students of the course include those enrolled on the Media & Broadcast Production degree, as well as students from other degree pathways such as Music & Audio Production, Sound Design and international students enrolled on Study Abroad programmes.

This chapter looks at the course's focus on emulating professional media production practices from commercial industry and public broadcasters, in particular the BBC radio 'magazine' format, as a method for students to explore a variety of talk segment techniques around a central theme or issue whilst experimenting with sequencing and structure. This chapter shares observations around the topics and issues chosen by students as prevalent to their audiences, including broadly themed shows around mental health and environmentalism, as well as specialist shows such as 'Worth the Weight', a female weightlifting podcast and a documentary podcast about the musical sub-genre 'Hyperpop'.

This chapter also looks at the development of assessments based on industry practices, such as pitching, proposals, audio and other deliverables as assessments, as well as skills development through continuous peer feedback around regular formative assessment on mini podcasting tasks.

Reflective commentary from graduates who previously studied on the module offers insights into the student perspective of the teaching and assessment of this podcast production curriculum, highlighting what aspects were most transferable to their current work in the media industry. This chapter also looks at the wider impact of the course through links to the University's student radio station, development of an additional departmental media production team and national student award wins and nominations for a number of the podcasts produced on the course.

This chapter reviews these contexts and experiences with the aim of sharing some learning and best practices for developing podcasting curricula and developing communities of media producers within higher education.

Course Context

In 2017, this Radio and Podcast Production course was developed at Queen's University Belfast as part of the launch of a new undergraduate degree in Media & Broadcast

DOI: 10.4324/9781003677253-8

Production. At this time, the University already had a student radio society dating back to 1953, with its current station, Queen's Radio, established in 2003. It also had a strong track record in teaching and research in the field of creative audio technologies at the Sonic Arts Research Centre and a Master's degree in Broadcast Literacy. 2017 also marked the launch of LawPod, a conversational podcast produced by colleagues and students in the University's School of Law. Following this, the medium of podcasting quickly grew in popularity amongst staff and students, with over 50 different podcast series launched to date. Amongst these are podcasts disseminating research (e.g. 'Bad Bridget', 'A History of Pandemics', 'The Science of Ageing Well') and creating spaces of conversation around education and campus matters ('The Degree Abroad', 'Alumni Anthologies', 'QUB Voices'). There have also been podcasts produced collaboratively between the University's researchers and the BBC, e.g. 'The Crisis Files' and 'QUB Talks 100 – The Partition of Ireland'. This institutional enthusiasm and investment echoes the wide movement across the sector in the growth of 'scholarly podcasts'.[1]

The local and regional podcasting context of Belfast and Northern Ireland predominantly reflects the radio broadcasting industry's public, commercial and community sectors. The major public broadcaster BBC Northern Ireland produces a number of podcasts mainly derived from its radio schedule along with some original regional commissions for BBC Sounds. Reflecting the broader podcasting landscape, the popular formats include long-form interview/conversation shows, documentaries and news reportage. The BBC podcasting format that perhaps most interestingly maps from their radio output is the magazine format.

The magazine format, like any of the others, might cover a broad genre (news, history, comedy) or a niche theme (finance, gardening, cookery), but is made distinctly a magazine show by the sequenced structure of a variety of contrasting short items that explore the broad theme through different topics. The magazine radio format originated in commercial radio in the USA in the 1930s[2] and became popular in the UK on BBC radio, particularly on stations focused on speech-led content, such as Radio 4.[3] The format has translated well to the podcasting era at the BBC. One of the longest-running magazine radio shows, BBC Radio 4's 'Women's Hour', now doubles as a podcast. BBC Northern Ireland creates a range of podcasts in a magazine format including 'Gardener's Corner', 'Cheat Code: Gaming & Tech', 'Inside Business', 'On Your Behalf' and 'Blas Pod' (Irish language).

The commercial radio sector in Northern Ireland (e.g. stations Downtown, Cool FM, U105 and Q Radio) primarily broadcasts music formats on-air, with stations typically podcasting packaged highlights of speech segments and interviews as podcasts. The community sector is similar, though demonstrating more specific community voices as might be expected, e.g. Raidió Fáilte's Irish language and Juice Radio's LGBT community.

It is perhaps due to the prevalence of music formats on commercial and community radio in Northern Ireland that many of these stations and organisations do not heavily pursue podcasting. In their place, independent producers and companies have led in podcasting. Recent independent podcasts in Northern Ireland mostly adopt long interview/conversation formats. The most common topics are news ('BelTel'), history ('The Troubles'), local profiles ('Best of Belfast'), sports ('Kicking Match' and 'The Score') and comedy, e.g. 'The Mudblood Podcast', Shane Todd's 'Tea with Me' and perhaps the longest-running podcast in Northern Ireland, 'General Banter', established in 2013.

Internationally, the podcasting industry exhibits examples of magazine formats in shows produced by a number of commercial outlets (e.g. Wondery, The Ringer, iHeartRadio).

Andok notes that magazine format is just one of the many cross-disciplinary aspects that have converged in the development of the new medium of podcasting.[4]

Course Content

This new Radio and Podcast Production course would become the University's first credited module for podcast production. Aimed at developing a variety of skills in research, writing, presenting, audio engineering and post-production, the course was pitched to students in their second year, building on core technical skills gained in the first year. Aiming to reflect the local and national radio and podcast landscape, the course would cover a range of speech genres, formats and programming structures. Central to this was conversation and storytelling, inviting students to develop skills both in their own verbal delivery of narrative and also in effective interview techniques to invite narrative development from their guests.

The course content was designed to share with students a broad range of examples of podcast and radio production that illustrated the development of creative approaches, technologies and key figures across the history of the media. This included study of early radio history prior to the podcasting era,[5] the broadening of radio practices across media forms in the digital era[6] and the development of the podcasting practices and industry.[7] Whilst many notable examples can be drawn from the USA, the course would also point to local practices in the UK[8] and other nations.[9]

Some key textbooks were adopted to provide definitions for genres of speech programming[10] and technical and practical best practice.[11] Additional texts provided advice and instructions around particular elements of production, such as use of the voice,[12] conducting interviews,[13] scriptwriting,[14] storytelling,[15] use of offensive language[16] and the magazine format.[17]

Through the first six weeks of the 12-week course, the students would be presented with weekly reading lists and listening playlists to build their knowledge of (and taste for) varying genres of podcasts (conversational, storytelling, drama, documentary), honing in on the magazine format in the latter weeks.

Given its adaptability and ability to incorporate a wide variety of topics and segment styles, the magazine format was chosen as a key point of focus for the students to learn from and model within their assignments. The versatility of the magazine format would allow students to explore either a general show theme or a niche topic through a series of items they would produce in-studio (interview, monologue, live performance, game), on-location (interviews, vox pops, mixed packages) and interacting with the audience (listener questions, suggestions, polls etc). Looking at the UK landscape, the magazine format thrives on BBC Radio 4 with shows including Woman's Hour, The Food Programme, You and Yours, Click On, Inside Health, Money Box and The Media Show. Locally, BBC Northern Ireland produces a number of magazine shows including The Arts Show, On Your Behalf, Inside Business, Your Place and Mine, Kintra and Blas.

During the second six weeks, the students would form groups in which they would learn in more detail the step-by-step strategies and techniques for producing a podcast. Weekly workshops would focus on the varying aspects of production (research, writing, interviews, voice, music, sound design, editing, mastering, publishing).

Weekly classes would be structured as a mix of lecture and tutorial/workshop time. The lecture portions would cover the topical focus of the particular weeks as noted above, and the tutorial/workshops would focus on particular tasks or discussions related to the lecture content, e.g. following the lecture covering scriptwriting, the task would be to draft a script for a specific purpose.

On some weeks, tutorials would host a visit from an industry professional from local public or commercial broadcasting. These were typically producers, researchers or presenters. Each year, the course would host two to four industry professionals for these Q&A sessions. These discussions were facilitated by me as module convenor, starting with my guiding the Q&A through talking points related to the course content so far and then opening to students' questions which might dig into specific aspects of media production, or relate to the wider topic of careers within the media. In end-of-semester module evaluations, students highly praised these Q&A sessions for giving them a broader and deeper understanding of both production craft and industry career prospects.

Throughout the course, the students would also be introduced to a range of equipment and software they could use to carry out the production, e.g. digital-audio-workstations like Pro Tools, Reaper and Audacity; our radio studio control room and live room with mixer and microphones; field recorders and reporter mics for location work. Most of the students would have learned to use the software and on-location equipment in their first year, with radio studio engineering skills being the new addition to their technical knowledge. To facilitate this technical learning, on certain weeks during tutorials, students would form small groups and rotate between tasks, allowing each group to get supervised practice time with different studio spaces and types of equipment. Technical walkthrough instruction handouts were also produced to provide students with instructions when practising in the studio in their own time.

To assess their learning, students would undertake three assignments, after which this chapter takes its title:

- Pitch: A proposal for a new podcast series in the magazine format.
- Practice: A portfolio of micro-podcasts about varying aspects of the podcast and radio industry.
- Podcast: Groups choose one of the pitched podcast ideas to develop and produce a pilot episode.

Pitch!

The Pitch assignment was developed to assess the students' learning on the podcasting and wider media industry, with a specific focus on the BBC's commission practices and UK broadcasting regulations. Students present a five-minute proposal for a BBC Sounds podcast series in a magazine format. The restriction to the magazine format provokes students to develop ideas for contrasting items that can cover different sub-topics (relevant to their broader show's topic) within a 30-minute programme structure that can sustain week to week.

The assessment criteria included their presentation communication skills (verbal, pitch-deck, timing, structure and clarity), and most importantly, the concept and detail of the proposed idea. In order to reflect industry practices, these aspects of the criteria were drawn from a professional commissioning brief. During the course's development, these briefs within the podcasting sector were not publicly available, so a range of criteria was drawn from the BBC Radio 4 commissioning brief for speech programming,[18] e.g.:

- Editorial Concept and Innovation (BBC requires 'Editorial' and 'Digital' innovation).
- Audience Strategy (BBC requires 'strategies to appeal to younger and diverse audiences').
- Capacity to Sustain (BBC requires 'efficient production process' and 'sustainability of plan').
- Ability to Comply with BBC Editorial Guidelines[19] and relevant UK legislation and regulations set by UK broadcasting regulator Ofcom, the Office of Communications.[20]

Whilst independent podcasts are not currently subject to Ofcom regulations, we introduce awareness of compliance as best-practice approaches so that students are prepared for related industry work which may be subject to compliance.

Students would develop their pitches during the first five weeks of the module and present them in class during Week 6. One of the main challenges in convening this assessment has been the formative assessment stage. Students are invited to share draft proposals and draft slide-decks in advance for formative assessment and feedback, which often helps students refine their concepts from broader topics to more specific angles, and to develop more detail in their examples for items, audience strategies, potential compliance risks etc. However, for large class sizes, providing timely feedback mid-semester can be very difficult for time management.

Another challenge in facilitating this assignment was scheduling the individual student pitch presentations during and outside of class time. This varied year-to-year depending on the class enrolment size, where large cohort sizes led to the scheduling of additional presentation timeslots and the development of fast and efficient methods for notating and distributing feedback.

During the first five years of the course, there were 150 students who made pitches for this assignment. 63% of students pitched shows for a general audience, with 31% aiming their shows at Youth audiences. Six students specifically targeted middle-aged audiences, one student aimed at an older audience, and one specifically aimed at a young family listenership.

The most popular topics were Music (19 students), Sports (16) and Film & Television (12). Some students pitched shows around current affairs (10), and issues related to specific audiences such as students and teens (10), and women (9). Other topics included History (7), Travel (6), Life Stories/Oral Histories (5), Literature (5), Video Games (4), Arts (4), Horror (3), Cars (3), Fashion (3), Food (2), Environment (2), Spirituality (2), Local Issues, Business, Life Advice, True Crime, Tech, Psychology and Conspiracy Theories (1 each). These pitches typically adopted varying styles of interviews and conversations in their items, though two other shows focused on dramatised segments for storytelling, one adopted a game show format and another proposed a structure based around children's bedtime stories for family listening at bedtime.

Perhaps what I find most interesting about the mix of topics and target audiences for the student pitches was the sense of compromise between what the students perceived to be 'generic' or 'niche'. It often seemed that the initial impulse of many students was to aim for 'broad audiences' as a way to achieve as many potential listeners as possible, but they would later find more innovative ideas by leaning into niche topics where they could develop more specific tangible concepts.

Over the first five years of the course, I noticed a general trend for student pitches to include more unique ideas for their show concepts and branding, and more specific ideas for items. I attribute this to the development of the Practice Portfolio assignment that runs in parallel with the Pitch Proposal assignment, which provokes students to analyse a variety of professional podcast productions, and is detailed below.

Practice!

The second assignment assessed the students in both their understanding of the podcasting landscape and their growing practical skills in the realm of vocal and audio work. The assignment is a portfolio of four micro-podcasts:

- 'A Review' – choose two shows on the same topic and compare production style, hosts etc.
- 'Conversation about Conversation' – interview someone on the topic of what makes a good conversation on a podcast.
- 'A Story' – write and perform an audio narrative based on the true story of a podcast, a network or an individual host of your choice.
- 'Coming up...' – record an introductory segment previewing the items for a prospective episode of an existing magazine radio show or podcast.

For each of the tasks, students were assessed on their vocal performance, their writing style/use of language, the accuracy of their research and the insight and evaluation in their analysis of their chosen podcasts.

This assignment was developed in 2020 following the initial runs of the course where the students produced a short mixed-package for their assessment which could feed into their final show. However, it was observed that whilst the initial approach helped the students develop research into their topic for their final assessment and develop some practical skills, it did not assess the students' learning about the existing media production landscape and it was not conducive to an environment for formative assessment where students would develop their voice and writing skills in advance of the final podcast assessment. Thus, the initial mixed-package assignment was removed and replaced with the Practice Portfolio, aiming to meet these two needs of the course.

The four micro-podcasts are produced week-by-week at the start of the semester, with each tutorial session offering an opportunity for students to listen back to each other's micro-podcasts in small groups and share feedback. I found this approach helped students build their confidence in sharing their work and raised the overall standard of on-mic vocal delivery amongst the cohort. In the end-of-semester module evaluation, students praised this opportunity for reflection on their own tasks and the helpfulness of continual feedback.

In their micro-podcasts, students were invited to analyse existing professional production of their choice, and I found that they analysed a wide variety of both radio and podcast shows, presenters and networks. Whilst some students focused on local programming such as productions by BBC Northern Ireland, local commercial broadcasters and independent comedians, many shared examples of productions based on the students' interests such as sports, gaming, lifestyle etc.

Perhaps the assignment most revealing of the students' personal listening habits, interestingly there were often not many cohorts in which clusters of students chose similar podcasts to analyse. It is not clear whether this relative individuality of chosen podcasts is representative of the students' own personal podcast listening diet, or if the majority of students made concerted efforts to choose distinctive podcasts not found by others. Either way, I feel this variety in their choices reflects the abundance of productions in the podcasting landscape and their appeal to young listeners.

In their analyses, students often discussed aspects they admired about certain podcasts, and often found aspects to critique where they would state how certain productions could be improved in one way or another. They brought this developing taste and insight into their final assignment, the Podcast Production project detailed below.

Podcast!

The final assignment on the course is the Podcast Production – a group project to produce a pilot episode of a podcast aimed at BBC Sounds in a magazine format. This project assesses the culmination of the student's learning through a number of key criteria:

- Editorial Value and Innovation – The overall concept, originality and creativity as well as adherence to BBC editorial guidelines and Ofcom regulations.
- Research – The breadth, depth and accuracy of research into topics covered in the production.
- Structure - The suitability of the format, running order, organisation and sense of flow.
- Audience – The relevance of content to the specified target audience, as well as calls to action and opportunities for interaction.
- Language – The clarity, style and flair of the language used in both scripted and non-scripted speech by hosts.
- Voice – The intelligibility and enthusiasm of hosts.
- Sound – Suitable audio quality, suitability of sound design and music elements – all sounds should be royalty-free or used with permission of the original artist unless falling under 'fair use'.

Whilst the above criteria assess the result of the group production work, students are also assessed on their individual work on the project via three criteria:

- Communication – Communication, Support and Cooperation with other group members.
- Participation – Participation, Engagement and Enthusiasm during planning and collaboration.
- Contribution – Quality of work contributed to the development and production of the project.

Finally, students also submit documentation notes sharing relevant deliverables, production notes and illustrative material, e.g. log-line, target audience, running order, script, signed contributor release forms, screenshots of audio editing, photographs of the production process etc.

To look more closely at the student work produced for this assignment, I will focus on the class of 2022 which produced 13 podcasts on a wide variety of topics. These included lifestyle podcasts: 'Taboo Podcast' (health for young women), 'Saved In Chat' (issues relating to female students) and 'Going Out Out' (student nightlife issues). There were also a number of music podcasts: 'Brutal Measure' (mini features about heavy metal songs), 'Studio Soundbytes' (highlighting local music producers), 'The Music Mixtapes' (local indie music magazine) and 'How To Survive Your Music Exams' (advice for young music students). Other podcasts covered media: 'Cinematic Catastrophes' (b-movies), 'Shrimp Chimpin' (video games) and 'Pat, Peggy & Pisstakes' (soap opera EastEnders). 'Baking Sense' shares items on baking recipes and local bakers, 'Extra Time' covered a recent football tournament and 'Worth the Weight' shared stories and advice from women bodybuilders.

Like all years of the course, the final podcasts produced by the students showcased a mix of fandoms and enthusiasms amongst the cohort. What is notable about this year was the seeming culmination of the development of the module content and skills provision over the initial years of the course, resulting in an overall high level of creativity of the students across the board in 2022. At this stage, the productions all displayed a creative mix of engaging items, ideas, audio production and arguably marketable identities.

Encouragingly, the student podcast productions from the course have been sustaining a relatively high quality, with at least one student podcast production nominated at the Irish SMEDIA Awards each year since 2020.

Reflections and Outlook

The development of the course over its first five years offered many learning points for the provision of podcasting education to take forward into the coming years, when there will no doubt be continual evolutions within the industry.

A key learning point has been around the importance of formative assessment and feedback. Observations from the early delivery module found that students required more practice to build confidence with their writing and their vocal delivery, and that the development of their creative ideas benefited greatly from any opportunities for conversations amongst themselves, the module convenor, teaching assistants and in some cases industry professionals. These observations echo the ethos of the Transforming the Experience of Students Through Assessment (TESTA) framework which emphasises opportunities for formative assessment and quick feedback.[21] The continual development of the Radio and Podcast Production course introduced more formal opportunities for students to submit work-in-progress and receive feedback throughout the course, and helped shape best practice examples for a TESTA study of the broader BA Media & Broadcast Production course at the University.[22] The key takeaway here is that much of the creative and technical skills development in podcasting can happen effectively through short iterative tasks, such as those in the Practice Portfolio assignment detailed earlier.

Another key learning point is in the role of facilities (studio space and equipment) in the learning process and the quality of the final production outputs. The early years of the course included the lockdown periods of the COVID-19 pandemic, and thus the course's lifespan offers an interesting sample of students using various forms of equipment both in campus studios and at home. As might be expected, the overall audio quality of the student podcasts was much higher when they used the recommended microphone setups in the campus studio space. Other setups such as ad-hoc microphones used in other studios, in the field or at home often resulted in hiss, distortion etc. I acknowledge that the ideal setup is not always available and that there are many prohibitive factors to getting time in a great sound studio. I would typically advocate for all aspiring podcasters to get started using whatever equipment is available, and that the most important aspect is ultimately the vocal expression and speech content. However, whilst students showed great capacity for creativity when using a range of different equipment, there was a subtle but noticeable trend for the projects produced in ideal studio conditions to have stronger vocal performance and content. This could perhaps be attributed to a general confluence of skills development, but I wonder perhaps if there is something about the quiet and controlled atmosphere of the sound studio that intangibly elevates the performance of the student to create more expressive vocal delivery and engaging verbal communication.

Adaptability and sustainability are two key areas of consideration, and a key takeaway here is that the course has had to continually adapt to sustain, whether that be responding to the changing radio and podcasting landscape, technological updates or worldwide pandemics. Whilst some courses can be repeated annually with fairly simple replication, teaching this course requires continual update to listening examples, reading, potential tech updates and scheduling. The involvement of industry professionals in visiting Q&A sessions requires continual tending to the relationships with those individuals and cultivating new ones.

Another observation is that the fragmented media landscape at which the students look for examples and inspiration is wide-ranging in terms of style, production values and ethics. Whilst the course in its UK context looks to the BBC and Ofcom for editorial and ethical frameworks and codes, the content that the students often consume does not follow such codes. Thus, it can be hard for students to calibrate towards a sense of 'quality' when so many popular productions lack the characteristics that many professionals and educators would consider to be representative of high quality. The main method of 'quality calibration' I have adopted is group listening, where the class and instructor(s) listen to both professional and student podcasts and critique the strengths and weaknesses of production. These conversations offer interesting insights into the aesthetic tastes and ethical considerations of the students, and allow a knowledge sharing of students with different tastes and experiences to learn from each other and the instructor.

I have found that podcasting in education thrives best when there is a scene of student and staff practitioners all creating and publishing work of varying kinds at the same time. At times when staff are producing podcasts and the student radio station is highly active, a wider impact appears to be that the students enrolled on the Radio & Podcast Production course are more engaged and performing at a higher level. A takeaway for others starting to teach podcasting in educational settings would be to try to build some sort of scene around the podcasting course or try to build the course around some activity already garnering some momentum. Building a podcasting scene helps newcomers network with others, fosters knowledge sharing and invites the learners to engage in more activities which will inspire more of the practice and iteration so crucial to developing as a podcaster.

Looking forward, the course will continue to develop, incorporating emergent research on the podcasting field as it firmly establishes itself as a key player in the media landscape. In just the past two years, the number of relevant texts for podcasting students has greatly expanded including a general textbook[23] and more specific writing on podcast journalism,[24] podcasting in education[25] and commercialisation and 'platformization'.[26] The course may also benefit from increasing transparency within the industry, particularly around commissioning processes.

A final uncertain thought for the outlook of this course, of education in podcasting and of the entire media landscape, is the consideration of generative artificial intelligence tools in the creation of media content. At the time of writing, early examples of AI-generated podcasts are still quite discernible from human-made ones, and cheap or free AI tools readily available to most students cannot create speech content that would pass as their own work, effectively engage an actual listening audience or receive a good grade on a course. However, with the fast rate of technological development, one might predict that we will soon reach a tipping point. We could imagine an AI generative speech processing tool capable of automating scriptwriting and voice synthesis that might be truly convincing to the ear – an effective, engaging listening experience, or indeed perceived as quality evidence of achieving the kinds of learning outcomes we currently use. An immediate fear might be that generative AI might outpace our media literacy, taste and trends. However, I imagine that we listeners, educators and creators will continue to constantly reconfigure our practices of consumption, perception, conception and production of audio media. I posit that educators will continue to adapt resources and facilities to keep pace with the shifting sands of podcasting by keeping open minds and open ears.

Notes

1 Cook, Ian M., *Scholarly Podcasting: Why, What, How?* (Taylor & Francis, 2023).
2 Brown, Michael, "Radio Magazines and the Development of Broadcasting: *Radio Broadcast* and *Radio News*, 1922–1930." *Journal of Radio Studies* 5, no. 1 (1998): 68–81.
3 Starkey, Guy, *Radio in Context* (Bloomsbury, 2014), 119.
4 Andok, Mónika, "Podcast—The Remediation of Radio: A Media Theoretical Framework for Podcast Research." *Journalism and Media* 6, no. 1 (2025): 7.
5 Parker, Linda Busby and Donald Parker. *The Art and Science of Radio* (Allyn and Bacon, 1984); Crisell, Andrew. *Understanding Radio* (Routledge, 1994); VanCour, Shawn, *Making Radio: Early Radio Production and the Rise of Modern Sound Culture* (Oxford University Press, 2018).
6 Edmond, Maura, "All Platforms Considered: Contemporary Radio and Transmedia Engagement." *New Media & Society* 17 (2015): 566–1582.
7 Berry, Richard, "Part of the Establishment: Reflecting on 10 Years of Podcasting as an Audio Medium." *Convergence: The International Journal of Research into New Media Technologies* 22 (2016): 661–671; Llinares, Dario, Neil Fox and Richard Berry, *Podcasting: New Aural Cultures and Digital Media* (Springer, 2018).
8 Berry, Richard, "Radio, Music, Podcasts – BBC Sounds: Public Service Radio and Podcasts in a Platform World." *Radio Journal: International Studies in Broadcast & Audio Media* 18 (2020): 63–78; Berry, Richard, "No Longer the Only Game in Town: British Indies, Podcasts and the New Audio Economy of Independent Production." *Interactions: Studies in Communication & Culture* 12 (2021): 51–64.
9 Hand, Richard J. and Mary Traynor, *Radio in Small Nations: Production, Programmes, Audiences* (University of Wales Press, 2012); Cwynar, Christopher, "More Than a "VCR for Radio": The CBC, the Radio 3 Podcast, and the Uses of an Emerging Medium." *Journal of Radio & Audio Media* 22 (2015): 190–199.
10 Chignell, Hugh, *Key Concepts in Radio Studies* (Sage Publications, 2009).
11 Kern, Jonathan, *Sound Reporting: The NPR Guide to Audio Journalism and Production* (University of Chicago, 2008); Starkey, Guy, *Radio in Context* (Bloomsbury, 2014); McLeish, Robert and Jeff Link, *Radio Production* (Focal Press, 2016); Sauls, Samuel J. and Craig A. Stark, *Audio Production Worktext: Concepts, Techniques, and Equipment* (Focal Press, 2016).
12 Fisher, Jeremy and Gillyanne Kayes, *This Is a Voice: 99 Exercises to Train, Project and Harness the Power of Your Voice* (Wellcome Collection, 2016).

13 Grobel, Lawrence, *The Art of the Interview: Lessons from a Master of the Craft* (TBS, 2004); Beaman, Jim, *Interviewing for Radio* (Routledge, 2011); Hudson, Gary and Sarah Rowlands, *The Broadcast Journalism Handbook* (Routledge, 2018).
14 Evans, Colin Haydn, *Writing for Radio* (Allison & Busby, 1991); Boyd, Andrew, Peter Stewarts and Ray Alexander, *Broadcast Journalism: Techniques of Radio and Television New* (CRC Press, 2012).
15 Abel, Jessica, *Out on the Wire: Uncovering the Secrets of Radio's New Masters of Story with Ira Glass* (Crown, 2015); McHugh, Siobhán. *The Power of Podcasting: Telling Stories Through Sound* (UNSW Press, 2022).
16 Ofcom, *Research Report: Attitudes to Potentially Offensive Language on TV and Radio* (Ofcom, 2016).
17 Barbour, Pamela, "Some Notes on Planning and Producing a Radio Magazine Programme." *Caribbean Quarterly* 47, no. 1 (2001): 69–79.
18 BBC, *BBC Radio 4 Commissioning Brief No: 47138, Round 3, 2020/21: A PROGRAMME ABOUT FOOD* (BBC, 2019).
19 BBC, "BBC Editorial Guidelines 2025." Last modified June, 2025, https://www.bbc.co.uk/editorialguidelines/guidelines.
20 Ofcom, "The Ofcom Broadcasting Code (with the Cross-promotion Code and the On Demand Programme Service Rules)." Last modified June 12, 2025. https://www.ofcom.org.uk/tv-radio-and-on-demand/broadcast-standards/broadcast-code.
21 Jessop, Tansy, Yassein El Hakim and Graham Gibbs. "TESTA in 2014: A Way of Thinking about Assessment and Feedback." *Educational Developments* 15, no. 2 (2014): 21–24.
22 D'Arcy, John. *Use of TESTA to Explore Assessment and Feedback Practices of BA Media & Broadcast Production* (Queen's University Belfast report, 2014).
23 Morris, Jeremy Wade, *Podcasting* (Polity, 2024).
24 Bird, Dylan and Mia Lindgren. "Podcast Journalism: Storytelling Experimentation and Emerging Conventions." In *The Oxford Handbook of Radio and Podcasting*, edited by Michele Hilmes and Andrew J. Bottomley. Oxford University Press, 2023.
25 Lemanczyk, Sarah, *The Podcaster's Manifesto* (Cognella Academic Publishing, 2023).
26 Kammer, Aske and Thomas Spejlborg Sejersen, *The Institutional Development of Podcasting From Participatory Practice to Platform Content* (Routledge, 2025).

References

Abel, Jessica. *Out on the Wire: Uncovering the Secrets of Radio's New Masters of Story with Ira Glass*. Crown, 2015.

Andok, Mónika. "Podcast—The Remediation of Radio: A Media Theoretical Framework for Podcast Research." *Journalism and Media* 6, no. 1 (2025): 7.

Barbour, Pamela. "Some Notes on Planning and Producing a Radio Magazine Programme." *Caribbean Quarterly* 47, no. 1 (2001): 69–79.

BBC. "BBC Editorial Guidelines 2025." Last modified June, 2025. https://www.bbc.co.uk/editorialguidelines/guidelines.

BBC. *BBC Radio 4 Commissioning Brief No: 47138, Round 3, 2020/21: A PROGRAMME ABOUT FOOD*. BBC, 2019.

Beaman, Jim. *Interviewing for Radio*. Routledge, 2011.

Berry, Richard. "Part of the Establishment: Reflecting on 10 Years of Podcasting as an Audio Medium." *Convergence: The International Journal of Research into New Media Technologies* 22 (2016): 661–671.

Berry, Richard. "Radio, Music, Podcasts – BBC Sounds: Public Service Radio and Podcasts in a Platform World." *Radio Journal: International Studies in Broadcast & Audio Media* 18 (2020): 63–78.

Berry, Richard. "No Longer the Only Game in Town: British Indies, Podcasts and the New Audio Economy of Independent Production." *Interactions: Studies in Communication & Culture* 12 (2021): 51–64.

Bird, Dylan and Mia Lindgren. "Podcast Journalism: Storytelling Experimentation and Emerging Conventions" (pp. 420–439). In *The Oxford Handbook of Radio and Podcasting*, edited by Michele Hilmes and Andrew J. Bottomley. Oxford University Press, 2023.
Boyd, Andrew, Peter Stewarts and Ray Alexander. *Broadcast Journalism: Techniques of Radio and Television New*. CRC Press, 2012.
Brown, Michael. "Radio Magazines and the Development of Broadcasting: *Radio Broadcast* and *Radio News*, 1922–1930." *Journal of Radio Studies* 5, no. 1 (1998): 68–81.
Chignell, Hugh. *Key Concepts in Radio Studies*. Sage Publications, 2009.
Cook, Ian M. *Scholarly Podcasting: Why, What, How?* Taylor & Francis, 2023.
Crisell, Andrew. *Understanding Radio*. Routledge, 1994.
Cwynar, Christopher. "More Than a "VCR for Radio": The CBC, the Radio 3 Podcast, and the Uses of an Emerging Medium." *Journal of Radio & Audio Media* 22 (2015): 190–199.
D'Arcy, John. *Use of TESTA to Explore Assessment and Feedback Practices of BA Media & Broadcast Production*. Queen's University Belfast report, 2014.
Edmond, Maura. "All Platforms Considered: Contemporary Radio and Transmedia Engagement." *New Media & Society* 17 (2015): 566–1582.
Evans, Colin Haydn. *Writing for Radio*. Allison & Busby, 1991.
Fisher, Jeremy and Gillyanne Kayes. *This Is a Voice: 99 Exercises to Train, Project and Harness the Power of Your Voice*. Wellcome Collection, 2016.
Grobel, Lawrence. *The Art of the Interview: Lessons from a Master of the Craft*. TBS, 2004.
Hand, Richard J. and Mary Traynor. *Radio in Small Nations: Production, Programmes, Audiences*. University of Wales Press, 2012.
Hudson, Gary and Sarah Rowlands. *The Broadcast Journalism Handbook*. Routledge, 2018.
Jessop, Tansy, Yassein El Hakim and Graham Gibbs. "TESTA in 2014: A Way of Thinking about Assessment and Feedback." *Educational Developments* 15, no. 2 (2014): 21–24.
Kammer, Aske and Thomas Spejlborg Sejersen. *The Institutional Development of Podcasting From Participatory Practice to Platform Content*. Routledge, 2025.
Kern, Jonathan. *Sound Reporting: The NPR Guide to Audio Journalism and Production*. University of Chicago, 2008.
Lemanczyk, Sarah. *The Podcaster's Manifesto*. Cognella Academic Publishing, 2023.
Llinares, Dario, Neil Fox and Richard Berry. *Podcasting: New Aural Cultures and Digital Media*. Springer, 2018.
McHugh, Siobhán. *The Power of Podcasting: Telling Stories Through Sound*. UNSW Press, 2022.
McLeish, Robert and Jeff Link. *Radio Production*. Focal Press, 2016.
Morris, Jeremy Wade. *Podcasting*. Polity, 2024.
Ofcom. *Research Report: Attitudes to Potentially Offensive Language on TV and Radio*. Ofcom, 2016.
Ofcom. "The Ofcom Broadcasting Code (with the Cross-promotion Code and the On Demand Programme Service Rules)." Last modified June 12, 2025. https://www.ofcom.org.uk/tv-radio-and-on-demand/broadcast-standards/broadcast-code.
Parker, Linda Busby and Donald Parker. *The Art and Science of Radio*. Allyn and Bacon, 1984.
Sauls, Samuel J. and Craig A. Stark. *Audio Production Worktext: Concepts, Techniques, and Equipment*. Focal Press, 2016.
Starkey, Guy. *Radio in Context*. Bloomsbury, 2014.
VanCour, Shawn. *Making Radio: Early Radio Production and the Rise of Modern Sound Culture*. Oxford University Press, 2018.

Chapter 7

Teaching Visual Podcasting for Higher Education and Industry Readiness

Nathan Dodzo and Patrice Seuwou

Introduction

Podcasting has evolved from its origins as a niche form of on-demand audio content, content that can be consumed wherever and whenever the user desires, independent of traditional broadcast schedules. This approach emphasises user flexibility and control, illustrating how digital radio expanded reach, interactivity, and relevance[1] into a dynamic, multimedia medium that blends audio storytelling with compelling visual elements. This development has given rise to *visual podcasting*, a format that combines the intimacy and narrative depth of traditional podcasting with the engagement and reach of video.[2] As visual podcasts gain prominence across entertainment, education, and professional sectors, their potential to shape both media consumption and academic and professional sector-specific learning is becoming increasingly evident.

In higher education, this evolution presents both opportunities and challenges. On one hand, visual podcasting offers educators an innovative tool for fostering creativity, critical thinking, and digital literacy. On the other hand, it requires the integration of complex technical skills, creative competencies, and industry-standard production values into the curriculum. For students aspiring to enter the media industry, the capacity to produce high-quality visual podcasts that engage audiences and meet professional expectations is now a critical employability skill.[3] The central pedagogical challenge, and the focus of this chapter, is on how to design and deliver teaching that aligns academic learning outcomes with the realities of professional visual podcast production. Drawing on practice-based teaching within an undergraduate visual podcasting module, this chapter offers a framework for balancing creative storytelling, technical proficiency, and industry relevance. It seeks to contribute to scholarship on media education by demonstrating how iterative, industry-informed teaching strategies can prepare graduates to produce audience-centred content that is both academically rigorous and commercially viable.

Historical and Industry Context of Visual Podcasting

The term *podcast* was first coined in 2004 by journalist Ben Hammersley. However, the concept dates back to 2001 when software developers Adam Curry and Dave Winer created a method for downloading radio broadcasts to an iPod.[4] Initially emerging as 'on-demand radio', early podcasts were audio-only and primarily accessed via desktop computers or portable media players. Their popularity skyrocketed in the mid-2000s, fuelled by developments such as Apple's integration of podcasts into iTunes, a media

DOI: 10.4324/9781003677253-9

management application used to organise and play digital audio and video, particularly on Apple devices; high-profile adoption by public figures; and the emergence of successful independent creators. Over the following decade, the medium matured, aided by the proliferation of smartphones and streaming platforms that made content more accessible and personalised.

Visual podcasting represents a significant shift within this trajectory, blending traditional audio storytelling with video components designed to enhance engagement. Unlike standard YouTube videos, visual podcasts retain the narrative structure and pacing of audio podcasts while adding carefully integrated visual elements, such as in-studio recordings, interview footage, and supporting imagery, to complement the audio experience (*summarised in* Table 7.1). The rise of visual podcasting has been driven by the growing dominance of video platforms, demand for visually enriched content, and diversification of news and entertainment formats. Crucially, both visual podcasting and YouTube video publishing benefit from a low barrier to entry, enabling a wide range of creators to produce and share content with minimal technical or financial constraints. In the case of YouTube, its powerful search engine further amplifies this accessibility by enhancing discoverability and audience reach, making it an especially attractive platform for emerging voices and independent producers.

Industry analysis projects sustained growth in the sector, with the global podcasting market expected to increase from approximately US$32.54 billion in 2025 to US$173.49 billion by 2032, representing a compound annual growth rate of around 27%.[5] Visual podcasts are particularly well-positioned within this expansion, attracting 'video-first' audiences, supporting cross-platform distribution, and enabling richer monetisation strategies through sponsorships, advertising, and merchandise. In addition to these commercial advantages, the integration of live streaming, interactive features, and artificial intelligence (AI) tools is reshaping production workflows. AI-driven solutions now offer tangible efficiencies by automating repetitive tasks and reducing the manual labour traditionally associated with content creation. These include automated topic and script generation, streamlined storyboarding, guest research, and even post-production editing processes. Such innovations not only accelerate turnaround times but also lower

Table 7.1 Summary of the distinctions between visual podcasts, traditional podcasts, and standard YouTube content

Feature	*Traditional Podcast (Audio-Only)*	*Visual Podcast*	*Standard YouTube Video*
Format	Niche, on-demand audio content.	Blends audio storytelling with video components.	Primarily video content.
Structure	Emphasises user flexibility and control.	Retains the narrative structure and pacing of audio podcasts.	Varies, often prioritising visual flow.
Visuals	None (accessed primarily via desktop or portable media players).	Features carefully integrated visual elements to complement the audio experience.	Visuals are the dominant element.
Origin	Emerged as 'on-demand radio'.	Represents a significant shift from the audio-only trajectory.	Generally video-first content.

entry barriers for independent creators, allowing for more agile and scalable production models. Furthermore, AI-enhanced translation tools improve accessibility for global audiences, while advanced analytics refine audience targeting, thereby maximising engagement and reach.

Bridging Industry Standards and Higher Education Learning Outcomes

A central challenge in teaching visual podcasting is to ensure that student-produced work not only satisfies academic learning outcomes but also meets the rigorous expectations of professional media production. In the design and delivery of visual podcasting modules in an academic setting, this is effectively addressed through an intentional alignment of assessment criteria with industry standards.[6]

According to Sauls and Stark (2022), professional evaluation criteria in educational podcasting that reflect standards used in commercial media environments typically include the following:

- Clarity and Consistency of Message: Just as in commercial broadcasting, the podcast must communicate its core message clearly and maintain consistency in tone, style, and purpose throughout episodes.
- Audience Engagement and Relevance: Content should be tailored to the target audience's interests and expectations, with measurable engagement indicators such as listener retention, feedback, and interaction.
- Production Quality: High standards are expected in audio fidelity, editing precision, and overall technical execution, mirroring industry benchmarks for sound design, mixing, and mastering.
- Narrative Structure and Flow: Commercial media prioritises compelling storytelling. Podcasts should demonstrate coherent narrative arcs, effective pacing, and strategic use of suspense or emotional resonance.
- Brand Identity and USP: A strong and recognisable brand presence, including a clear unique selling proposition (USP), is essential for differentiation and audience loyalty, just as it is in professional media.
- Visual Integration (for video podcasts): In visual formats, alignment between spoken content and visual elements, such as graphics, transitions, and camera work, is evaluated for coherence and aesthetic appeal.
- Compliance and Ethical Standards: Adherence to copyright, privacy, and ethical guidelines is critical, reflecting the legal and reputational considerations of commercial media production.

These evaluation criteria mirror those applied in commercial media environments,[7] aiming to prepare students for careers in media or communications. However, it is important to note that direct empirical evidence linking this specific pedagogical approach to graduate employment outcomes remains limited in the scholarly literature. While industry professionals consulted during curriculum development affirmed the relevance of these competencies, rigorous longitudinal studies tracking graduate career trajectories would strengthen our understanding of this approach's long-term efficacy. This represents an important direction for future research in media education scholarship.

This deliberate alignment between academic requirements and professional benchmarks profoundly shapes the pedagogical approach. Teaching emphasises practical skill acquisition alongside a deep theoretical understanding. Students gain hands-on experience in operating professional recording equipment, applying visual composition principles, managing audio quality, and developing a coherent visual identity for their podcasts. This practice-based teaching methodology is designed to replicate industry workflows, ensuring that students are prepared for the demands of the professional world.

Equally vital is fostering the capacity to adapt content for target audiences beyond the academic environment, which ensures that students are equipped to produce work that is competitive and audience-centred in a saturated media market.

Academic and industry-informed feedback mechanisms are integrated throughout the learning process to reinforce this blend of academic and industry standards. For instance, student projects often receive formative feedback that addresses specific issues critical in professional contexts, such as inconsistent branding, audio-visual synchronisation errors, or a lack of visual variety. By engaging in iterative feedback cycles, students refine their technical and creative output, internalising a professional mindset that values precision, coherence, and strong audience connection, and successful habits of iterative self-evaluation and continuous improvement. This process also transforms raw recordings into polished content ready for commercial or public distribution.

Furthermore, preparing graduates for an evolving market requires addressing the challenges and opportunities presented by emerging technology. While AI tools can streamline production workflows through automated tasks like script generation or post-production editing, students must be trained in their responsible integration in academic practice. Appropriate use includes leveraging AI for idea generation or refining grammar and style. Conversely, verbatim copying of AI-generated content or relying on it for critical thinking is strictly prohibited as a form of academic dishonesty. Modules must also anticipate and prepare students for emerging opportunities in augmented reality (AR) and virtual reality (VR), which are opening new possibilities for immersive, interactive podcast experiences.

Pedagogical Framework: Iterative Learning and Production Cycles

A practical approach to teaching visual podcasting is to replicate, as closely as possible, the workflows and quality expectations found in professional production environments. Within this context, *iterative learning*, where students engage in repeated cycles of production, review, and refinement, serves as a core pedagogical strategy. This process mirrors the dynamic nature of industry workflows, in which content is rarely produced in a single pass but instead evolves through structured feedback and continuous improvement.[8] This pedagogical approach is closely aligned with Kolb's Experiential Learning Cycle, a well-established framework where learning occurs through repeated engagement, reflection, abstraction, and application.[9]

Kolb's Experiential Learning Cycle consists of four interrelated stages:

- Concrete Experience (CE): Students encounter or carry out a new experience, or reinterpret an existing one. In visual podcasting modules, this stage involves students actively engaging in the practical steps of content creation, from initial planning and scripting to the actual recording and preliminary editing of their visual podcast episodes.

- Reflective Observation: Students review and contemplate that experience, noting inconsistencies between experience and understanding. This corresponds to students receiving targeted formative feedback from tutors and peers on their produced content. This feedback prompts them to critically analyse their work, identifying technical flaws or creative shortcomings.
- Abstract Conceptualisation: Students formulate new concepts or hypotheses based on their reflections, integrating insights into logical frameworks. At this point, students process the received feedback, internalising the principles of effective visual podcast production (e.g. the importance of consistent audio levels, narrative pacing, or visual coherence) and developing strategies for improvement.
- Active Experimentation (AE): Students apply these conceptual insights to new situations, testing predictions and planning for future actions. This is demonstrated as students implement the learned concepts and feedback into subsequent production cycles, refining their scripts, improving technical aspects, and enhancing overall visual storytelling, thereby demonstrating a direct application of their evolving understanding.

These stages form a continuous cycle: experimentation leads to new experience, which again fuels reflection and conceptualisation, and so on, resulting in increasingly refined understanding and action.

The framework is structured across the semester to ensure scaffolded skill development, as evidenced in the Sample Module Schedule (Table 7.2):

Table 7.2 Sample module schedule

Week	*Content Delivery Focus*	*Key Task/Practical Application*	*Assessment & Feedback*
1	Introduction to visual podcasting, history, and trends	Analysing popular visual podcasts	Individual task: Research a case study for Assessment Part 1
2	Identifying target audience, developing concepts, and content planning	Group task: Write a proposal and develop a pitch presentation	Group formation and role allocation
3	Introduction to podcasting equipment (cameras, microphones, lighting)	Hands-on session with recording equipment	Individual task: Create an equipment checklist
4	Copyright, legal, and ethical considerations	Scripting, storyboarding, and running order creation	Assessment Part 1: Research analysis of case study submission. Submit detailed script for peer review.
5	Creating a cohesive brand identity (logos, typography, style guides) and social media promotional strategies	Develop a brand kit and social media plan	Group task: Develop a brand kit and marketing plan
6	Preparing for interviews, including questioning types (open, probing, closed) and active listening	Conducting mock interviews. Plan and record an interview segment for practice	Formative feedback on interviewing techniques and segment content

(Continued)

Table 7.2 (Continued)

Week	*Content Delivery Focus*	*Key Task/Practical Application*	*Assessment & Feedback*
7	Best practices for audio and video recording, setting up a recording environment	Group task: Record a short practice episode	Formative feedback and Active Experimentation begins
8	Basics of video editing software, cutting, transitions, and effects	Group task: Edit practice episode footage	Continued iteration and refinement
9	Advanced video editing techniques, colour correction, sound design	Revise your edited episode with advanced techniques	Planning for the main episode recording
10	Publishing platforms, distribution strategies, and monetisation options	Set up distribution accounts; create a monetisation plan	Assessment – Content creation of final episode
11	Dedicated production time for final content creation and refinement	Focused production and post-production work	Final episode production continues
12	Finalising technical quality and preparing for showcase	Apply final advanced editing techniques to the episode and submit to a platform to gauge feedback	Submission preparation and final checks
13	Finalise the episode ready for submission	Final submission to a platform to gauge feedback	Assessment Part 2: Present final podcast episode and submit individual reflection

The module structure ensures that CE involves practical steps, such as the hands-on session with recording equipment in Week 3. AE is deeply embedded, with students recording and refining practice episodes between Week 7 and Week 9. This production structure ensures that skill development is grounded in real-time problem-solving. Examples from student projects underscore that embedding structured review points enables students to see tangible improvements over time.

Beyond skill acquisition, iterative learning fosters reflective practice, a hallmark of both academic and professional development. By analysing their work against industry exemplars and peer feedback, students begin to internalise professional-quality benchmarks and adapt their creative strategies accordingly. This approach not only enhances technical competency but also builds resilience, adaptability, and collaborative problem-solving skills, attributes highly valued in the media sector.[10]

Core Components of Teaching Visual Podcasting

Teaching visual podcasting in higher education requires the integration of technical expertise, creative storytelling, and professional media standards into a coherent curriculum. The production process is broken down into clearly defined stages, each offering opportunities for practical skill development supported by theoretical understanding. This section outlines the core components of an industry-aligned teaching framework, summarised in Table 7.3.

Table 7.3 Summary of core components in teaching visual podcasting. SEO, search engine optimisation

Component	*Key Focus Areas*	*Industry Relevance*
Planning and concept development	Defining purpose, target audience analysis (demographics & psychographics), USP creation, content strategy, storytelling techniques.	Aligns content with audience needs, strengthens brand positioning.
Scripting and storyboarding	Scriptwriting for clarity and flow, visual planning of shots, camera angles, and sequences.	Ensures narrative cohesion, improves audience engagement through planned visual design.
Equipment and set-up	Microphone and camera selection, lighting techniques, essential accessories, software choices.	Produces professional-grade audio-visual quality that meets industry technical standards.
Recording techniques	Pre-production preparation, optimal mic placement, soundproofing, camera positioning, troubleshooting.	Reduces technical flaws, maintains consistent quality in professional environments.
Roles and collaboration	Clear role allocation (producer, director, audio engineer, presenter), teamwork, project management.	Replicates industry production workflows and collaborative skill demands.
Post-production editing	Editing workflow, audio balancing, colour correction, transitions, branding integration.	Produces polished final outputs ready for commercial or public distribution.
Branding and visual identity	Logo, thumbnails, style guide, typography, consistent intro/outro, lower thirds.	Enhances brand recognition and professionalism across platforms.
Audience engagement and promotion	Social media strategies, SEO, audience interaction, promotional content calendar.	Builds audience loyalty and increases discoverability across digital platforms.
Publishing and distribution	Hosting platform selection, RSS feed management, cross-platform distribution, monetisation models.	Expands reach, supports sustainable content production through revenue opportunities.

Planning and Concept Development

Practical podcasting begins with meticulous planning. It is essential for students to be introduced to strategies for defining the podcast's purpose, identifying target audiences, and articulating a USP.[11] Audience analysis involves examining both demographic factors such as age, gender, and location, and psychographic variables like interests, values, and lifestyle. Tools such as surveys, interviews, and analytics platforms are recommended for gathering relevant audience insights.

Idea generation is supported through techniques such as mind mapping, freewriting, and visual brainstorming.[12] Once initial concepts are formed, students conduct feasibility assessments and apply SWOT analysis to identify strengths, weaknesses, opportunities, and threats. Developing a clear USP is emphasised as central to audience attraction, brand recognition, and content direction.

Content planning involves establishing an editorial calendar, selecting appropriate episode formats (e.g. monologue, interview, hybrid), and structuring narratives for maximum engagement. Storytelling principles, such as narrative flow, character relatability, emotional resonance, and suspense, are reinforced through both audio and visual cues, including the integration of B-roll, infographics, and graphical overlays.

Scripting, Rundown, and Storyboarding

While some podcasts rely on loose conversational outlines, visual podcasting benefits significantly from structured scripting. A well-crafted script enhances clarity, consistency, and narrative flow, ensuring that both audio and visual elements are seamlessly integrated.[13] Students should be guided in developing scripts that go beyond dialogue, incorporating scene descriptions, timing cues, and technical directives such as camera movements or lighting changes. This approach helps align the spoken content with the intended visual presentation, resulting in a more cohesive and professional production.

Storyboarding complements scripting by offering a visual framework for planning each episode. It allows students to map out camera angles, shot sequences, transitions, and visual pacing in relation to the script.[14] Through this process, they can pre-visualise the composition and rhythm of their podcast, anticipate audience engagement strategies, and ensure that the visual storytelling supports the narrative structure. Together, scripting and storyboarding form the backbone of effective visual podcast planning, equipping students with the tools to produce compelling and coherent content.

Equipment and Set-up

Creating and launching a high-quality visual podcast starts with choosing the right gear and crafting a strategic budget. Instruction should stress that audio quality often has a greater impact on audience retention than video fidelity,[15] while helping students balance performance with affordability.

Core Equipment Essentials

Students should explore key categories of podcasting equipment, focusing on functionality and format suitability:

- Microphones
    - Dynamic: durable, excellent noise rejection
    - Condenser: studio-grade clarity
    - USB: plug-and-play ease for beginners
    - Lavalier: discreet, mobile interviews
    - Shotgun: directional capture in controlled settings
- Cameras
  From budget webcams to DSLRs and mirrorless models, students should consider resolution, frame rate, and lens adaptability (Owens, 2023).[16]
- Lighting
  Effective lighting elevates video quality. Teach three-point lighting and introduce LED panels, ring lights, and soft boxes.
- Accessories
  Tripods, boom arms, pop filters, shock mounts, and audio interfaces enhance professionalism and stability.

Strategic Budgeting

Budgeting is a core skill. Modules should guide students in identifying production needs and allocating resources wisely.

Influencing Factors

- Content Format: Solo, interview, or group set-ups require different gear
- Recording Environment: Studio, home, or mobile locations affect choices
- Quality Goals: Desired production value shapes investment levels

High-Impact Investments

Focus spending on elements that most affect quality:

- Microphone: Crucial for clear audio
- Camera: Should match visual goals and budget
- Lighting: Often overlooked but transformative
- Software: Must support efficient editing and streaming

Accessory Allocation

Budget for tools that improve usability:

- Stands and mounts for stability
- Pop filters and shock mounts to reduce noise
- Headphones for live monitoring and troubleshooting

Cost-Saving Strategies

Help students stretch budgets without compromising quality:

- Start Small: Begin with essentials, upgrade over time
- DIY Solutions: Repurpose household items for soundproofing or lighting
- Second-Hand Gear: High value at lower cost
- Free Software: Tools like Audacity and OBS reduce expenses

Balancing Quality and Cost

Budgeting should be taught as an evolving process. Modules should reinforce:

- Strategic investment in core components
- Gradual upgrades as resources grow
- Informed decisions through research and comparison

By combining smart equipment choices with thoughtful budgeting, students can build a professional-grade set-up that supports both their creative vision and financial realities.

Recording Techniques

Effective recording techniques are fundamental to producing high-quality visual podcasts, and a well-structured module should ensure that students master these essential skills. The pedagogical approach in visual podcasting modules ought to strongly emphasise pre-production preparation as a cornerstone of professional output. This involves guiding students to systematically work through a comprehensive checklist before recording begins.

Key areas for pre-production guidance that modules should address include:

- Ensuring all cameras, microphones, and other hardware are functioning correctly.
- Properly configuring audio recording environments and visual illumination.
- Creating an appropriate and professional visual backdrop for the recording.
- A final check of the script or outline to ensure clarity and readiness.

For audio recording, modules should teach students best practices such as correct microphone placement, typically 6–12 inches (approximately 15–30 cm) from the speaker at a 45-degree angle. The importance of using pop filters to minimise harsh ‘p’ and ‘b’ sounds and implementing basic soundproofing measures to reduce unwanted background noise should also be covered.

Regarding video recording, guidance should include maintaining an eye-level camera position and ensuring even lighting to create a professional and engaging visual presentation.[17] These practices contribute significantly to audience retention and overall production quality.

It is crucial for modules to train students in troubleshooting common problems that can arise during recording, such as background noise, ‘plosives’ (harsh consonant sounds), and digital artefacts. Students should also be instructed to conduct short test recordings prior to the main session, enabling them to verify and ensure technical quality before committing to a full take. By integrating these practical steps, visual podcasting modules can effectively prepare students to manage the technical demands of live recording environments and achieve industry-standard results.

Roles and Collaboration

Visual podcasting is inherently collaborative, requiring multiple roles such as producer, director, presenter, scriptwriter, videographer, audio engineer, and social media manager.[18] Group-based assignments should be designed to replicate industry production teams, with assessment criteria addressing not only the final product but also teamwork, role clarity, and task delegation.

Examples from student projects previously discussed illustrate how team dynamics significantly influence production quality. For instance, a project that initially presented issues such as inconsistent branding, structural pacing issues, and uneven audio levels also faced challenges with uneven member participation. Conversely, another project, which demonstrated clear progression over multiple episodes, successfully applying feedback on lighting, audience engagement, and branding, also showcased strong collaboration, underscoring teamwork as a critical employability skill.

The differing outcomes between these groups can often be attributed to how effectively teams manage the core aspects of collaboration outlined in the assessment criteria. The group that struggled with uneven participation stemmed from a lack of clear initial role allocation and task delegation, potentially coupled with varying levels of commitment among team members and insufficient internal communication to address these disparities. In contrast, the group demonstrating strong collaboration successfully established clear responsibilities, effectively delegated tasks, and maintained consistent teamwork, leading to a more cohesive and professionally presented final product.

Strategies for Enhancing Collaboration and Teamwork

To support students in this critical area, a module tutor can implement several strategies:

- Tutors should guide groups in the initial phases to explicitly define individual roles and responsibilities, and to delegate tasks clearly from the outset. Encouraging the creation of a team charter or agreement can help set expectations for participation and accountability.
- Integrate opportunities for students to reflect on their group dynamics and collaborative processes throughout the production cycle. This could involve structured check-ins or peer feedback sessions focused specifically on teamwork, allowing for early identification and resolution of issues such as uneven participation.
- Continually highlight that effective collaboration, role clarity, and task delegation are critical employability skills highly valued in the media sector, and that these are key components of professional readiness and success, directly impacting the quality and coherence of the final output.

Post-Production Editing

Post-production is the crucial stage where raw recordings are transformed into polished, broadcast-ready content. Visual podcasting modules should therefore provide comprehensive guidance to equip students with the skills necessary to excel in this area. The pedagogical approach should cover a structured editing workflow, ensuring students understand each phase of refining their audio-visual material.

Key areas of instruction that modules can address in post-production editing include:

- Editing Workflow: Students should be guided through the complete editing process, from importing and organising their raw footage and audio to creating a rough cut, refining it into a fine cut, and conducting a final review before export. This structured approach mirrors industry practice, promoting efficiency and attention to detail.
- Audio Refinement: A significant focus should be placed on achieving high-quality audio. This involves teaching students how to normalise audio levels across different segments, reduce unwanted background noise, and balance sound effects effectively to create a cohesive listening experience. Reference to established practices in video editing can reinforce these techniques.[19]
- Visual Enhancements: Modules should cover techniques for improving the visual quality of the podcast. This includes instruction on colour correction to ensure consistent and appealing visuals, effective use of transitions between shots, and the seamless integration of B-roll footage to enhance visual storytelling and maintain audience engagement.

- Branding Integration: To ensure a professional and recognisable output, students must learn how to integrate branding elements effectively. This encompasses adding lower thirds for speaker identification, designing and implementing title cards, and consistently incorporating introductory and outro sequences that reflect the podcast's visual identity.

It is vital that visual podcasting modules provide targeted feedback to students on common post-production pitfalls. This includes addressing issues such as inconsistent audio levels, abrupt visual cuts, overuse of visual effects, and a lack of clear storytelling focus in the final edit. By identifying and rectifying these issues, students can significantly enhance the professional quality and audience appeal of their visual podcasts.

Branding and Visual Identity

A strong visual brand is essential for audience recognition and retention.[20] Students develop logos, thumbnails, colour palettes, typography, and style guides to maintain brand consistency. Feedback frequently addresses the absence or inconsistency of such elements, reinforcing their importance in professional presentation.

Audience Engagement, Promotion, and Self-Evaluation

In visual podcasting, promotion is not a post-production afterthought; it is a core component of the creative process. Students are taught to integrate audience engagement strategies from the outset, including interactive Q&A sessions, targeted social media campaigns, newsletters, and behind-the-scenes content that fosters community and transparency. Lessons on search engine optimisation for titles and descriptions, as well as keyword targeting, are embedded to enhance discoverability and long-term reach.[21]

However, for students, many of whom will be self-employed content creators, the ability to evaluate their own success and iterate based on feedback is paramount. To support this, the curriculum must emphasise the development of personalised models for self-evaluation and continuous improvement. Students should be encouraged to track and interpret key performance indicators such as

- Audience retention and drop-off rates
- Engagement metrics (likes, shares, comments, saves)
- Search visibility and keyword performance
- Demographic and geographic reach
- Conversion rates (e.g. newsletter sign-ups, merchandise sales)

These metrics can be accessed through platforms like YouTube Analytics, Spotify for Podcasters, Google Search Console, and social media insights dashboards. Students must learn to use these tools not just to measure success, but to identify areas for growth, test new strategies, and refine their content and promotional approach.

To ensure students are applying these tools effectively, assignments and workshops include:

- Reflective analysis reports on campaign performance
- Iterative content planning based on analytics feedback

- Peer review and critique sessions focused on engagement strategy
- Goal-setting exercises tied to measurable outcomes

By embedding data literacy and self-assessment into the creative workflow, students gain the autonomy and insight needed to thrive in a competitive digital landscape. Success becomes not just a matter of talent, but of informed, adaptive practice.

Publishing, Distribution, and Monetisation

When teaching visual podcasting, it is just as important to introduce students to the practicalities of hosting and distributing visual podcasts, beginning with platform selection, such as Podbean, Buzzsprout, and Anchor, and the management of RSS feeds. Students need to be guided through the process of syndicating content across major platforms including YouTube, Apple Podcasts, Spotify, and Rumble, ensuring broad accessibility and discoverability.

Monetisation should be explored not merely as a financial goal, but as a strategic extension of content creation. Students need to examine models such as sponsorship, merchandise sales, paid subscriptions, and live events, evaluating their suitability based on audience size, content genre, and long-term brand development. Emphasis should be placed on aligning monetisation with authentic engagement and sustainable growth, drawing on market insights and evolving digital trends.[22]

This also encourages students to think entrepreneurially, equipping them with the tools to build viable, independent media ventures.

Legal and Ethical Considerations

Teaching visual podcasting requires more than the transmission of technical and creative skills; it also demands a thorough understanding of the legal and ethical frameworks that govern professional media production. Adherence to these principles is not only a matter of compliance but is also central to maintaining credibility, building audience trust, and sustaining professional longevity. One of the most significant areas of concern is copyright compliance, as all original works, including scripts, audio, visuals, and music, are automatically protected under copyright law. Using copyrighted material without permission can result in legal consequences and reputational damage, making it essential for students to either create their own assets or work with licensed material.[23] While the fair use doctrine allows for limited use of copyrighted material in contexts such as criticism, commentary, teaching, and research, its application is determined on a case-by-case basis and is often subject to interpretation, requiring careful judgement.[24]

Where fair use is not applicable, Creative Commons (CC) licensing offers a flexible alternative by enabling creators to share their work under specified conditions. Understanding the nuances between licence types, such as attribution-only (CC BY), non-commercial use (CC BY-NC), or no-derivatives (CC BY-ND), is crucial for ensuring lawful use of third-party material. When neither fair use nor an appropriate CC licence applies, obtaining explicit permission from the copyright holder, ideally in writing, is the most secure course of action. Alongside intellectual property concerns, privacy and confidentiality are fundamental. Students must secure informed consent before recording or sharing personal information about contributors, guests, or audiences, and they should employ secure storage and responsible handling of such data in compliance with relevant data protection regulations.

Ethical storytelling is another cornerstone of professional podcasting. It involves representing subjects fairly, avoiding stereotypes, and providing sufficient context to prevent misrepresentation.[25] Fact-checking is central to this responsibility, requiring verification of all information through credible sources and the prompt correction of inaccuracies. Transparency is also essential when dealing with sponsorships, paid promotions, or product placements. Regulatory guidelines, such as those of the Federal Trade Commission,[26] stipulate that such relationships must be disclosed clearly to audiences to prevent deception. Finally, adherence to the content policies of hosting and distribution platforms is a non-negotiable aspect of professional practice, covering areas such as copyright enforcement, hate speech, misinformation, and monetisation eligibility. Failure to comply can

Table 7.4 Summary of legal and ethical considerations in visual podcasting

Consideration	*Key Elements*	*Industry Relevance*
Copyright compliance	Understanding copyright scope; respecting ownership of scripts, audio, visuals, music.	Avoids infringement disputes; upholds professional credibility.[a]
Fair use doctrine	Limited use for criticism, commentary, news, teaching, scholarship, research; four-factor analysis.	Supports creative reuse within legal boundaries; mitigates legal risks.
Creative Commons licensing	Identifying licence types (e.g. CC BY, CC BY-SA, CC BY-NC); proper attribution; licence compliance.	Expands content options; encourages ethical content sourcing.
Obtaining permissions	Contacting rights holders; securing written agreements; negotiating usage terms.	Ensures lawful use of protected material; strengthens industry relationships.
Privacy and confidentiality	Protecting personal information; securing consent before sharing identifiable details.	Builds audience trust; meets legal requirements under data protection laws.
Ethical storytelling	Balanced representation; informed consent; avoiding stereotypes and exploitation.	Maintains integrity, social responsibility, and audience trust.[b]
Fact-checking	Verifying all shared information through credible sources; correcting errors promptly.	Preserves accuracy, reliability, and public credibility.
Plagiarism and attribution	Giving credit for external sources; maintaining originality in content creation.	Upholds academic and professional integrity.[c]
Sponsored content transparency	Disclosing advertisements, sponsorships, and paid promotions clearly.	Meets advertising regulations; maintains audience confidence.[d]
Platform policy compliance	Adhering to hosting and distribution platform rules; avoiding prohibited content.	Prevents removal, demonetisation, or suspension from platforms.

[a] Aufderheide and Jaszi, *Reclaiming Fair Use*.
[b] Ward, *Ethics and the Media*.
[c] Charles Lipson, *Doing Honest Work in College: How to Prepare Citations, Avoid Plagiarism, and Achieve Real Academic Success* (University of Chicago Press, 2004).
[d] 'Commission Enforcement Policy Statement on Deceptively Formatted Advertisements | Federal Trade Commission'.

lead to content removal, demonetisation, or account suspension, underscoring the necessity of embedding legal and ethical awareness into media education. Table 7.4 summarises the Legal and Ethical Considerations in Visual Podcasting.

Challenges and Opportunities in Teaching Visual Podcasting

While the integration of visual podcasting into higher education offers transformative learning potential, it also presents a series of challenges that educators must address to ensure effective delivery. One of the most persistent barriers is the issue of resources. Producing professional-quality visual podcasts requires access to suitable microphones, cameras, lighting, and editing software, alongside appropriate recording environments. In many institutions, budget constraints limit the availability of such resources, resulting in disparities in production quality among students. Addressing these limitations may involve phased investments, shared facilities, or the strategic use of cost-effective alternatives and open-source software solutions.

A second challenge lies in the diverse technical skill sets required for visual podcasting. Students must develop competencies across a wide spectrum, including audio engineering, video composition, editing, colour correction, and post-production workflows. Given the varying levels of digital literacy among students, curricula must be scaffolded to allow for differentiated learning, with additional support sessions and practice opportunities for those requiring extra guidance. At the same time, the rapid growth of the podcast industry has led to a saturated market, meaning that students must be equipped to differentiate their work through unique branding, innovative formats, and consistently high production values in order to stand out. Despite these challenges, the field offers rich opportunities for innovation and professional growth. Technological developments such as AR and VR are opening new possibilities for immersive, interactive podcast experiences, while AI is streamlining processes including transcription, translation, audio clean-up, and targeted audience recommendations. Furthermore, multi-platform integration, adapting content for streaming services, social media, and dedicated podcast platforms, has become a key strategy for maximising audience reach and diversifying revenue streams. By anticipating and incorporating these trends into curricula, educators can ensure that students are not only prepared for the current media landscape but are also equipped to thrive in its future iterations. In doing so, visual podcasting education can serve as both a creative outlet and a pathway to industry readiness, bridging academic learning with the demands of a rapidly evolving professional environment.

Conclusion

The integration of visual podcasting into higher education represents both an innovative pedagogical opportunity and a direct response to the evolving demands of the media industry. As the medium continues to expand, driven by technological advances, shifting audience preferences, and the convergence of audio and video content, it offers educators a powerful means of fostering creativity, technical expertise, and professional readiness among students. This chapter has outlined how teaching visual podcasting can be structured to combine creative storytelling with rigorous technical training, all while embedding industry-aligned standards and ethical awareness.

Central to this approach is the emphasis on iterative, practice-based learning, enabling students to engage in multiple production cycles where feedback directly informs improvement. By experiencing the full production pipeline, from planning and scripting to recording, editing, branding, distribution, and promotion, students develop not only technical competence but also the critical thinking, adaptability, and collaborative skills necessary for professional success. Aligning academic assessment criteria with industry expectations ensures that graduates leave with a portfolio of work that reflects both creative innovation and technical precision.

At the same time, this chapter has underscored the importance of embedding legal and ethical considerations into the curriculum. Awareness of copyright, licensing, fair use, privacy, and responsible storytelling is essential for producing credible, lawful, and trustworthy content. These principles, alongside an understanding of platform policies and sponsorship transparency, safeguard both professional integrity and audience trust.

While challenges such as resource constraints, technical skill disparities, and market saturation remain, they can be mitigated through strategic curriculum design, institutional investment, and the adoption of emerging technologies. The future of visual podcasting in education is particularly promising, with developments in AI, AR, VR, and multi-platform distribution offering new ways to enhance production, broaden audience reach, and deepen engagement.

While this pedagogical framework offers significant benefits, it is important to acknowledge its limitations. First, the resource-intensive nature of visual podcasting may reproduce existing educational inequalities, potentially disadvantaging students from under-resourced institutions or backgrounds. Second, our emphasis on industry alignment may inadvertently socialise students into accepting commercial media's status quo rather than critically examining it. Third, the iterative approach requires substantial time investment that may not be feasible in all curricular contexts. Fourth, by focusing primarily on technical and professional competencies, we may underemphasise broader humanistic education in media ethics, media history, and critical cultural analysis. Finally, in a rapidly saturating market, training more content creators raises ethical questions about sustainable career pathways and the environmental impact of increased digital production. These limitations suggest that visual podcasting pedagogy works best as one component within a broader, more critical media education – not as a standalone solution to preparing students for the media industries.

In preparing students to navigate and contribute to this dynamic media landscape, educators play a pivotal role in shaping the next generation of content creators. By integrating creative practice, technical mastery, industry alignment, and ethical responsibility, teaching visual podcasting can bridge the gap between academic learning and professional achievement, equipping graduates to produce high-quality, audience-centred work that thrives in an ever-changing digital environment.

Notes

1 'Radio on Demand: New Habits of Consuming Radio Content - Tal Laor, 2022', accessed 3 December 2025, https://journals.sagepub.com/doi/10.1177/17427665211073868.

2 Richard Berry, 'Podcasting: Considering the Evolution of the Medium and Its Association with the Word "Radio"', *Radio Journal:International Studies in Broadcast & Audio Media* 14, no. 1 (2016): 7–22, https://doi.org/10.1386/rjao.14.1.7_1.

3 Jim Owens, *Video Production Handbook* (Routledge, 2023); Samuel Sauls and Craig Stark, *Audio Production Worktext: Concepts, Techniques, and Equipment* (Routledge, 2022).
4 Berry, 'Podcasting'.
5 Coherent Market Insights Pvt Ltd, 'Podcasting Market Size to Worth USD 173.49 Billion by 2032, Says Coherent Market Insights', GlobeNewswire News Room, 9 April 2025, https://www.globenewswire.com/news-release/2025/04/09/3058669/0/en/Podcasting-Market-size-to-worth-USD-173-49-Billion-by-2032-says-Coherent-Market-Insights.html.
6 Sauls and Stark, *Audio Production Worktext.*
7 Sauls and Stark, *Audio Production Worktext.*
8 Owens, *Video Production Handbook*; Sauls and Stark, *Audio Production Worktext.*
9 David A. Kolb, *Experiential Learning: Experience as the Source of Learning and Development* (Prentice-Hall, 1984).
10 Berry, 'Podcasting'.
11 Owens, *Video Production Handbook.*
12 Stephanie Torta and Vladimir Minuty, *Storyboarding: Turning Script to Motion* (Mercury Learning & Information, 2011).
13 Sauls and Stark, *Audio Production Worktext.*
14 Torta and Minuty, *Storyboarding.*
15 'The Complete Guide to Podcasting Audio Equipment', Podcastle Blog, 6 July 2023, https://podcastle.ai/blog/podcasting-equipment/.
16 Owens, *Video Production Handbook.*
17 Owens, *Video Production Handbook.*
18 Sauls and Stark, *Audio Production Worktext.*
19 Steven E. Browne, *Video Editing: A Postproduction Primer* (Focal Press, 2002).
20 Owens, *Video Production Handbook.*
21 Lucas Graves, *Deciding What's True: The Rise of Political Fact-Checking in American Journalism* (Columbia University Press, 2016).
22 Ltd, 'Podcasting Market Size to Worth USD 173.49 Billion by 2032, Says Coherent Market Insights'.
23 Patricia Aufderheide and Peter Jaszi, *Reclaiming Fair Use: How to Put Balance Back in Copyright* (University of Chicago Press, 2011).
24 Stephen Fishman, *The Copyright Handbook: What Every Writer Needs to Know* (Nolo, 2024).
25 Hanna Meretoja, *The Ethics of Storytelling: Narrative Hermeneutics, History, and the Possible* (Oxford University Press, 2018); Stephen J. A. Ward, *Ethics and the Media: An Introduction* (Cambridge University Press, 2011).
26 'Commission Enforcement Policy Statement on Deceptively Formatted Advertisements | Federal Trade Commission', accessed 3 December 2025, https://www.ftc.gov/legal-library/browse/commission-enforcement-policy-statement-deceptively-formatted-advertisements.

References

Aufderheide, Patricia, and Peter Jaszi. *Reclaiming Fair Use: How to Put Balance Back in Copyright.* University of Chicago Press, 2011.

Berry, Richard. 'Podcasting: Considering the Evolution of the Medium and Its Association with the Word "Radio"'. *Radio Journal: International Studies in Broadcast & Audio Media* 14, no. 1 (2016): 7–22. https://doi.org/10.1386/rjao.14.1.7_1.

Browne, Steven E. *Video Editing: A Postproduction Primer.* Focal Press, 2002.

'Commission Enforcement Policy Statement on Deceptively Formatted Advertisements | Federal Trade Commission'. Accessed 3 December 2025. https://www.ftc.gov/legal-library/browse/commission-enforcement-policy-statement-deceptively-formatted-advertisements.

Fishman, Stephen. *The Copyright Handbook: What Every Writer Needs to Know.* Nolo, 2024.

Graves, Lucas. *Deciding What's True: The Rise of Political Fact-Checking in American Journalism.* Columbia University Press, 2016.

Kolb, David A. *Experiential Learning: Experience as the Source of Learning and Development.* Prentice-Hall, 1984.

Lipson, Charles. *Doing Honest Work in College: How to Prepare Citations, Avoid Plagiarism, and Achieve Real Academic Success.* University of Chicago Press, 2004.

Ltd, Coherent Market Insights Pvt. 'Podcasting Market Size to Worth USD 173.49 Billion by 2032, Says Coherent Market Insights'. GlobeNewswire News Room, 9 April 2025. https://www.globenewswire.com/news-release/2025/04/09/3058669/0/en/Podcasting-Market-size-to-worth-USD-173-49-Billion-by-2032-says-Coherent-Market-Insights.html.

Meretoja, Hanna. *The Ethics of Storytelling: Narrative Hermeneutics, History, and the Possible.* Oxford University Press, 2018.

Owens, Jim. *Video Production Handbook.* Routledge, 2023.

Podcastle Blog. 'The Complete Guide to Podcasting Audio Equipment'. 6 July 2023. https://podcastle.ai/blog/podcasting-equipment/.

'Radio on Demand: New Habits of Consuming Radio Content - Tal Laor, 2022'. Accessed 3 December 2025. https://journals.sagepub.com/doi/10.1177/17427665211073868.

Sauls, Samuel, and Craig Stark. *Audio Production Worktext: Concepts, Techniques, and Equipment.* Routledge, 2022.

Torta, Stephanie, and Vladimir Minuty. *Storyboarding: Turning Script to Motion.* Mercury Learning & Information, 2011.

Ward, Stephen J. A. *Ethics and the Media: An Introduction.* Cambridge University Press, 2011.

Part C

Podcasts as a Tool for Community Engagement

Chapter 8

Doing It for Themselves

The Use of Participatory Podcasting to Empower Community Voices

Adam Gratton and Nicola Gratton

'Podcasting is a platform for telling stories that wouldn't be heard otherwise. It's a way to give a voice to the voiceless'.

This quote, widely attributed to Sarah Koenig, host of the podcast 'Serial', highlights the potential of podcasting to democratise knowledge, information, and stories, giving voice to marginalised communities and challenging the gatekeepers present in more traditional forms of media and education. One of the widely recognised benefits of podcasting is that it provides those with the means of producing a podcast with a potential global audience. However, while these means are available for many, more marginalised communities, including those facing multiple disadvantages, such as a history of homelessness, substance misuse, domestic violence, or poverty, are less likely to listen to or have access to podcasts, either as consumers or creators. Socio-economic inequalities and the digital divide mean that while some can utilise this platform, others face a complexity of barriers. Often, limited access to technology is just one of the challenges. Moreover, a lack of confidence, social capital, and more broadly a general lack of awareness of podcasting as a form of communication can mean that establishing a podcast series is not as easy as providing technology to seldom heard and underrepresented communities and supporting them to identify a theme.

This chapter introduces a model of Participatory Community Podcasting designed by The Community Cast, an innovative digital company based in the West Midlands in the UK.

The Community Cast uses digital media to empower communities. Its work challenges traditional journalism by asking: what if seldom-heard voices had the skills and confidence to tell their own stories through podcasting? Through building relationships with residents and community groups, it aims to support and enable them to create awareness and generate conversations about the issues which matter most. Using a combination of cocreated methods built around digital, journalistic, and media practices, The Community Cast works alongside and empowers a diverse range of individuals and groups. Using digital and traditional media training, it works with people to provide access to learning outside of conventional educational routes, as well as working alongside existing organisations with the aim of placemaking.

The Participatory Community Podcasting model was designed as a way of overcoming digital barriers and empowering communities to understand the benefits of podcasting in highlighting causes. It also builds the skills, confidence, and technical knowledge to create a high-quality communication through podcasting, with a dual purpose: to amplify the voices of the hosts to a potentially global audience and build a cohesive, complementary,

DOI: 10.4324/9781003677253-11

and skilled team, with the ability to 'do it for themselves' from identifying the episode topics to development, publication, and promotion.

We will open the chapter with an introduction to some of the present-day inequities of access to digital technologies and podcasting specifically, followed by the role of community engagement in addressing some of these inequities. Following an outline of two case studies from practice, we will draw together our learning into a model of Participatory Community Podcasting, including the challenges and benefits of the approach. We will conclude the chapter with a discussion on the future aspirations of the team to reconcile participatory approaches with high-quality, industry-standard podcasting.

Digital Inequities

In 2025, podcasts are expected to reach an estimated 15.5 million listeners in the UK,[1] although distribution of listenership is uneven. Ofcom[2] states that although a fifth of adults listen to podcasts each week, reach is higher among younger people and those in higher socio-economic groups. Podcast consumption and exposure, therefore, are not equitable across all ages and socio-economic groups. While 26% of people in higher socio-economic groups and an equal percentage of people living in the South of England listen to podcasts on a regular basis, only 14% of people in semi-skilled or manual jobs or on state benefits do the same. Equally, individuals over the age of 55 are less likely to listen to podcasts regularly than their younger counterparts.[3] Elsewhere, studies have reported that podcast listeners typically have a higher-than-average wage with an academic education and middle-class background.[4]

There is also a seemingly growing educational divide. Higher education is becoming increasingly expensive, with university degree fees again increased in mid-2025 by £285 per year, meaning it now costs a possible £28,605 for an undergraduate degree. It is necessary to point out that with this, maintenance loans will also increase. However, with fuel, food, and energy prices remaining high, this will be of little consolation to students who are already feeling the pinch. Even the slightest increase in these costs can be a proverbial straw on the back of the camel, before we even factor in the likes of broadband, mobile phone, and equipment costs. Added to this are people and communities who, due to multiple disadvantages and other socio-economic impacts, could not consider such traditional educational routes.

It is therefore clear that access to and the use of podcasting is not equitable across communities. Jundi and Gratton[5] highlight the interconnected nature of poverty and digital exclusion. In a project aimed at improving digital exclusion in a post-industrial town in the West Midlands of the UK, they identified the impact of digital exclusion on communities. With so much of our work and social lives now online, those who are unable to access it are becoming increasingly socially and economically isolated.

Media is evolving and changing at ever greater speed and frequency, and with it the privilege of opportunity. It is not cheap to access the equipment or resources to get online and, in the face of ever-increasing cost of living, it is unaffordable to many. While finances are a challenge for some and the rising cost of living has prevented some people from getting online,[6] a lack of motivation is a significant barrier to individuals accessing the online world[7,8] including a lack of understanding of the benefits that being online, or in our case accessing podcasts, can bring. To compound this, Jundi and Gratton point to Quek's mapping of digital inclusion projects, indicating that there is an overwhelming lack of projects that focus on individuals' motivations as a means of addressing issues of digital exclusion.

It is clear then that some communities are much less likely to include listening to podcasts as part of their everyday lives. While it may be the case that a significant proportion of society has a smartphone, it is not the case that everyone is able to, or wants to use these to access podcasts, either as consumers or producers. Inequalities of poverty and social opportunity restrict equitable and equal chances to digital communication, such as podcasting, as a way of telling stories, building social value, inclusion, and developing educational opportunities. It therefore begs the question, whose voices are we hearing? And importantly, who is missing?

Podcasting, Community Engagement, and Coproduction

There is growing evidence of the value of podcasting in empowering communities to share their realities, engage in the civic arena,[9] and create spaces which 'broker the relationship between marginalised communities and wider publics'.[10]

Jundi and Gratton[11] highlight the need for community engagement principles to underpin any digital inclusion work. They embedded a participatory approach throughout the project, replacing technology experts with digital champions, providing equipment and learning opportunities at a pace that was right for their audiences, and putting together a team of 'Community Connectors' to reach the most digitally excluded people. They argue that their project 'was not a digital project, but a community engagement project that provided a model of digital support'.[12] By framing the work in this way, they were able to access people for whom digital engagement seemed a distant hope.

How to reach individuals through good community engagement practices is just one element of effectively engaging marginalised communities to share their lived experiences and elevate their own voices. How we work with communities once we have reached them is of equal importance. Although definitions of coproduction are broad and varied, a common feature of all these practices is acknowledgement of the value of involving people with lived experience of a particular situation, condition, or experience in decision making about the services [or] support they receive.[13,14] While the practice of coproduction is evident across a broad range of services and organisations, including the NHS,[15] charity and voluntary sector organisations,[16] and funders,[17,18] there is little evidence of what good coproduction practice looks like, let alone how to effectively work with communities to coproduce media that will elevate their voices, and in doing so, tackle issues of societal inequality.

Participatory Community Podcasting recognises the inequalities in access to podcasting and the implications this has for whose voices become dominant in the podcasting arena. It also presents a model of coproduction that places ownership of the podcast firmly with communities. It utilises core community engagement and coproduction practices to reach unheard groups, build their confidence and skills, provide educational opportunities, and ensure the content of the podcasts they produce is impactful and meaningful for their communities.

Examples from Practice

The Community Cast's approach to Participatory Community Podcasting was first launched in 2021 and has delivered six iterations between 2022 and 2025. Each programme has been refined to meet the needs of the specific group. Outlined below are two examples of the Participatory Community Podcast programme delivered with two distinct groups and using two distinct approaches, demonstrating the scope of the work. The first case study outlined here is Expert Citizens CIC. Expert Citizens were the first group to receive the Participatory Community Podcasting programme. The second group is the Young Leaders Podcast with YMCA North Staffordshire. This work remains ongoing at the time of writing.

Expert Citizens CIC

Expert Citizens is a Community Interest Company based in Stoke-on-Trent, in the West Midlands, with a national UK reach. They are led by and for people with lived experience of multiple disadvantage, including homelessness, mental ill-health, addiction, and experience of the criminal justice system. In early 2021, The Community Cast was approached by the organisation's CEO about supporting the Expert Citizen team to develop skills around communication and digital technologies, with a view to helping Expert Citizens promote its work, empower its community, learn new skills, and raise their voice through storytelling.

The Community Cast initially delivered a two-day Podcasting 101 programme to 12 individuals. This was well received and motivated the group and the management team to do a more in-depth programme, called Podcast 'Bootcamp', which became the first Participatory Community Podcast programme.

Fourteen Expert Citizens were recruited to the Bootcamp. All had some experience of multiple disadvantage, including substance misuse, homelessness, domestic violence, or mental ill-health. While some of the members had some awareness of what podcasts were, none had any experience of either listening to or creating podcasts, reflecting the wider challenges of people experiencing multiple disadvantages in accessing digital equipment, skills, and tools.[19,20] Given the voluntary nature of the programme, the informal approach adopted by facilitators, and the composition of the group, irregular attendance was commonplace. Consistency was therefore challenging. However, a core group of four members was present at all sessions. This group provided some stability for the programme, supporting fewer regular members to engage with the content and ultimately becoming the main production team for the Expert Citizens Podcast.

An eight-week programme was devised to provide some structure for the groups' learning. As this was a new endeavour, there was a period required for writing the course content and designing teaching materials. The facilitator knew some members of the group from previous work and therefore was able to ensure the materials were well-suited to the learning preferences of the group. While there was some structure to ensure all the ethical and skills-based content was covered, The Community Cast ensured most of the course content was interactive and engaging. The course content was supported by a backdrop of presentation slides, supporting the participants' ability to retain information.[21] This allowed the teaching to be informal and conversation-based while ensuring the core learning content was clearly visible. This was particularly important for topics such as ethical journalistic practices and technical skills.

In the early stages of the programme, there was a strong focus on building relationships and trust, both between the facilitator and group, and within the group itself. This consisted of informal conversations to allow the group members to learn more about each other, extended coffee breaks, and taking the first sessions at the pace of the group. This deliberate use of informal dialogue is crucial in cementing relationships.[22] The conversations were often brought back to the content of the podcasts they were producing, but this was done at a slow and gradual pace. The trust that this period established ensured people were not only engaged with the programme and felt comfortable attending sessions but also helped to build the confidence and skills within the group to push themselves outside of their comfort zones.

For this reason, it was also important to minimise established and traditional power dynamics of teacher/student. The facilitator worked with the group to gradually develop an equitable footing where the group took increasing amounts of control of the sessions. The first step towards this was for the group to agree on their own ground rules and identify their individual aspirations for the course. As the course progressed, the group were able to take an increased level of control of the direction and output of the podcast. Setting this dynamic in an organic way attempts to ensure that everyone feels included and that the programme is peer-focused and led.

The Bootcamp opened with an introduction to podcasting, including fundamental information such as identifying what a podcast is and what is required to create one. Over time, it moved on to hardware and technical needs, and how to use the newly acquired equipment. As this approach and method are about widening inclusion and access, this began with introducing the concept of equipment at a basic level. The facilitator started with the approach that all you need is 'your voice' and a smartphone. It is from this that the discussion evolved to the inclusion of more technical (and potentially intimidating) equipment and how to use it.

Following the session on equipment, the group moved on to planning, including writing, scripting, and structuring their own podcast episodes and series and then moved on to recording and editing. To conclude the programme, the facilitator worked with the group to design their own branding, artwork, and publicity, and supported the group to publish the podcast series they had produced. The end of the Bootcamp was marked by a celebration event, where participants came together, reflected on their successes, and were congratulated by The Community Cast team and Expert Citizens management team.

The Bootcamp was delivered through a joint funding venture between Expert Citizens CIC and The Community Cast and resulted in the purchase of equipment, which would remain and belong to Expert Citizens for them to continue their podcasting journey. The Community Cast advised the Expert Citizen management team on the equipment required, not only for the training but also with a view to their community setting up and continuing their podcast and series, ensuring a long-term, sustainable approach to podcasting.

The expected outcomes of the group were achieved. The group created, developed, and launched their own organisational podcast: The Expert Citizens Podcast. However, the impact on the group reached far deeper. The core group sustained their podcast for approximately one year after their initial launch.

The most noticeable results were in individual confidence in learning new skills such as editing and how they worked together as a group. They also adopted specific roles which spoke to them on an individual basis, honing their specific transferable skills, for example hosting, editing and writing, and researching. Crucially, the group were able to step into an unfamiliar digital world and elevate their voices to share their own stories and experiences, reducing stigma and building empathy.

YMCA North Staffordshire, Young Leaders Podcast

The Community Cast was approached by the Creative Director of YMCA North Staffordshire to explore opportunities for collaboration to support the voices of young people across Stoke-on-Trent and North Staffordshire while also providing essential skills training and learning to the YMCA Youth Governance Team (YGT). The YGT is a group of staff, volunteers, and residents who want to represent young people and give them a chance for their voice to be heard across Stoke-on-Trent and beyond.

To date, six young people from the YMCA YGT have been involved in the programme. They have invited numerous guests to appear on the podcast and have produced two series of the Young Leaders Podcast, with series three now underway. Those who took part had either never listened to podcasts before or had only engaged briefly with the format. None of the participants had any experience of ever being involved in the creation of a podcast or the skills and knowledge required.

Following a period of getting to know the group to build relationships and establish trust, the programme was launched. For this iteration of the programme, although the core principles and model remain the same, unlike the previous case study which followed a more structured and linear approach to delivery, this collaboration was based on more of a 'learn as you work' approach which delivered a more creative, relaxed, and fun learning environment in which they were more comfortable to develop the idea and develop a young person-centred community action narrative.[23] In this case, the outputs were produced throughout the programme with the podcast episodes going live from day one. The Community Cast adapted and delivered an approach which integrated the methodology in an unintrusive way to ensure participants felt at ease and learning was experiential throughout the programme.

Given the group's limited interaction with podcasts, it was essential to support participants to feel comfortable with the concept of podcasting and talking into a microphone in the early stages. All sessions involved a period of informal conversations that were gently guided towards the podcast episode that was the focus of that day's session, ensuring the group were aware of the process to take place and had an opportunity to include their key points. Where young people were feeling nervous, the facilitator talked to them about their own experiences, reminding them that no one knows the subject area better than they do.

Each person involved in the podcast sessions or additional training sessions received training in communication, both digital and face-to-face, script writing, use of digital equipment, and digital audio editing. They were also coached in hosting and presenting, planning and time management, interviewing and publishing. The group were also supported to create the artwork for their podcast and to disseminate their podcast to a wide audience.

During the first series, The Community Cast took responsibility for editing each episode, with the team focusing more on the pre-production of the show. However, to expand their group's expertise, The Community Cast ran a two-day workshop on editing and audio production. The group are now able to edit their own podcast, drawing on support from The Community Cast as needed.

The core YGT team, taking the lead with podcast hosting and production, was also working full-time for the YMCA. As such, time management was a key consideration, and the programme had to be flexible around the availability not only of the team but also of podcast guests. The approach was streamlined by ensuring all training and engagement were completed during the recording of episodes.

The YGT developed confidence, knowledge, and the skills to grow an established podcast series. They have had an increased sense of social value and have learnt new and transferable skills in digital and interpersonal communication, writing scripts, numerical skills through timings and managing audio gain levels, editing, teamwork, digital artwork, the process of podcasting, online publishing, planning, time management, interviewing, and project management.

To date, they have produced two podcast series and, at the time of writing, are about to embark on a third with reduced input from The Community Cast. In support of this, the YMCA has recently invested in a podcasting room through which young people can record and produce their podcasts. The team will continue to work together to learn and teach new participants, develop their content, and be a platform for the voice of their community in the future. This demonstrates the value of Participatory Community Podcasting in establishing a sustainable approach to empowering marginalised communities to elevate their own voices through podcasting.

Learning

These case studies have resulted in significant learning for The Community Cast team, allowing for an evolution of the Participatory Community Podcasting approach over time. During this time, the benefits of the approach have become clear. Using podcasting, an ever-growing and increasingly popular and accessible medium for communication and storytelling, a multitude of skills and knowledge can be brought into play, from written and verbal communication, planning, project management, art, digital skills, recording equipment, editing software, online publishing platforms, and social media. Participatory Community Podcasting develops an increased sense of social value through empowering and training community members, building confidence through mentoring and support, developing knowledge and confidence to create a podcast series from scratch, placing lived experience at the heart, nurturing a culture of respect and inclusion to ensure their voice is at the forefront, and instilling genuine control and ownership over the process.

The Community Cast's approach to Participatory Community Podcasting has provided an educational alternative, creating learning opportunities outside of traditional educational routes. Moreover, it has contributed to addressing the digital divide for those who face social, health, or economic barriers. It has provided an opportunity for marginalised communities to gain digital communication skills and improve their confidence and self-worth. By doing so, it helps bridge the gap between those who have access to traditional education and digital technologies and those who do not, ensuring that everyone has the chance to learn and grow.

However, the approach is not without its challenges. Participatory work is inherently time-consuming and intensive. It requires a significant investment of time to build relationships, understand community dynamics, and facilitate meaningful participation. This often means that timelines need to be extended beyond initial expectations. The slow, organic, and informal nature of the work, combined with the complex lives of some of the group members, means that getting a consistent membership can be challenging. However, it has been made clear that with a relaxed and informal facilitation approach, combined with taking sufficient time to build trust with and within the group, this inconsistency can be managed. A core 'production team' group established itself in both case studies. These members developed a strong passion for the work and became the team to carry the podcast forward beyond the involvement of The Community Cast. It has also been found that, once established, the group members hold one another to account, strengthening the group's commitment and responsibility to the programme. The end goal of creating an actual, live podcast also strengthens the collective ownership of their journey. The Community Cast provides a supportive guide, offering the right tools to the participants who are the craftspeople in control of their voice and message.

Core to all programmes has been the need to establish trust and long-term relationships both with and within the groups, reflecting the core principles of community engagement, youth work, and asset-based community development approaches.[24,25] This helped to create a community around the subject areas, allowing group members to not only get learning support from The Community Cast team but also from each other. Time was invested in establishing strong relationships with the group at all stages of the programmes. Key to this, there have been activities such as informal conversations before, during, and after the programme sessions, hosting celebration events to recognise successes and attending community meals to meet informally with group members. In addition, small acts of ensuring groups are facilitated well with conflicts managed effectively and all members having an equal role to play, completing tasks for the group on time, and creating a safe environment for all members to tell their own stories without judgement are vital to the relationship-building process. Strong relationships also make challenging inappropriate or discriminatory behaviours within the group easier.

The programme has been responsive to the needs of the groups and individuals within them. Building relationships has been central to ensuring the programmes are appropriate for the group members and individual needs are accounted for, including mental ill-health, poverty-based exclusions, social anxiety, and additional learning needs. Adopting a flexible approach has therefore been essential.

This is illustrated in the two case studies. With Expert Citizens, the approach needed to respond to their varying levels of engagement due to ongoing individual circumstances. This required a more focused and easily replicable type of training prior to the launch of the podcast. On the other hand, YMCA had a more consistent membership, allowing the podcast series to be launched after a shorter training period and for a more experiential and reflective learning process. Despite the two very different approaches, both responded to the needs of the group, delivered the same core content, and produced similar outcomes in the form of sustained podcast series.

The need to maintain the community-led elements of the programmes, while ensuring the process and outputs are ethical, professional, fact-checked, and inclusive of diverse voices, has resulted in the programme embedding ethical journalistic practices at the heart of the training and mentoring sessions. The programme includes direct training sessions on verification, understanding sources, and tackling misinformation and disinformation.[26] In addition, the groups are made aware that they have their own editorial guidelines, including accuracy of information, ethical reporting, and critical thought. Fostering a safe space through which the group can test ideas and make mistakes without judgement, again supported by the investment in building relationships with and between the group, means these potentially challenging topics are streamlined into the programme delivery.

A Model of Participatory Community Podcasting

The work has been, and will continue to be, adapted to the needs of the individuals and groups involved. However, there is a set of core fundamental principles and techniques that underpin the approach, which have been translated into a model of Participatory Community Podcasting (Figure 8.1).

The Community Cast's Participatory Community Podcasting model offers a unique and inclusive approach to education, especially for those who may not have access to traditional educational routes, thereby providing potential to reframe educational pathways. This method empowers individuals and communities by providing them with the tools and skills needed to create their own podcasts, thereby fostering a sense of ownership and control over their learning journey. It provides an opportunity for people and communities who are not able to access more conventional channels of education to not only learn new digital communication skills but also to do it for themselves.

The approach is unique and inclusive, embracing the holistic learning that podcasting brings.[27] By supporting individuals and communities with the confidence, tools, and skills needed to create their own podcasts, it fosters a sense of ownership and control over their learning journey.

Participatory Community Podcasting is loosely based on the concept of Participatory Journalism which is a bottom-up approach to news and information dissemination through which citizens play an active role.[28] While the approach democratises news, it has also been criticised for its risk of misinformation, legitimacy, and ethics.[29,30,31] Our model of Participatory Community Podcasting acknowledges and addresses these risks through a model that is underpinned by ethics, relationships, and training. The model is outlined in Figure 8.1. It has been developed over four years of delivery of participatory

Figure 8.1 The Community Cast's Participatory Community Podcasting model.

podcasting programmes with a range of groups whose voices are not traditionally heard within the podcasting sphere.

The Participatory Community Podcasting model is comprised of five core elements. The model is based on four years of working with communities to develop their own podcasts. The model is deliberately presented as 'bottom up', starting with the need for effective community engagement and coproduction to ensure those voices who are least likely to be heard are reached and supported.

Community engagement and coproduction – To reach communities who are unheard and underserved, the model advocates using community engagement techniques appropriate to the group and creating access to educational opportunities which offer skills with 'real world' applications. All Participatory Community Podcast programmes are coproduced, with the group taking increasing control over the programme as it progresses.

Trust and relationships – Time is invested in establishing relationships and trust, both with and within the group. This trust becomes the vehicle through which confidence is built, the group supports each other through the learning and podcast production, equity is established between the facilitator and the team, transparency is maintained, and ethical journalistic practices are embedded within the programme.

Respect and inclusion – Group-negotiated ground rules and open and honest dialogue help to establish positive group dynamics between the participants as well as between the trainer and the group. Facilitators are consistently reviewing the accessibility of the programme, and the question 'who aren't we hearing?' is continually addressed. The group are encouraged to include and promote different voices.

Training and mentoring – A significant part of the model is the training and mentoring programme. The training for each programme is adapted to the needs of the group but always includes increasing confidence through incremental increases in responsibility and delivery, development of digital and technical skills and knowledge, and ethical journalistic practices, such as safe practice and inclusive storytelling. Embedding journalistic ethics and integrity helps to tackle the mis/disinformation challenges of community journalism. The need for solid fact-checking and rigour in sourcing and context is focused on as a core discipline to protect participants and develop their skills. Throughout this part of the process, providing ongoing support which challenges without inhibiting or stifling is crucial. Balancing industry standards with lived experience and storytelling, while not being detrimental to building confidence, is key to an equal and equitable learning experience.

Lived experience and voice – The Participatory Community Podcasting model ultimately aims to raise and share the voices of underserved communities in an ethically responsible way, which protects them from recourse while emboldening their storytelling, confidence, and sense of social value and worth. In doing so, the approach can frame podcasting as a potentially radical space,[32] reducing stigma and 'connecting underserved [people's] lived experience with the world in which they live'.[33]

Conclusions

This chapter has outlined an approach to Participatory Community Podcasting, illustrated through two case studies and learning drawn from these. The Participatory Community

Podcasting model has been created to work with communities that are typically unfamiliar with the use of podcasting to share their lived experiences and support them to create podcasts of industry standard while not losing their authentic voice. The approach is collaborative and based on coproduction, through which the podcast professional plays the role of facilitator, supporting community voice, rather than being the mouthpiece themselves. However, central to all Participatory Community Podcast programmes is a training and mentoring programme delivered by a trained professional that embeds journalistic ethics and integrity. This ensures the stories elevated through podcasting are not only authentic and steeped in lived experience but are also accurate, fact-checked, and delivered in ethical and non-extractive ways.

The model has been refined and adapted over four years and will continue to respond to the needs of the groups who benefit from it. However, the model is not without its challenges and limitations. To date, the model has been tested with a relatively small number of participants, from a predominantly white working-class background and a defined geographical area. The relational, bespoke, and flexible nature of the approach means that the model, while providing guidance for practitioners, should not be considered as a 'one size fits all' methodology. The audiences for this work may have had negative experiences of education and conventional learning environments. All of this combined requires adaptive training that strikes a careful balance between ensuring the course content is robust and accommodates individual needs in relation to how the group reacts to the work.

The model also requires a longer time frame than more traditional training methods, allowing time and space for sustained and trusting relationships to develop. This necessitates additional staff resources as well as longer-term engagement for community members. While this can be an obstacle in and of itself, it also poses challenges for the scalability of the approach. To date, all Participatory Community Podcasting sessions have been with relatively small, in-person groups to maintain the ability to form strong relationships between the group and facilitator and to avoid exclusion of members through a lack of access to digital equipment. While there may be potential to develop an online Participatory Community Podcasting programme, careful consideration would need to be made to how relationships remain central to the model and how the experience remains coproduced, experiential, and interactive. The team have identified potential areas for future development, including diversifying the reach of podcasting to further seldom-heard communities, and the potential for community advisory groups to inform the content of future podcast episodes and series. These would provide The Community Cast with further opportunity to test and develop the model with a diverse range of participants. Central to any future development of the approach will be the question of whose voices are included and whose are missing?

The Participatory Community Podcasting model presented in this chapter provides practitioners and academics with clear guidance on how to support communities to design and create podcasts to share their stories, raise awareness, and develop the skills to 'do it for themselves'. It presents a way of delivering industry-standard training using participatory approaches in a way that is conducive to working with communities with limited access to the tools, skills, and knowledge that are required to produce high-quality podcasting.

Notes

1 Leu, P. *Podcasts in the UK – Statistics & Facts*. 2025. Accessed on 26.08.2025 https://www.statista.com/topics/6908/podcasts-in-the-uk/.
2 Ofcom. *Audio Listening in the UK*. 2024. Accessed on 26.08.2025 https://www.ofcom.org.uk/siteassets/resources/documents/research-and-data/data/statistics/2024/audio-report-2024/ofcom-audio-report.pdf?v=320716.
3 Ofcom. *Audio Listening in the UK*. 2024. Accessed on 26.08.2025 https://www.ofcom.org.uk/siteassets/resources/documents/research-and-data/data/statistics/2024/audio-report-2024/ofcom-audio-report.pdf?v=320716.
4 Galily, Y., Laor, T. and Samuel-Azran, T. It's the Platform, Stupid (-; the Elitist Nature of Sport Podcast Listeners. *Online Information Review*. 47(5). 906–924. 29 August 2023. https://doi.org/10.1108/OIR-12-2021-0684
5 Jundi, D. and Gratton, N. Addressing Digital Poverty Through Community Engagement. In: *Action on Poverty in the UK. Sustainable Development Goals Series*. Palgrave Macmillan. Cham, 2023, 235–248. https://doi.org/10.1007/978-3-031-37182-0_13.
6 Lloyds Bank. *Consumer Digital Index: The UK's Largest Study of Digital and Financial Lives*. 2022. https://www.ipsos.com/sites/default/files/ct/publication/documents/2022-11/221103-lloyds-consumer-digital-index-2022-report.pdf.
7 Lloyds Bank. *Consumer Digital Index: The UK's Largest Study of Digital and Financial Lives*. 2024. https://www.lloydsbank.com/assets/media/pdfs/banking_with_us/whats-happening/lb-consumer-digital-index-2024-report.pdf.
8 Jundi, D. and Gratton, N. Addressing Digital Poverty Through Community Engagement. In: *Action on Poverty in the UK. Sustainable Development Goals Series*. Palgrave Macmillan. Cham, 2023, 235–248. https://doi.org/10.1007/978-3-031-37182-0_13.
9 Bruce, B. (Chip) and Lin, C.-C. Voices of Youth: Podcasting as a Means for Inquiry-Based Community Engagement. *E-Learning and Digital Media*. 6(2). 230–241. 2009. https://doi.org/10.2304/elea.2009.6.2.230.
10 Vrikki, P and Malik, S. Voicing Lived Experience and Anti-Racism: Podcasting as a Space at the Margins for Subaltern Counter Publics. *Popular Communication*. 17(4). 273–287. 2019. https://doi.org/10.1080/15405702.2019.1622116.
11 Jundi, D. and Gratton, N. Addressing Digital Poverty Through Community Engagement. In: *Action on Poverty in the UK. Sustainable Development Goals Series*. Palgrave Macmillan. Cham, 2023, 235–248. https://doi.org/10.1007/978-3-031-37182-0_13.
12 Jundi, D and Gratton, N. Addressing Digital Poverty Through Community Engagement. In *Action on Poverty in the UK. Sustainable Development Goals Series*. Palgrave Macmillan. Cham, 2023, 235–248. 246. https://doi.org/10.1007/978-3-031-37182-0_13.
13 Goodwin, G. The Problem and Promise of Coproduction. *Politics, History, and Autonomy*. 122. World Development, 2019, 501–513.
14 Mitlin, D. With and Beyond the State, Co-production as a Route to Political Influence, Power and Transformation for Grassroots Organizations. *Environment and Urbanisation*. 20(20). 339–360. 2008.
15 Coalition of Personalised Care. *Coproduction*. Accessed on: 27.11.25. https://www.england.nhs.uk/always-events/co-production/.
16 Mind. *Coproduction – Deciding together*. 2023. https://www.mind.org.uk/workplace/influence-and-participation-toolkit/how/methods/co-production/.
17 National Lottery Community Fund. *A meeting of Minds: How coproduction benefits people, professionals and organisations. Insights and inspirations from five strategic investments in England*. 2019. https://www.tnlcommunityfund.org.uk/media/A-Meeting-of-Minds_How-co-production-benefits-people-professionals-and-organisations.pdf?mtime=20190919092658&focal=none.
18 UK Research and Innovation. *Co-production in Research*. 2023.https://www.ukri.org/manage-your-award/good-research-resource-hub/research-co-production/.
19 Lloyds Bank. *Consumer Digital Index: The UK's Largest Study of Digital and Financial Lives*. 2024. https://www.lloydsbank.com/assets/media/pdfs/banking_with_us/whats-happening/lb-consumer-digital-index-2024-report.pdf.

20 Jundi, D. and Gratton, N. Addressing Digital Poverty Through Community Engagement. In *Action on Poverty in the UK*. Sustainable Development Goals Series. Palgrave Macmillan. Cham, 2023, 235–248. https://doi.org/10.1007/978-3-031-37182-0_13.
21 Qasserras, L. The Role of Visual Learning Aids across Diverse Learning Styles in High School Education. *European Journal of Applied Linguistics Studies*. 7(2): 68–80. 2024. https://doi.org/10.46827.
22 Hammon, M. and McArdle, E. Conversation in Youth Work: A Process for Encounter. *Child and Youth Services*. 45(1). 140–160. 2023. https://doi.org/10.1080/0145935X.2023.2279305.
23 Bruce, B. and Lin, C.-C. Voices of Youth: Podcasting as a Means for Inquiry-Based Community Engagement. *E-Learning and Digital Media*. 6 (2). 230–241. 2009. https://doi.org/10.2304/elea.2009.6.2.230.
24 Lansing, A.E., and Romero, N.J., Siantz, E. et al. Building Trust: Leadership Reflections on Community Empowerment and Engagement in a Large Urban Initiative. *BMC Public Health*. 23. 1252. 2023. https://doi.org/10.1186/s12889-023-15860-z.
25 McMullin, C. Building Relationships with Young People: A Model for Practice. *Relational Social Work*. 2(2). 50–60. 2018. https://doi.org/10.14605/RSW221805.
26 Broda, E. and Strömbäck, J. Misinformation, Disinformation, and Fake News: Lessons from an Interdisciplinary, Systematic Literature Review. *Annals of the International Communication Association*. 48(2). 139–166. June 2024. https://doi.org/10.1080/23808985.2024.2323736.
27 Bruce, B. and Lin, C.-C. Voices of Youth: Podcasting as a Means for Inquiry-Based Community Engagement. *E-Learning and Digital Media*. 6 (2). 230–241. 2009. https://doi.org/10.2304/elea.2009.6.2.230.
28 Smith, S. Participatory Journalism as a Way of Knowing. In: *Discussing the News. Palgrave Studies in Science, Knowledge and Policy*. Palgrave Macmillan, Cham, 2017, 9–25. https://doi.org/10.1007/978-3-319-52965-3_2.
29 Broda, E. and Strömbäck, J. Misinformation, Disinformation, and Fake News: Lessons from an Interdisciplinary, Systematic Literature Review. *Annals of the International Communication Association*. 48(2). 139–166. June 2024. https://doi.org/10.1080/23808985.2024.2323736.
30 Dvořák, V. But Whose Harm? Towards the Ethics of Participatory Advocacy Journalism with Unhoused Populations. *Journalism*. 26(1). 169–186. 2024. https://doi.org/10.1177/14648849241228093.
31 Porlezza, C. From Participatory Culture to Participatory Fatigue: The Problem With the Public. *Social Media + Society*. 5(3). 1–4. 2019. https://doi.org/10.1177/2056305119856684.
32 Vrikki, P. and Malik, S. Voicing Lived Experience and Anti-Racism: Podcasting as a Space at the Margins for Subaltern Counter Publics. *Popular Communication*. 17(4). 273–287. 2019. https://doi.org/10.1080/15405702.2019.1622116.
33 Bruce, B. and Lin, C.-C. Voices of Youth: Podcasting as a Means for Inquiry-Based Community Engagement. *E-Learning and Digital Media*. 6 (2). 230–241. 2009. https://doi.org/10.2304/elea.2009.6.2.230.

References

Broda, E. and Strömbäck, J. Misinformation, Disinformation, and Fake News: Lessons from an Interdisciplinary. *Systematic Literature Review*. 48(2). 139–166. *Annals of the International Communication Association*, June 2024. https://doi.org/10.1080/23808985.2024.2323736

Bruce, B. and Lin, C.-C. Voices of Youth: Podcasting as a Means for Inquiry-Based Community Engagement. *E-Learning and Digital Media*. 6(2). 230–241. 2009. https://doi.org/10.2304/elea.2009.6.2.230

Coalition of Personalised Care. *Coproduction*. Accessed on: 27.11.25. https://www.england.nhs.uk/always-events/co-production/

Dvořák, V. But Whose Harm? Towards the Ethics of Participatory Advocacy Journalism with Unhoused Populations. *Journalism*. 26(1). 169–186. 2024. https://doi.org/10.1177/14648849241228093

Galily, Y., Laor, T. and Samuel-Azran, T. It's the Platform, Stupid (-; the Elitist Nature of Sport Podcast Listeners. *Online Information Review.* 47(5). 906–924. 29 August 2023. https://doi.org/10.1108/OIR-12-2021-0684

Goodwin, G. The Problem and Promise of Coproduction. *Politics, History, and Autonomy.* 122. World Development, 2019, 501–513.

Hammon, M. and McArdle, E. Conversation in Youth Work: A Process for Encounter. *Child and Youth Services.* 45(1). 140–160. 2023. https://doi.org/10.1080/0145935X.2023.2279305

Jundi, D. and Gratton, N. Addressing Digital Poverty through Community Engagement. In *Action on Poverty in the UK. Sustainable Development Goals Series*: Palgrave Macmillan. Cham, 2023, 235–348. https://doi.org/10.1007/978-3-031-37182-0_13

Lansing, A.E., Romero, N.J., Siantz, E. et al. Building Trust: Leadership Reflections on Community Empowerment and Engagement in a Large Urban Initiative. *BMC Public Health.* 23. 1252. 2023. https://doi.org/10.1186/s12889-023-15860-z

Leu, P. *Podcasts in the UK – Statistics & Facts.* 2025. Accessed on: 26.08.2025 https://www.statista.com/topics/6908/podcasts-in-the-uk/

Lloyds Bank. *Consumer DIGITAL INDEX: The UK's Largest Study of Digital and Financial Lives.* 2022. https://www.ipsos.com/sites/default/files/ct/publication/documents/2022-11/221103-lloyds-consumer-digital-index-2022-report.pdf

Mind. *Coproduction – Deciding Together.* 2023. https://www.mind.org.uk/workplace/influence-and-participation-toolkit/how/methods/co-production/

McMullin, C. Building Relationships with Young People: A Model for Practice. *Relational Social Work.* 2(2). 50–60. 2018. https://doi.org/10.14605/RSW221805.

Mitlin, D. With and Beyond the State, Co-Production as a Route to Political Influence, Power and Transformation for Grassroots Organizations. *Environment and Urbanisation.* 20(20). 339–360. 2008.

National Lottery Community Fund. *A Meeting of Minds: How Coproduction Benefits People, Professionals and Organisations. Insights and Inspirations from Five Strategic Investments in England.* 2019. https://www.tnlcommunityfund.org.uk/media/A-Meeting-of-Minds_How-co-production-benefits-people-professionals-and-organisations.pdf?mtime=20190919092658&focal=none

Ofcom. *Audio Listening in the UK.* 2024. Accessed on: 26.08.2025 https://www.ofcom.org.uk/siteassets/resources/documents/research-and-data/data/statistics/2024/audio-report-2024/ofcom-audio-report.pdf?v=320716.

Porlezza, C. From Participatory Culture to Participatory Fatigue: The Problem With the Public. *Social Media + Society.* 5(3). 1–4. 2019. https://doi.org/10.1177/2056305119856684

Qasserras, L. The Role of Visual Learning Aids across Diverse Learning Styles in High School Education. *European Journal of Applied Linguistics Studies.* 7(2). 68–80. 2024. https://doi.org/10.46827

Smith, S. Participatory Journalism as a Way of Knowing. In: *Discussing the News. Palgrave Studies in Science, Knowledge and Policy:* Palgrave Macmillan. Cham, 2017, 9–25. https://doi.org/10.1007/978-3-319-52965-3_2

UK Research and Innovation. *Co-production in Research.* 2023.https://www.ukri.org/manage-your-award/good-research-resource-hub/research-co-production/

Vrikki, P. and Malik, S. Voicing Lived Experience and Anti-Racism: Podcasting as a Space at the Margins for Subaltern Counter Publics. *Popular Communication.* 17(4). 273–287. 2019. https://doi.org/10.1080/15405702.2019.1622116

Chapter 9

Public Engagement through Podcasting

Putting Theory into Practice in a University Module on Globalisation and Diversity

Duncan Lees, Stephanie Schnurr, Matthew W. Turner, Joel Agius, Diana Wang, VC Zhang, Marianna Patrick and Yvette Yitong Wang

As the department's name suggests, a key concern in Applied Linguistics at the University of Warwick is putting theory into practice by applying language-related research to real-world situations. For staff, one of the great joys of this is helping students understand how linguistic and intercultural research can not only shed light on important issues that arise in countless institutional, professional, and social situations, but also provide tools to tackle them. However, translating this real-world applicability into assignments that are genuinely meaningful for students can be a challenge – especially in the context of a UK higher education system that does not necessarily have flexibility and spontaneity at the heart of its assessment and quality assurance processes. This chapter will show how a focus on podcasting has been introduced to one postgraduate module in order to enable students to apply theory to practice, while making it easier for staff to give more targeted support and feedback as they do so. This chapter will share details of the overall module revision project, to which podcasting is central, and emphasise the importance of collaboration at every stage of the process, providing examples of how such projects can enact genuine staff-student co-creation. It will then discuss what was involved in introducing podcasting to a module/course that does not have a specific media focus, and what podcasting can offer students and staff in such contexts. Finally, it will show how podcasting is a particularly powerful activity for students of applied linguistics and intercultural communication, while suggesting how these disciplines might be able to inform other uses of podcasting within education.

Background: The Need for Module Revision and Podcasting as a Potential Solution

The module referred to in this chapter is one that was previously called "Globalisation and Diversity in the Workplace": an optional module which is offered on the University of Warwick's MSc in Intercultural Communication for Business and the Professions (MSc ICBP). This module required students to identify a local impact of globalisation and diversity, and then work in groups to come up with an intervention that helps address it. Over the years, this has led to some fascinating, innovative projects, which have seen the students – who are almost always from outside the local area, and typically also from abroad – engaging in various ways with local individuals and communities, from elderly residents of Coventry to recent immigrants to the UK. The most effective projects often

DOI: 10.4324/9781003677253-12

involved the production of some form of media, including websites, videos, and indeed podcasts. Such projects allowed students to take account of and even directly feature the voices of the people they were engaging with in a format that could then be shared more widely with interested parties across and beyond the university. However, it gradually became apparent that many students needed additional practical skills and knowledge in order to create more "professional" videos, websites, and podcasts. This in turn suggested a need for the module's teaching staff to offer a diverse and shifting range of training and scaffolding activities, which they had neither the time nor the practical and professional experience to deliver in all cases.

The teaching staff on the module had been debating how to address this problem when in late 2024 a possible solution presented itself in the form of a funding call issued by the Warwick Institute of Engagement (WIE).[1] This was offering up to £2000 for the purposes of redeveloping existing modules to include new elements of public or community engagement.[2] The module's requirement that students address a local impact of globalisation and diversity fitted nicely with this emphasis on public engagement, which the WIE defines as:

> [H]ow people working and studying at universities interact with external publics/partners to share knowledge, research, and expertise; foster collaboration on new ideas; or collectively co-produce new research, or new ways of working. Its aim is to create spaces that enable curiosity, exploration and conversation for a broad cross section of society. Through these interactions everyone gains valuable insights, in turn contributing to societal development and progress.[3]

Several aspects of this conception (interacting with external publics, working collaboratively, creating spaces that enable conversation) are well-suited to podcasting, and the specifics of the WIE's funding call pointed towards concrete steps that could be taken to introduce podcasting to a module like this, which had no specific media focus. Most importantly, the WIE could provide industry-informed podcasting training (which the module's staff were not themselves qualified to deliver), while the funding would allow purchase of the necessary equipment (which the department did not have). Although requiring students to produce a podcast would mean limiting some of their choices – previously they could have produced other forms of media, or none at all – it became apparent that this requirement could be a form of "enabling constraint",[4] freeing students up to engage in the task's most meaningful aspects. As will be discussed below, it is hoped that this shift will allow future students on the module (now called "Globalisation, Diversity and Public Engagement") to focus even more on engaging with relevant people and communities as they learn how to produce high-quality podcasts – something staff will also be able to support more effectively thanks to the WIE's industry-informed training.

Collaboration and Co-creation in (and around) Podcasting

Before discussing the process of introducing podcasting to this module, it is important to highlight the staff-student collaboration that characterised the project as a whole. Working collaboratively to create podcasts can provide students with interactive, dynamic learning experiences, which can bridge cultural and geographical divides.[5] This was certainly relevant for the highly international MSc ICBP cohort and their intercultural focus, but the fact that the pilot podcasts in this project emerged from collaborations between Master's and PhD students had additional benefits. As one of the MSc team members noted:

> It was great to work alongside an experienced PhD student who asked us tricky (but the right) questions to edge us MSc students in the right direction. We were quite competent, but bouncing ideas off a PhD student made me think deeper about my choices and even how I operate in a team.

The benefits went both ways, as Marianna Patrick, who joined the team as a PhD student and is now a Research Fellow in the department, has noted. Having worked as a graduate teaching assistant on "Globalisation and Diversity", Marianna's research interests in place and migration had already helped shape teaching and learning on the module. However, creating a podcast with MSc students "opened up fresh ways of looking at the module material", allowing her to "think about how the topics we explore in class play out in the real world". As well as contributing to the direction of future teaching and learning on the module, such new perspectives also illustrate how podcasts in educational contexts can offer opportunities for creating "new collaborative knowledge" that cuts across disciplinary divides[6] – something which is again highly relevant for this module, its students, and the wider MSc ICBP.

In fact, beyond the production of the podcasts themselves, every stage of this module revision project was underpinned by an ethos of staff-student co-creation, which Bovill et al.[7] define as "when staff and students work collaboratively with one another to create components of curricula and/or pedagogical approaches". This co-creative approach initially came out of the WIE's stipulation that applications for their funding scheme should involve some form of staff-student collaboration. While including students familiar with the module in the process of revising it suggested some obvious benefits, involving students in this time-consuming, bureaucratic procedure also posed challenges in terms of institutional factors and questions of inclusivity.[8] With MSc ICBP students completing their degree in one year, "last year's students" would not be available, but obviously having students involved in revising a module they were still completing assessment for could raise all kinds of problems. The timeline for the WIE funding helped, as successful projects were to be implemented in Terms 2 and 3 – meaning current "Globalisation and Diversity" students could be recruited, as they would already have submitted their final assignments at the end of Term 1. Nevertheless, asking students to take on so much extra work voluntarily, when they already had so much of their own MSc work to do, risked placing an unfair burden on participants, and potentially excluding anyone who could not make this kind of voluntary commitment (e.g. due to caring responsibilities, needing to do paid work while studying etc).

Here the WIE's funding call offered another solution, as paying students for their work was one of the permitted uses of the £2000 budget. The importance of this cannot be overstated. It meant that student collaborators could be recruited according to their enthusiasm and suitability for the project (rather than just their availability for unpaid work), and that there would be greater transparency and accountability in terms of how much work would be required and how this would be rewarded. Recognising the students' work *as work* seemed only fair given the extent and importance of their contributions, which far exceeded what could have been asked of volunteers. In the end, the WIE

Table 9.1 "Globalisation and diversity" module revision project team members and responsibilities

	Joel Agius	*Diana Wang*	*VC Zhang*	*Marianna Patrick*	*Matthew Turner*	*Yvette Wang*	*Duncan Lees*	*Stephanie Schnurr*
	PGT	*PGT*	*PGT*	*PGR*	*PGR*	*PGR*	*Staff*	*Staff*
Applying for WIE funding; contributing to follow-up report	✓	✓	✓	✓	✓	✓	✓	✓
Researching student perspectives on module revision	✓	✓	✓					
Writing up module revision documents							✓	✓
Planning podcasts	✓	✓	✓	✓	✓	✓	✓	✓
Recording / editing podcasts	✓	✓	✓	✓		✓		
Reviewing podcasts					✓		✓	✓
Presenting at EPOD 2025	✓	✓			✓		✓	
Co-authoring chapter for EPOD Book Two	✓	✓	✓	✓	✓	✓	✓	✓

funding allowed the creation of a team (see Table 9.1) made up of two staff, three MSc/taught postgraduate students (PGTs), and three postgraduate researchers (PGRs). This team then worked together on everything from developing the initial funding bid to following it up by producing academic outputs – including this chapter. Table 9.1 provides further illustration of the extent of co-creation featured in this project, with only one task – the bureaucratic matter of completing the module revision proposal and related documents – being done by the teaching staff alone (although even this drew heavily on the students' contributions).

Given the range of responsibilities they took on, the student members eventually fulfilled all four roles that Bovill et al.[9] suggest are commonly adopted by students in the co-creation of learning and teaching:

- *Students as consultants*: In this role, students are involved in "sharing and discussing valuable perspectives on learning and teaching",[10] which the PGTs did in team meetings by reflecting on their experiences of the "Globalisation and Diversity" module, and on what changes would be appealing and meaningful for students.
- *Students as co-researchers*: This involves students "collaborating meaningfully on teaching and learning research or subject-based research with staff".[11] For this project, the PGTs ran focus groups, using their position as peers and "insiders" to collect feedback from fellow "Globalisation and Diversity" students that was qualitatively different from what the module tutors themselves could have elicited. Two of the PGTs (Joel Agius and Diana Wang) and one PGR (Matthew Turner) also co-presented a paper on the project with a staff member (Duncan Lees) at EPOD 2025. Finally, insights from all of the student members have been incorporated into this chapter (hence their recognition as *co-authors*).
- *Students as pedagogical co-designers*: This role sees students "sharing responsibility for designing learning, teaching and assessment".[12] As discussed above, this was already being done by the PGR who had taught on the module, but more generally the ideas shared by the PGTs fed into every aspect of the project (including the completion of the module revision documentation by the staff).
- *Students as representatives*: This is when "student voices [contribute] to decisions in a range of university settings",[13] and in this project the PGTs and PGRs contributed to the shaping of the funding application, decisions around the planning and production of the pilot podcasts, and the discussion of project outcomes – internally (e.g. in the follow-up report for the WIE) and externally (e.g. in this chapter).

Having established the crucial roles played by the student members throughout this module revision project, this chapter will next discuss what was involved in introducing podcasting to a module with no specific media focus.

Enabling Constraints and Industry-Informed Support: Introducing Podcasting to a Non-Media Module

As has been noted above, while previous student projects for the "Globalisation and Diversity" module often involved the production of some form of media, including the occasional podcast, this was not a requirement. Informed by various academic conceptions of globalisation, including Appadurai's notion of globalisation as being characterised by flows of people, finance, technology, media, and ideology,[14] the module has always encouraged students to draw upon their own interests and experiences when identifying what issues to address, and how to address them. As such, past student projects have approached local impacts of globalisation and diversity in a host of innovative ways, from organising community outreach events for immigrants with young families, to running cuisine-themed intercultural workshops for international students left isolated on campus over Christmas, and even staging an open-mic comedy event tackling cultural and racial stereotypes. Developing and deploying consistent assessment criteria is obviously quite complex when the projects involved are so radically different (e.g. what does "Presentation" mean for a poster campaign compared to an open-mic night?). However, a more intractable problem concerned how the teaching staff could properly support the students' development of projects that covered such different skills, knowledge, and criteria for excellence. The "professional" aspect of other modules on the MSc ICBP generally relates to things the module tutors already have direct experience of – such as working in Public Relations, or delivering Intercultural Training. However, providing more hands-on support for the diverse projects on this module – including podcasts – would often necessitate practical and technical expertise well beyond the staff's own academic and professional backgrounds.

Deciding how to address this without limiting students' choices was difficult, but the WIE's funding call showed how introducing a focus on podcasting could be a productive compromise. While requiring students to produce a podcast for their final assignment does involve a restriction of sorts, this project has shown how such requirements can function as a form of "enabling constraint", whereby imposing certain conditions actually helps learners to focus their time, energy, and creativity on the most meaningful aspects of an activity.[15] In previous years on the module, some student groups would spend so long debating the form that their intervention should take that they had insufficient time to implement that intervention properly. In future, requiring every group to produce a podcast should eliminate these debates, freeing time up for students to focus on engaging with the people and communities impacted by their chosen issue while producing high-quality, impactful podcasts. In the past, differences in students' backgrounds and experiences sometimes also resulted in one or two group members with specific skills and knowledge (e.g. in web design or video editing) facing undue pressure to take care of the technical aspects of everyone's work and/or sometimes having too much control over the group's project. While prior experience of podcasting will obviously give future students a head-start, the fact that the same equipment, training, and support will be available to everyone should make it easier for groups to make decisions and allocate tasks more equitably and efficiently. It should also create a more level playing field in terms of expectations around the quality of what students are asked to produce, in turn making it more straightforward for staff to mark and give fair, consistent feedback. The public engagement element of the assessment can in future be framed in terms of how each group identifies and interacts with their podcast's guests and how they tailor the podcast's structure, content, and style for their target audience, for example. Similarly, whereas in the past the assessment criteria for "Presentation" in particular had to be couched in vague, catch-all terms, in the future, students and staff will be able to refer to a clear, podcast-specific set of requirements and expectations related to hosting, interviewing, recording, editing, using music, and the like.

To make this shift towards podcasting a reality, the project needed input from people with the kind of practical and professional expertise in making podcasts that the module's teaching staff lacked. Within the team, this was provided by one of the PGRs, Matthew Turner, who is conducting PhD research on podcasting and language teaching,[16] and as a co-founder and co-presenter of TEFLology,[17] is himself an experienced podcaster. Matthew provided crucial input at various stages of the project, from practical advice during the development of the funding application (e.g. on what equipment we needed to budget for) to detailed feedback on the two pilot podcasts. Beyond the team, the WIE provided invaluable support. Attending a WIE training day run by a podcasting expert with industry experience allowed the student team members to grow in confidence as they learned knowledge and skills they could apply to their podcasts – and share with others, including staff. The WIE's industry-informed support also extended to advice on purchasing equipment. One example was a discussion about whether buying equipment (in our case a Zoom H6 Audio Recorder, USB microphones, headphones etc) was the best use of our budget when Warwick already has podcasting facilities. However, because these facilities need to be booked in advance by staff, it was decided that purchasing our own equipment would give the students more independence and flexibility. Portable equipment would also allow students to go out and engage with the relevant people and communities in their own spaces, rather than requiring them to come onto the unfamiliar and potentially intimidating territory of a university campus (or participate remotely using technology which might be equally unfamiliar and intimidating to some). Finally, engaging with the WIE and its resources is already building up real-world, industry-informed frames of reference amongst staff and students (e.g. talk of "beds", "stings", and multiple senses of "hosting") that will feed into future teaching and assessment on the "Globalisation and Diversity" module, and hopefully contribute to a wider culture of podcasting in the department.

The final word in this section goes to one of the students who did the hard work of creating a pilot podcast. Together with fellow PGT Diana Wang and PGR Yvette Wang, Joel Agius co-created "Gender, Representation and Linguistics", a podcast featuring interviews with women in academia, sharing their real-life stories of balancing family responsibilities with academic careers. Joel stressed that producing this podcast allowed its student creators to bridge theory and lived experiences, deepening their understanding of the real-world import of topics such as identity, representation, and inclusion in ways no written essay would. In Joel's words, "hearing voices makes them more grounded and relevant", and this added another dimension to the process of putting theory into practice, as their team "learned about how to represent sensitive stories fairly, accurately and ethically". All of the MSc ICBP students attend research methods sessions on conducting and analysing interviews – including from more interactional and reflexive perspectives[18] – but interviewing people for a podcast is a very different prospect. Doing these interviews gave Joel and the other PGT members additional practice in formulating and asking open, thoughtful questions, and having the confidence to guide conversations while listening carefully and "giving space" for interviewees "to share authentically". This was followed by learning how recorded interviews are edited into the narratives heard on podcasts, both technically (in this case by learning to use Audacity) and in terms of navigating the ethics of shaping how others' voices and views are represented. All of this complemented and reinforced what the PGTs were learning on the MSc ICBP, but as Joel highlights, creating a podcast gave them extra "confidence through doing", which had its own significance: "we created something professional and meaningful from scratch, which we are proud of, and proud of our speakers for participating in it, and developed creative ideas for the future".

Different Voices: Podcasting, Applied Linguistics, and Intercultural Communication

Significantly, Joel's comment in the previous section includes mention that he and his fellow podcasters were proud not only of their own efforts but also of the contributions made by their "speakers". This is another reminder of the importance of incorporating different voices into this project – in the podcasts, of course, but also across the whole module revision process. Returning to the concept of co-creation that was discussed earlier, it is significant that "voice" has been identified by Omland et al.[19] as one of four core concepts discussed in research on staff-student co-creation, along with "dialogue", "positioning", and "agency". As they note, "[v]oice can be used both literally to signal a person's actual speaking, and metaphorically to signal a sense of empowerment and agency experienced when one's voice influences situated circumstances (Cook-Sather, 2020)". The first, more literal sense is of obvious relevance when co-creating podcasts and will be returned to shortly. However, the more metaphorical sense of "voice" is also important, as this project has attempted not simply to report students' views but to allow students to express them directly and influence the project by doing so. Scholarly publications on co-creation (and other forms of collaboration, including podcasting) often feature quotes from people who have been brought into a project as co-creators, only for the final say on what it all means – and the authorial credit – to go solely to academic staff. In reaction to this, it has been a point of principle for this project that every member of the team has been able to contribute to its academic outputs and has received authorial credit accordingly.

This use of "voice" also relates to another core concept in staff-student co-creation: "positioning", which Omland et al. take to mean "how relations among people are socially constituted".[20] These relations can potentially become more equal and reciprocal as staff and students engage in co-creation. However, as Omland et al. stress, changes in positionality are not simply bestowed through isolated gestures or decisions (e.g. paying the students or crediting them as co-authors) but are negotiated through sustained, dialogic interaction. In the wider project, such interactions have spanned everything from team meetings and email exchanges to small talk during the lunch break at EPOD 2025. But most powerfully, they took place during the creation of the podcasts, as the students interacted with each other and their interviewees. An example of how shifts in positionality can be achieved in these interactions was shared by PGT member Diana Wang, who, together with Joel Agius (PGT) and Yvette Wang (PGR), co-created the aforementioned "Gender, Representation and Linguistics" podcast. For this, Diana spoke to an academic who had taught her on the MSc, but adopting the roles of interviewee and interviewer changed the staff-student dynamic and resulted in a conversation quite unlike their previous "institutional" interactions. In Diana's words:

> One of the most memorable moments for me was hearing one of my module professors – someone I had only encountered in formal academic contexts – share her struggle of juggling various roles in her academic and family life, which had remained hidden from us students. It prompted me to rethink broader gender issues discussed in our 'Globalisation and Diversity' module.

This interaction gave Diana a very different understanding of this one person – as a woman, a mother, and an immigrant, as well as an academic – and of how issues of gender and globalisation discussed on the module relate to the realities of academia in the UK and elsewhere.

While this was clearly a transformative experience for Diana herself, because the interview was for a podcast it can be shared publicly, and other people will be able to engage with Diana's interviewee as she recounts her experiences in her own words and in her own voice. This sense of the word "voice" is, of course, a fundamental element of podcasting, as discussed by University of Leeds Emeritus Professor Stephen Coleman in his plenary address at EPOD 2025, in which he described the voice as "a technology for self-disclosure".[21] Listeners to the team's pilot episodes and other podcasts will make meaning out of them not only on the basis of what the speakers are saying but also the voices with which they are speaking. In the case of Diana interviewing her tutor, while the two explicitly discuss some aspects of their identities, listeners will draw their own conclusions (rightly or wrongly) about other aspects, based on their accents and various other qualities of their voices. Here it should be noted that while they conversed in English, neither the interviewer nor the interviewee speaks English as their first language (which is Mandarin for the former, and Portuguese for the latter). Such interactions are a major focus of the research on intercultural communication that underpins the MSc ICBP, including the discipline of intercultural pragmatics. In Troy McConachy and Helen Spencer-Oatey's definition, intercultural pragmatics "aims to account for the ways that individuals from different cultural backgrounds use, interpret and evaluate language use".[22] This discipline provides students with tools to analyse how people draw upon all kinds of different linguistic and cultural resources as they make sense of, and in, interactions – including in relation to identities that may be indexed through the voice or made relevant by the participants. A moment-by-moment, micro-level understanding of how intercultural interactions work in the real world can therefore be helpful when students are participating in them and also when they need to analyse and interpret them – whether for research purposes or while editing a podcast.

Crucially, intercultural pragmatics approaches such interactions not as inherently difficult or problematic, but as examples of "normal communication", whereby "[i]nteractants [...] also have their successes and failures, just like any human beings who communicate".[23] Similarly, it typically rejects deficit perspectives in which people using anything other than their "first" language are treated as incomplete or inferior versions of an idealised "native speaker", seeing them instead as legitimate users of that language (and often skilled multilinguals, as are Diana and her interviewee). Such an approach to intercultural interaction is not merely a political aspiration but a recognition of the realities of today's world, in which interactions between people from different cultural and linguistic backgrounds are increasingly common – and the norm in many contexts. This is certainly the case at many of the UK's "superdiverse"[24] universities, with the team behind this chapter a case in point, only three of its eight members having English as their first language. In situations such as this, so-called "intercultural" interactions are simply everyday communication. Podcasting in this kind of context therefore represents an opportunity not only to assess language learners[25] or give them a chance to practise[26] but also to allow *all* students and staff to assert the legitimacy of their language use and of themselves as language users. This can be taken further still by embracing a translanguaging approach,[27] which moves beyond the idea of multilinguals' "code-switching" between discrete languages (which by implication have clear, fixed boundaries – including in relation to *whose* languages they are), instead framing such interactions as utilising speakers' own translingual repertoires.

Questioning what legitimacy means in terms of language use, language users, and indeed languages themselves, should also be extended to interrogating how speaking (and hearing) are so often privileged in our understandings of how communication occurs – including in podcasting.[28] An example from the other podcast produced for this module revision project, "Inclusion/exclusion in sports", produced by Marianna Patrick (PGR) and VC Zhang (PGT), illustrates this. Featuring interviews with people who had experienced being linguistic minorities in sporting contexts, the podcast explored how sport can become a site of both connection and exclusion due to linguistic and cultural factors, and related questions of access, belonging, and identity. Marianna notes:

> I spoke with a Deaf cricket player who shared his experiences playing in both Deaf and hearing teams, and the communication challenges that arose on and off the pitch. Hearing his story first-hand helped me consider issues of communication in sport in ways that no lecture ever could.

As she recounts, Marianna *spoke* to her interviewee and *heard* his answers as he *spoke* about his experiences – including the impact of being in sporting situations in which no British Sign Language interpreting was available. However, their discussion, in its content and form, is a reminder that privileging speaking and listening when we think about podcasts – and communication – risks excluding those who may need, or choose, to interact and engage in different ways. Again, this also shows how producing a podcast can help students of applied linguistics and intercultural communication – or other disciplines – to better understand how communication works in the real world and why this matters.

Conclusion

The comments from student team members featured in this piece echo Rachel-Ann Charles' observation, in a chapter on integrating podcasts into a media studies course with a decolonial focus, that assignments which allow "students to tackle real-world problems through media production" can empower them "to become culturally conscious emerging media professionals".[29] For students of applied linguistics and intercultural communication, such consciousness must involve understanding how language works in the real world, and this chapter has argued that podcasting represents a powerful way of achieving this. However, it has hopefully also shown what podcasting can offer students and staff of other academic disciplines, and how – even for courses with no specific media focus. While there is still a long way to go for this particular project – including, at the time of writing, publishing the pilot podcasts and preparing for the first iteration of the new "Globalisation, Diversity and Public Engagement" module – the project has already proved transformative. In addition to team members developing new skills and knowledge that they are eager to make use of in future podcasts, the experience of collaborating throughout the project has also prompted them to reconsider what is possible in higher education when staff and students step out of their normal roles and relationships and attempt genuine co-creation.

Notes

1 Warwick Institute of Engagement, *Warwick Institute of Engagement* (University of Warwick, August 29, 2025). https://warwick.ac.uk/wie/.
2 Warwick Institute of Engagement, *Public and Community Engagement Module Development Fund* (University of Warwick, August 29, 2025). https://warwick.ac.uk/wie/funding andgrantsupport/moduledevelopment/.
3 Warwick Institute of Engagement, *What Is Engagement?* (University of Warwick, August 29, 2025). https://warwick.ac.uk/wie/training/staff/skillsfestival-staff/whatisengagement.
4 Joe Winston, *Transforming the Teaching of Shakespeare with the Royal Shakespeare Company* (Bloomsbury Arden Shakespeare, 2015), 87–88.
5 Sam Coley, "Podcasting as a tool for internationalisation: past examples and future opportunities," in *Podcasting and Education: Concepts, Communities and Case Studies*, Eds. Carola Boehm, Tim Canfer and Camilo Salazar (Routledge, 2025), 51.
6 Jenny O'Connor and Robert O'Connor, "All ears: exploring epistemic living spaces in university podcasting," in *Podcasting and Education: Concepts, Communities and Case Studies*, Eds. Carola Boehm, Tim Canfer and Camilo Salazar (Routledge, 2025), 170.
7 C. Bovill et al., "Addressing potential challenges in co-creating learning and teaching: overcoming resistance, navigating institutional norms and ensuring inclusivity in student-staff partnerships." *Higher Education* 71 (2016): 196. https://link.springer.com/article/10.1007/s10734-015-9896-4.
8 Bovill et al., "Addressing potential challenges in co-creating learning and teaching." 201–204.
9 Bovill et al., "Addressing potential challenges in co-creating learning and teaching." 197–198.
10 Bovill et al., "Addressing potential challenges in co-creating learning and teaching." 197–198.
11 Bovill et al., "Addressing potential challenges in co-creating learning and teaching." 197–198.
12 Bovill et al., "Addressing potential challenges in co-creating learning and teaching." 197–198.
13 Bovill et al., "Addressing potential challenges in co-creating learning and teaching." 197–198.
14 Arjun Appadurai, *Modernity at large: cultural dimensions of globalization* (University of Minnesota Press, 1996).
15 Joe Winston, *Transforming the Teaching of Shakespeare with the Royal Shakespeare Company* (Bloomsbury Arden Shakespeare, 2015), 87–88.
16 Matthew W. Turner, "Podcasting as an approach to reflective practice for educators in the field of English language teaching," in *Podcasting and Education: Concepts, Communities and Case Studies*, Eds. Carola Boehm, Tim Canfer and Camilo Salazar (Routledge, 2025), 185–200.
17 The TEFLology Podcast, "The TEFLology podcast: a podcast about language teaching and applied linguistics." *The TEFLology Podcast*. September 1, 2025.
18 Steve Mann, *The Research Interview* (Palgrave Macmillan, 2016).
19 Maren Omland et al., "Co-creation in higher education: a conceptual systematic review." *Higher Education* (2025). https://doi.org/10.1007/s10734-024-01364-1.
20 Omland et al., "Co-creation in higher education."
21 Stephen Coleman, "What's in a voice?," (Conference paper, Education Through Podcasting Conference 2025, London, June 27, 2025).
22 Troy McConachy and Helen Spencer-Oatey, "Cross-cultural and intercultural pragmatics," in *The Cambridge Handbook of Sociopragmatics*, Eds. Michael Haugh, Dániel Z. Kádár and Marina Terkourafi (Cambridge University Press, 2021), 733.
23 Istvan Kecskes, *Intercultural Pragmatics* (Oxford University Press, 2014), 166.
24 Steven Vertovec, "Super-diversity and its implications." *Ethnic and Racial Studies* 30 (2007): 1024–1054. https://doi.org/10.1080/01419870701599465.
25 Simon Perry, "Podcasting as a form of assessment: increasing student motivation in academic English speaking assessment." *Language Testing in Asia* 14, No. 1 (2024): 1–24. https://doi.org/10.1186/s40468-024-00288-y.
26 Joanna Duchesne, "Try making this: a case study in podcasting as a language learning technique," in *Podcasting and Education: Concepts, Communities and Case Studies*, Eds. Carola Boehm, Tim Canfer and Camilo Salazar (Routledge, 2025), 79–92.
27 Olivia García and Li Wei, *Translanguaging: Language, Bilingualism and Education* (Palgrave Pivot, 2014). https://link.springer.com/book/10.1057/9781137385765.

28 Jenny O'Connor and Robert O'Connor, "All ears: exploring epistemic living spaces in university podcasting," in *Podcasting and Education: Concepts, Communities and Case Studies*, Eds. Carola Boehm, Tim Canfer and Camilo Salazar (Routledge, 2025), 170–184.
29 Rachel-Ann Charles, "Decolonising media studies through podcasting," in *Podcasting and Education: Concepts, Communities and Case Studies*, Eds. Carola Boehm, Tim Canfer and Camilo Salazar (Routledge, 2025), 111.

References

Appadurai, Arjun. *Modernity at Large: Cultural Dimensions of Globalization.* University of Minnesota Press, 1996.

Bovill, C., A. Cook-Sather, P. Felten, I. Millard, and N. Moore-Cherry. "Addressing potential challenges in co-creating learning and teaching: overcoming resistance, navigating institutional norms and ensuring inclusivity in student-staff partnerships." *Higher Education* 71 (2016): 195–208. https://link.springer.com/article/10.1007/s10734-015-9896-4.

Charles, Rachel-Ann. "Decolonising media studies through podcasting." In *Podcasting and Education: Concepts, Communities and Case Studies*, edited by Carola Boehm, Tim Canfer and Camilo Salazar, 105–115. Routledge, 2025.

Coleman, Stephen. "What's in a voice?" Paper presented at Education Through Podcasting Conference 2025, London, June 2025.

Coley, Sam. "Podcasting as a tool for internationalisation: past examples and future opportunities." In *Podcasting and Education: Concepts, Communities and Case Studies*, edited by Carola Boehm, Tim Canfer and Camilo Salazar, 50–63. Routledge, 2025.

Cook-Sather, Alison. "Respecting voices: How the co-creation of teaching and learning can support academic staff, underrepresented students, and equitable practices." *Higher education* 79 (2020): 885–901. https://doi.org/10. 1007/s10734-019-00445-w.

Duchesne, Joanna. "Try making this: a case study in podcasting as a language learning technique." In *Podcasting and Education: Concepts, Communities and Case Studies*, edited by Carola Boehm, Tim Canfer and Camilo Salazar, 79–92. Routledge, 2025.

García, Olivia and Li Wei. *Translanguaging: Language, Bilingualism and Education.* Palgrave Pivot, 2014. https://link.springer.com/book/10.1057/9781137385765.

Kecskes, Istvan. *Intercultural Pragmatics.* Oxford University Press, 2014.

Mann, Steve. *The Research Interview.* Palgrave Macmillan, 2016.

McConachy, Troy and Helen Spencer-Oatey. "Cross-cultural and intercultural pragmatics." In *The Cambridge Handbook of Sociopragmatics*, edited by Michael Haugh, Dániel Z. Kádár and Marina Terkourafi, 733–757. Cambridge University Press, 2021.

O'Connor, Jenny and Robert O'Connor. "All ears: exploring epistemic living spaces in university podcasting." In *Podcasting and Education: Concepts, Communities and Case Studies*, edited by Carola Boehm, Tim Canfer and Camilo Salazar, 170–184. Routledge, 2025.

Omland, Maren, Magnus Hontvedt, Fazilat Siddiq, Anja Amundrud, Hege Hermansen, Maiken A.S. Mathisen, Gudrun Rudningen and Frederik Reiersen. "Co-creation in higher education: a conceptual systematic review." *Higher Education* (2025): 1017–1047. https://doi.org/10.1007/s10734-024-01364-1.

Perry, Simon. "Podcasting as a form of assessment: increasing student motivation in academic English speaking assessment." *Language Testing in Asia* 14, No. 1 (2024): 15. https://doi.org/10.1186/s40468-024-00288-y.

TEFLology Podcast, The. "The TEFLology podcast: a podcast about language teaching and applied linguistics." *The TEFLology Podcast.* September 1, 2025.

Turner, Matthew W. "Podcasting as an approach to reflective practice for educators in the field of English language teaching." In *Podcasting and Education: Concepts, Communities and Case Studies*, edited by Carola Boehm, Tim Canfer and Camilo Salazar, 185–200. Routledge, 2025.

Vertovec, Steven. "Super-diversity and its implications." *Ethnic and Racial Studies* 30 (2007): 1024–1054. https://doi.org/10.1080/01419870701599465.
Warwick Institute of Engagement. *Public and Community Engagement Module Development Fund.* University of Warwick, August 29, 2025. https://warwick.ac.uk/wie/fundingandgrantsupport/moduledevelopment/.
Warwick Institute of Engagement. *Warwick Institute of Engagement.* University of Warwick, August 29, 2025. https://warwick.ac.uk/wie/.
Warwick Institute of Engagement. *What Is Engagement*? University of Warwick, August 29, 2025. https://warwick.ac.uk/wie/training/staff/skillsfestival-staff/whatisengagement.
Winston, Joe. *Transforming the Teaching of Shakespeare with the Royal Shakespeare Company.* Bloomsbury Arden Shakespeare, 2015.

Chapter 10

'Un-Podcasting' as Method

How Music and Running Podcasts Shaped a New Definition of Podcasting

Carola Boehm

Introduction

This chapter is the result of a specific experimental practice and its associated line of enquiry.[1] These have led me to propose a new definition of podcasting. Thus, one of the main outcomes of this research is an understanding not only of my own creative practice and its contexts, but also the evolutionary shift in how the terminology and the perception of what a podcast is have changed over the last two decades, as well as the factors that have influenced terminology, discourses, and perceptions around podcasting.

Besides my practice output and analysis, a key outcome for me was the positioning of the below new definition, which had the flexibility of including my podcast practice and future innovative ways for audio-based content production. At the risk of putting the outcome of my little research journey here first, I posit the new definition I developed for podcasts as:

> A Podcast is an audio-focused cultural form that is constructed by social innovation in content production.
>
> (Boehm at EPOD 2025)

The article has two main sections. The first section will focus on the podcast practice itself, using *CBDB Runs* Podcast as a case study. The last section will focus on the critical analysis of the evolution of these terms and on how the addition of music can be contextualised in terms of terminology, definitions, and the conceptual understanding of the phenomena of podcasting.

From Methodology to 'Un-Podcasting' Practice

The aim of this mini research project of mine is rather a luxurious one. In an academically indulgent manner, by creating a podcast (*CBDB Runs* on Mixcloud), I create an experimental space to explore definitional boundaries and ask what this may mean for my *un-podcasting* practice in the context of a learning and knowledge society. Along the journey, I will tether it to existing literature, including that of scholars who presented in EPOD'24 and contributed to the first book in our EPOD series, published by Routledge earlier this year.

DOI: 10.4324/9781003677253-13

The practice uses music immersion and reflective narrative not just for enjoyment, but as a vehicle for embodied learning, personal development, and community engagement.

My lenses add to this: Culture 3.0 supports this framing of podcasting as a participatory cultural practice, in which audiences are co-creators of meaning rather than passive consumers. My podcast exemplifies this shift by inviting listeners into a shared, experiential journey that is both personal and public. And University 3.0 concepts allow me to reflect on my perceived need to advocate and develop practices for creative, civic, and co-productive models of education. This is the kind of podcast that becomes a learning environment outside traditional classrooms, bridging formal and informal learning through immersive aural experiences, training guidance, and cultural critique.

Together, these frameworks position my work as a critical response to the tensions EPOD 2025 explores – how educational podcasting can remain authentic, inclusive, and innovative whilst navigating the expectations of media platforms and industry standards.

The research underpinning this presentation is grounded in a podcast-oriented, practice-led, exploratory methodology (practice as research) that draws from experimental creative practice. The methodology has been put forward, amongst others, by Nelson's seminal Practice As Research.[2] As usual, when adopting a Practice As Research methodology, my practice pulls along critical and conceptual insights.

It is 'PRAXIS', in the sense that it is theory imbricated within a practice. As such, I am not just doing a podcast; I am also exploring the limits around concepts and definitions, and in turn, this informs my podcasting practice. The podcast practice pulled along lines of enquiry around the evolving definitional boundaries of podcasting, both from the scholarly literature and other documentary sources in the public domain (news items, public discourses).

Thus, the research has all three classic elements that Nelson's methodology puts forward,[3] and this helps me develop a critical and conceptual framework around my podcasting practice, with:

- **Know How** – embodied knowledge, phenomenological experience, tacit knowledge, performer-doer-maker knowledge (e.g. podcasting practice, recording practice, creative practice)
- **Know What** – reflexive, critical reflections, explicit knowledge, practitioner action research etc (e.g. history of podcasting, history and facts around podcasting)
- **Know That** – conceptual frameworks, cognitive academic knowledge, tethering to critical discourses or lit reviews, audience research (e.g. analysis of factors influencing the evolution of definitions of podcasting)

For the critical and conceptual analysis (Know That), I often use an additional semiotic analysis, based on the Cultural Political Economy (CPE) framework[4] and expanded by me.[5] This supports the exploration of critical elements and structural conditions that interact to shape cultural practices, which is useful when exploring emerging phenomena such as podcasting and its definitional evolution as the form evolved. This is important as the type of podcasting practice I will discuss sits at the intersection of education, entertainment, and non-institutionalised learning journeys. In its present form, it also challenges conventional definitions of podcasting and opens up new conceptual spaces for understanding audio-based cultural practices.

My expanded CPE framework allows for the integration of multiple analytical lenses – structural (e.g. whether the podcast phenomenon is talk-oriented, or exclusive to Spotify), discursive (what the media, narratives, and academic outputs say), agential (who or which companies led on specific developments), and technological (what are the underlying technical frameworks) – to examine how podcasting practices are embedded in broader cultural and institutional contexts and how they evolve. For instance, the structural lens helps interrogate platform affordances and licensing regimes; the discursive lens explores how podcasting is framed in academic and public discourse; the agential lens considers the role of the prosumer switching from consumer to producer; and the technological lens highlights how platform-specific features shape the form and function of audio content and, with it, the perceived essence of what a podcast is (see Table 10.1).

Two conceptual lenses lie at the heart of its methodological expansion, and have proven particularly generative in my work: Culture 3.0[6] and University 3.0.[7] These lenses help reframe podcasting not merely as a media format but as a cultural and educational practice that reflects broader shifts in how knowledge is produced, shared, and experienced. Culture 3.0, for example, emphasises participatory, co-creative cultural engagement, whilst University 3.0 reimagines higher education as a permeable institution, emphasising engagement with society, industry, and collaborative knowledge production.

Together, these frameworks support a structured exploration of podcasting as a liminal space – a site where formal and informal learning, personal expression and public discourse, and entertainment and education converge. By situating my *un-podcasting*

Table 10.1 CPE example for one 'time slice' of the phenomenon podcast music and talk show

2025	*Mainstream*	*Spotify Music & Talk Shows*	*Mixcloud Shows*	*CBDB Runs*
Structural	Talk-oriented shows, episodic, narrative.	Exclusive to Spotify, licenses with labels in place.	Exclusive to Mixcloud, licenses with labels in place.	Exclusive to Spotify. Exclusive to Mixcloud.
Technological	mp3, rss	Anchor technology	Initially streaming only, now downloadable. No open RSS feeds (due to music licensing).	Requires significant music and audio post-production, metadata, workflow management, field recording, and miking.
Discourses	Audio first, episodic, narrative, talk shows	Music & chat shows, less known, no discourses emerging.	DJ site, still less known, not as popular with podcast audiences. No open RSS feeds.	Within health and running communities: Health unlocked, Strava, and Social media.
Agency	Independent podcasters, celebrity podcasters	Independent podcasters, anchor podcasters.	Independent DJs and community radio stations.	Self-agency as a runner, as a podcaster. Online running communities run by volunteers.

practice within this methodological constellation, I aim to contribute to a broader rethinking of what podcasting can be and do, particularly in relation to creative self-expression, embodied learning, and cultural critique.

The Contexts

This line of enquiry came about from different trajectories, bringing together both my professional and personal activities, each with its own personal long-term evolution and learning journeys that all relate to this podcast practice. My academic background is in music technology, holding degrees in music, electrical engineering, and computer science. My first decade as a researcher was spent exploring central music information database systems and music metadata, having worked with the Moving Picture Expert Group, which put forward the MP3 format, a key format for podcasts. Early on, I could see how podcasting would change the way we consume news, learning, media, and entertainment, and my early work on Culture 3.0[8] pointed towards podcasting as a form that had a lot of characteristic features of Culture 3.0 types of engagement.[9]

As an educator, I could also see how, in the era of the knowledge economy and knowledge societies, these decentralised, co-created learning and information ecosystems represented something that I called University 3.0.[10] Podcasting fits into these more permeably designed learning environments, with the current *CBDB Runs* podcast series representing a non-institutionally based, peer-to-peer learning environment.

The element which was the least integrated into my professional identity was my running. After ten years of suffering from the undiagnosed condition of Hashimoto's, my fitness, well-being, and weight management had degraded severely. Once diagnosed, I slowly ran my way back into a reasonable level of fitness, starting and finishing Couch to 5K. I continue to run and now podcast about this experience.

During my searches for how I could improve my health as a Hashimoto sufferer, I found HealthUnlocked (HU).[11] HU calls itself 'the largest social networking service for health', providing 'peer support for health conditions' and promoting 'patient empowerment by actively engaging people with their healthcare'. HU has around 400 forums with 2 million members, representing more than 300 patient organisations. Amongst these are five forums that are dedicated to supporting UK runners as part of various NHS/BBC fitness campaigns. This includes the supporting communities around various NHS apps and podcasts, including the NHS/BBC Couch to 5K app/podcast, guiding beginner runners through a nine-week plan to get to running 30 minutes continuously. Additionally, it includes the Active 10 Walking App, focusing on regular active walking, and the five-week-long audio-coached podcast plan for Strength & Flexibility.

The forums supporting these initiatives are volunteer-run by runners for runners, peer-to-peer, and, in my view, co-create insights that help all sorts of communities become confident in their fitness journeys. As one of the largest forums on HU, these five forums around running, walking, and fitness support around 170,000 members. By the end of this first year, I became one of the 20 volunteer admins who ensured that the five running forums on HU were safe for the community and kept people going in their running journeys. This worked for me. Since 2020, I have run three times a week, super slow (I call myself the Queen of Slow), and have experienced a regaining of various physical capabilities that I had been sure to have lost.

This is the context in which I started the *CBDB Runs* podcast, wanting to give back to specifically health-challenged runners, whose physical constraints are often not catered for in various alternative running communities. Additionally, the act of combining my podcasting with running created my own personal motivational factor to keep going.

The Podcast that Wasn't – CBDB Runs *(on Mixcloud)*

My current podcast practice, now functioning as my little experimental podcast lab, is now hosted on Mixcloud. Mixcloud is a streaming platform that supports long-form audio content such as DJ mixes, radio shows, and podcasts. It is one of the few platforms that offers legal music licensing, allowing podcasters (and DJs) to include full-length commercial music tracks in their shows without violating copyright laws. This makes it ideal for creators who want to blend music and spoken word in innovative ways.

The podcast is called *CBDB Runs*,[12] and it has existed as a show of 20 episodes on Spotify (until 2024) and is currently on Mixcloud (60+ shows). It constitutes a non-institutionalised peer-to-peer learning environment, and its design and shaping drew from existing conceptual frameworks I am familiar with, that of Sacco's Culture 3.0 and my own Uni 3.0.

It features training plans that make use of curated music lists and brief audio-coached instructions on when to run and when to walk, this run-walking often called Jeffing. Thus, the Mixcloud show started off with a Jeffing plan, but continued to have different jeffed or continuous runs. It explored different types of music-running-chat shows, with episodes that could be described as falling into different categories:

Category 1: Themed Jeffing Shows that Provide Audio Guidance on When to Walk and When to Run

Using the length of a song to dictate the duration of one running interval, these shows simply provided different lengths of runs that are jeffed. These shows often have a specific theme, where the music and the chat focus on this theme. Examples for this could be an R&B Christmas run, featuring bypasser's many seasonal wishes,[13] a run to celebrate World Book Day with songs about books,[14] or a show featuring songs about cooling and ice-cold topics to keep runners cool on hot summer runs[15] (Figure 10.1).

The shows also allowed runners to find the little bit of motivation to get out of the house when it is raining or when they do not feel like running. Running to the sound of songs about rain or clouds often provides just that tiny little motivational kick out the door, to banish the hardest gremlin of them all, that 5 cm high door threshold that – once beyond that – most runners keep on going.

Category 2: Training Plans that Provide an Incremental Audio-Coached Set of Runs over Several Weeks

Another set of shows is those associated with a running plan; the first one developed as part of the show was designed to get lapsed or beginner runners trained up to running 30 minutes continuously. A duration-based plan works well for those occasions where runners at different levels want to experience the same progress together in terms of duration of runs, but their different levels of fitness or ability allow them all to run at the paces

Songlist

1. Warmup Walk & Chat		- 00:00:00
2. Kelly Finnigan	- Santa's Watching You	- 00:02:01
3. Walk & Chat		- 00:03:36
4. The Twistin' Kings	- Xmas Twist	- 00:06:28
5. Walk & Chat		- 00:09:07
6. Rose Graham	- Black Christmas	- 00:11:44
7. Walk & Chat		- 00:14:30
8. Georgie Fame	- Ho Ho Ho	- 00:16:42
9. Walk & Chat // HALFWAY POINT		- 00:19:17
10. Sharon Jones & The DapKings	- God Rest Ye Merry Gents	- 00:22:24
11. Walk & Chat		- 00:24:28
12. Lavern Baker & The Gliders	- Tiny Tim	- 00:26:36
13. Walk & Chat		- 00:28:48
14. Sharon Jones & The DapKings	- Just Another Christmas (This time I'll Sing Along)	- 00:31:02
15. Walk & Chat		- 00:34:03
16. Santa Claus is Coming to Town	- Galactic, Anjelika 'Jelly' Joseph	- 00:35:21
17. Good Bye Until Next Time		- 00:38:24

Figure 10.1 CBDB's Christmas run to R&B, soul, and retro soul.

they are able and thus reach different distances. Thus, duration-based runs are perfect for virtual running communities, of which my show was a part. It allows solo runners to still feel part of a running community with shared and relatable experiences on each run.

As a first training plan, I launched a six-week running plan both on a forum webpage[16] and a series of Mixcloud shows.[17] The plan was one adapted from a six-week Runner's World Couch to 5K plan,[18] and whilst completing the runs on the plan, audio was recorded during the run in real-time.

Curated playlists, with each run having some themed collections, were put together, ensuring that the running sections were differentiated from the walking sections through the choice of songs. Walking sections included my recorded chatting over instrumental music. Thus, for instance, the second run in the plan, which has four repeats of two minutes of running and four minutes of walking intervals, incorporated well-known popular pop/rock songs for the two-minute intervals, fading into mediaeval-imagined instrumental cover versions for the four minutes of walking intervals, underlying my chatting (see Figure 10.2).

The training plans allowed runners to have some minimal guidance on when to run and when to walk, be immersed in a curated playlist of songs, and be entertained by short conversations that keep runners company. The latter was particularly important for me as a slow runner, as often 'back-of-the-pack' runners enjoy running solo, as running with groups can mean that they experience their low speed physically in their position in the pack. Thus, going by my own experience of not wanting to engage in running clubs, Park runs, or official races that might have cut-off points too short for me to finish in time, the audiences I had foremost in mind were again like-minded back-of-the-pack runners with health or weight challenges, keeping these solo runners company but still being able to gain confidence in running consistently.

This plan and the podcasting learning journey allowed me to carry out my first experiments with mic placements, processing of stepping and breathing sounds, and environmental acoustic characteristics.

Songlist

1.	WARMUP WALK & CHAT		- 00:00:00
2.	Breathe – Medieval Bardcore Version	- Beedle the Bardcore	- 00:00:37
3.	Africa – Medieval Style	- Bard to the Core, The Tavern	- 00:03:37
4.	Africa	- TOTO	- 00:07:30
5.	Wonderwall	- Stantough	- 00:09:31
6.	Wonderwall	- Oasis	- 00:13:33
7.	Bohemian Rhapsody	- Bardcore	- 00:15:33
8.	Bohemian Rhapsody	- Queen	- 00:19:33
9.	Bye Bye Bye	- Stantough	- 00:21:33
10.	HALFWAY POINT		- 00:22:21
11.	Bye Bye Bye	- NYSNC	- 00:25:33
12.	The Final Countdown	- Bardcore	- 00:27:33
13.	The Final Countdown	- Europe	- 00:31:33
14.	Take On Me	- Joseph C. Phaze	- 00:33:33
15.	Ob-La-Di, Ob-La-Da	- Stary Olsa	- 00:37:13
16.	Riders on the Storm	- Chalmeris	- 00:39:26
17.	COOLDOWN AND GOODBYE UNTIL NEXT TIME		- 00:42:16
18.	You Spin Me Right Around	- Middle Ages	- 00:44:36

Figure 10.2 CBDB's Week 1, Run 2 of the six-week plan.

Category 3: Beats per Minute Runs with Curated Songs with a Certain BPM for Syncing Your Cadence

Once finished with the plan, I continued recording continual or Jeffed runs, often with themes. However, I had already piloted specific 'BPM runs'. These curated shows are a list of songs with specific tempos or beats per minute (BPM) that allow runners to sync their steps to the beat.

Many runners enjoy running to music and trying to sync their cadence (leg turnover) to the beat. But, after having run regularly to music over the past five years, my experience suggested that although I was able to train up to a cadence of 160, with the average leg turnover for professional runners of 180 being simply unreachable for me, a comfortable recovery run cadence for me was in the sweet spot of between 145 and 155 BPM. Over the years, I had put together various Spotify playlists[19] that allowed me to 'train up to' 160 BPM, by using songlists in 10 BPM ranges from 120 to 170 BPM, each list having songs within a 10 BPM range. For instance, Pop & Rock 130–140 BPM or Classical 140–150 BPM.

These were put together initially by measuring via metronomes, but later through additional web services that came on board once they could access Spotify's metadata (e.g. Chosic or Sort Your Music).

For the Mixcloud show *CBDB Runs*, it was obvious to try out BPM runs, focusing on leg turnover and featuring songs with a specific range of beats. These focus on slower cadences of up to 160 BPM for slower runners to use for their runs and allow them to train up to 160 BPM (see Figure 10.3).

Additional Categories

As the podcast grew, additional categories were added as I experimented with different fitness-music-talk shows. These included:

- **Walks**, which feature a walking partner and me chatting to music we listen to whilst on a walk. Some walk shows also feature a lower BPM rate for those walkers who want to walk to a beat.

Figure 10.3 CBDB's BPM-curated song lists. BPM, Beats per Minute.

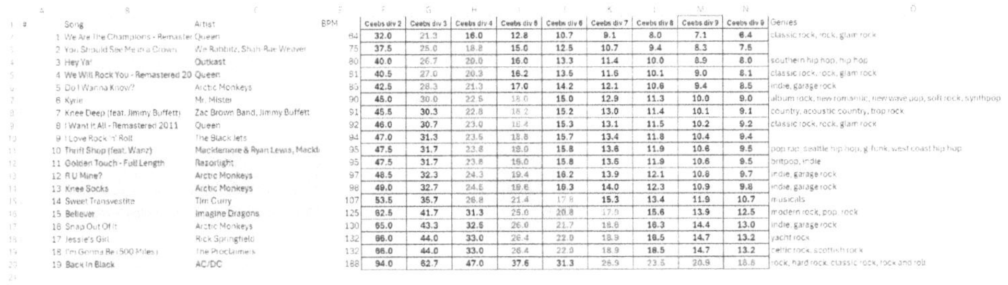

#	Song	Artist	BPM	Ceebs div 2	Ceebs div 3	Ceebs div 4	Ceebs div 5	Ceebs div 6	Ceebs div 7	Ceebs div 8	Ceebs div 9	Ceebs div 10	Genres
1	We Are The Champions - Remaster	Queen	64	32.0	21.3	16.0	12.8	10.7	9.1	8.0	7.1	6.4	classic rock, rock, glam rock
2	You Should See Me in a Crown	We Rabbitz, Shah-Rae Weaver	75	37.5	25.0	18.8	15.0	12.5	10.7	9.4	8.3	7.5	
3	Hey Ya!	Outkast	80	40.0	26.7	20.0	16.0	13.3	11.4	10.0	8.9	8.0	southern hip hop, hip hop
4	We Will Rock You - Remastered 20	Queen	81	40.5	27.0	20.3	16.2	13.5	11.6	10.1	9.0	8.1	classic rock, rock, glam rock
5	Do I Wanna Know?	Arctic Monkeys	85	42.5	28.3	21.3	17.0	14.2	12.1	10.6	9.4	8.5	indie, garage rock
6	Kyrie	Mr. Mister	90	45.0	30.0	22.5	18.0	15.0	12.9	11.3	10.0	9.0	album rock, new romantic, new wave pop, soft rock, synthpop
7	Knee Deep (feat. Jimmy Buffett)	Zac Brown Band, Jimmy Buffett	91	45.5	30.3	22.8	18.2	15.2	13.0	11.4	10.1	9.1	country, acoustic country, trop rock
8	I Want It All - Remastered 2011	Queen	92	46.0	30.7	23.0	18.4	15.3	13.1	11.5	10.2	9.2	classic rock, rock, glam rock
9	I Love Rock 'n' Roll	The Black Jets	94	47.0	31.3	23.5	18.8	15.7	13.4	11.8	10.4	9.4	
10	Thrift Shop (feat. Wanz)	Macklemore & Ryan Lewis, Mackl	95	47.5	31.7	23.8	19.0	15.8	13.6	11.9	10.6	9.5	pop rap, seattle hip hop, g funk, west coast hip hop
11	Golden Touch - Full Length	Razorlight	95	47.5	31.7	23.8	19.0	15.8	13.6	11.9	10.6	9.5	britpop, indie
12	R U Mine?	Arctic Monkeys	97	48.5	32.3	24.3	19.4	16.2	13.9	12.1	10.8	9.7	indie, garage rock
13	Knee Socks	Arctic Monkeys	98	49.0	32.7	24.5	19.6	16.3	14.0	12.3	10.9	9.8	indie, garage rock
14	Sweet Transvestite	Tim Curry	107	53.5	35.7	26.8	21.4	17.8	15.3	13.4	11.9	10.7	musicals
15	Believer	Imagine Dragons	125	62.5	41.7	31.3	25.0	20.8	17.9	15.6	13.9	12.5	modern rock, pop, rock
16	Snap Out Of It	Arctic Monkeys	130	65.0	43.3	32.5	26.0	21.7	18.6	16.3	14.4	13.0	indie, garage rock
17	Jessie's Girl	Rick Springfield	132	66.0	44.0	33.0	26.4	22.0	18.9	16.5	14.7	13.2	yacht rock
18	I'm Gonna Be (500 Miles)	The Proclaimers	132	66.0	44.0	33.0	26.4	22.0	18.9	16.5	14.7	13.2	celtic rock, scottish rock
19	Back In Black	AC/DC	188	94.0	62.7	47.0	37.6	31.3	26.9	23.5	20.9	18.8	rock, hard rock, classic rock, rock and roll

Figure 10.4 My calculation of which songs can be used for 20 SPM (data from Chosic, using Spotify data). Red indicates a perfect fit; green indicates a workable range. Yellow indicates 18 SPM for warmup and cooldown sections. SPM, Strokes per Minute.

- **Rows** that feature a similar style of show for indoor rowers, with interval rowing periods being a song's length and rowing to a specific BPM, with 30-second resting (and chatting) intervals. This type of interval training is well known in the indoor rowing world, so it made sense to experiment with this format for rowing. However, what was more challenging was the different calculation of cycles, which in the rowing world is measured by Strokes Per Minute (SPM). This tends to be much slower than for running. Thus, typical rowing SPM figures are between 18 and 28, with a limit at the lower end being 14, and a limit at the higher end being around 40. This makes the identification of appropriate songs more challenging, and I needed to use some more extensive spreadsheet calculations that would allow me to identify appropriate songs (see Figure 10.4). Additionally, the 'swoooshhhh .... swoooss-hhh' of a rowing machine, in contrast to the 'step step step' sound of a run, provided additional challenges of how to count your strokes in, how to give guidance to a beat, or how to help your listening and rowing audience to sync their strokes to the beat.

These different categories of shows on Mixcloud's *CBDB Runs* demonstrate the ongoing experimentation, aimed at finding that Goldilocks overlap between a song's beat and physical repetitive activity that can be made more enjoyable by syncing a beat to it.

The Music Podcast – an Oxymoron?

Music podcasts remain rare. Early podcasting emerged from audiophile communities, where enthusiasts recognised its potential but faced licensing challenges. First-generation podcasters (Table 10.2) navigated limited options: negotiating individual song licenses (Coverville), using Podsafe Music archives, or performing original works (*A Folk Song A Day*). These constraints pushed many towards talk-based formats, shaping early definitions of podcasting as primarily spoken word.

This limited the range of music podcasts and made entry difficult. A second generation adapted by composing original music, as in 36 Questions (2017), the first musical podcast, and *Composer Quest* (2013–2017), which featured creator-owned works. Others simplified licensing by focusing on one song per episode, exemplified by *Song Exploder* (2014–). Another model was *We Didn't Start the Podcast* (2016), which humorously covered Billy Joel's discography over 13 episodes. It incorporated humming, singing, and short song snippets, relying on risky fair use principles to illustrate commentary. Finally, *Sleeve Notes* (2013–) began with licensed music but later adopted Spotify's Music & Chat format, reflecting a shift towards platform-based solutions for integrating music legally. Spotify's Music & Talk feature (2020–2024) marked a turning point, enabling licensed music integration but tying such podcasts to platform exclusivity.[20] The Music & Talk innovation aimed to merge music and spoken word content within a unified advertising ecosystem, allowing creators to embed licensed music directly into podcast episodes. Despite these advances, sustaining hybrid models seemed to remain a challenge, as shown by Spotify discontinuing Music & Talk in 2024. And that created a conundrum for a handful of 'running podcasters' that had delightfully leaned into the music & chat format (See Table 10.3).

Table 10.2 History of music podcasts

Coverville: The Cover Music Show (2004–now). One of the first music podcasts, and still running, hosted by Brian Ibbott, showcases creative and often surprising cover versions of pop, rock, and country songs by both emerging and established artists, celebrating the art of reinterpretation since 2004. Brian Ibbott himself advocated for better licensing for podcasting and contacted major performance rights organisations – ASCAP, BMI, and later SESAC – to secure the necessary licenses for legally podcasting copyrighted music. This made Coverville one of the pioneering podcasts in establishing a legal framework for music podcasting, helping to adapt traditional licensing models to the emerging podcast format. It is probably due to his podcast and efforts that licensing organisations adapted their non-interactive license to include podcast licensing shortly thereafter (Wikipedia, 2025b).
***Rock and Roll Geek Show* (2004–now)**. Another first music podcast, known for its raw, independent style and deep engagement with rock music culture, hosted by Michael Butler. It used podsafe music and acquired direct permissions from well-known musicians and songwriters.
***A Folk Song A Day* (2010–2011)**. A unique project by English folk singer Jon Boden, recording and releasing one folk song each day for one year.

Table 10.3 Third generation of music podcasts, using Spotify for music, chat, and running

Wood On The Run (January 2021–July 2022). Hosted and recorded on the run by Manchester-based Jack Wood, it used music from the Spotify catalogue and followed a single-hosted chat show format whilst on a run.
Rob Deering's Running Tracks Radio Hour (July 2021–2024). Comedian and podcaster (Running Commentary) hosted this show solo, recorded on each run with a themed and curated list of music from the Spotify catalogue.
CBDB Runs (August 2023–April 2024). Solo-hosted by Carola Boehm, this show used a jeffing format (run to music, walk to talk) and used music from the Spotify catalogue.

The challenges around not having platform-wide agreements for music licensing had pushed music-centric independent podcast shows initially towards Spotify, and then Mixcloud (or SoundCloud). Mixcloud, having pushed innovation in the field of disseminating DJ mixes, advanced its licensing framework in 2017 and 2018 by partnering with Merlin (a global digital rights agency), Universal Music Group, and Warner Music Group, thereby legitimising its role as a music distribution platform.[21]

YouTube itself had secured licensing agreements in 2017 with the three major record labels – Warner Music Group, Sony Music Entertainment, and Universal Music Group.[22] These agreements introduced revenue-sharing models based on advertising views and streaming metrics, laying the groundwork for more integrated music-media experiences. Meanwhile, YouTube continued to evolve its podcasting capabilities. By 2023, YouTube Music began supporting podcast integration, building on its earlier licensing agreements from 2017.[23]

But before these licensing agreements were struck by Spotify, Mixcloud, and YouTube, it is apparent that early podcasting posed major challenges for music-focused creators due to the absence of streamlined licensing, and many shifted to talk-based formats, producing content about music rather than with music. This, in turn, shaped early perceptions (and, with it, definitions) of podcasting as primarily spoken word. Later, legal and technological solutions enabled music integration but tied it to platform exclusivity. This pushed music-centric shows outside the open podcasting ecosystem towards platforms like Spotify Music & Chat, Mixcloud, and SoundCloud, which supported music streaming and DJ-style content.

This move further blurred the boundaries between music streaming and podcasting, providing easier integration into what were called 'podcasts' by their platforms, but that did not have open RSS feeds or other characteristics of mainstream podcasting, such as being episodic, talk-focused etc.

Despite initial enthusiasm, Spotify discontinued the Music + Talk feature in 2024. And that is when I also moved from a Music, Chat and Run show on Spotify to one on Mixcloud.

When Is a Podcast Not a Podcast – The Evolution of Definitions?

So, what to call my podcast? How to define *CBDB Runs*? *CBDB Runs* is a creative, community-oriented 'show' hosted on Mixcloud (originally on Spotify), designed to support individuals – particularly those with health conditions such as hypothyroidism – in learning how to run and sustaining the habit. Sometimes framed as a 'jeffing companion playlist', it blends personal narrative, fitness guidance, and experimental song curation. Rather than polished production, the podcast embraces an exploratory, inclusive ethos aligned with lifelong learning and decentralised peer-to-peer engagement. It exemplifies podcasting as a cultural form rooted in co-production and everyday creativity, reflecting the participatory values of Culture 3.0.

Developing *CBDB Runs*, a music and chat show recorded on the run, raised questions (that I folded into my experimental lab). Its unconventional design required hosting on a platform geared towards DJ mixes and radio shows, without a shareable RSS feed due to music licensing. Thus, it defied traditional definitions, including my own from last year's EPOD conference: 'an audio-first show, made available via RSS feeds…'.[24]

Nevertheless, this was an audio-first experience. And the only reason for it not to have RSS feeds was not of a technical or audio production nature, but legal reasons. Thus, considering the shift towards conceptualising podcasting as cultural rather than technological, calling it a podcast seemed appropriate. Reflecting on its validity allowed me to unpick accepted meanings, inspiring the term 'un-podcasting'. Scholars have long debated podcast terminology. As Sharon[25] notes, 'over the past decade, scholars and journalists have been struggling with pinning down the exact meaning of the word podcast'. Most attempts differentiate between podcasting as a medium (technological), a practice (social-cultural), or a genre (formalistic).

The following analysis (Tables 10.4 and 10.5) views podcasting as a phenomenon shaped by discourses, technologies, social-cultural factors, and individual agency, changing across time slices. Understanding these shifts illuminates how definitions evolve and why, as Berry[26] observes, we 'immediately detect' podcast qualities, even without consensus on what they are.

The challenge of defining what podcasting is relates to the era we inhabit, marked by rapid shifts in cultural production. Today, we live in a knowledge society where creativity is characterised by co-creation and immersive participation, which Sacco calls Culture 3.0. This model leverages digital tools and connectivity for decentralised content creation, bypassing traditional gatekeepers. It thrives on open platforms and social media, generating value socially through participation rather than solely economically. Cultural production is now embedded in everyday life. In contrast, the UK's music and audio industry remains rooted in Culture 2.0, reliant on copyright-based models. However, podcasting, with its grassroots, collaborative nature, clearly embodies Culture 3.0 principles.[27] This shift also explains podcasting's meteoric rise: its technology democratised content creation, disrupting traditional media and enabling an expanding community of producers. Yet this paradigm brings friction between old and new norms, as corporations seek to preserve market share. As technologies like RSS move mainstream, they fade from public attention, similar to HTTP or TCP/IP, because their use becomes effortless. Sullivan[28] notes declining Google searches for 'RSS', but I would note this is not due to obsolescence but ubiquity. Likewise, podcasting's cultural meanings evolve as technical infrastructures recede in novelty.

In short, podcasting is now ubiquitous, but its purposes and practices shift as we advance into co-creative modes of production. Several distinct eras, or 'Imaginaries', capture these changing perceptions (see Tables 10.4–10.6).

From Constraints to Creativity: Redefining Podcasting through Music and Running

The exploration of how technology, agency, and structural elements shape podcasting definitions shows that this process is ongoing. My own practice revealed a striking

Table 10.4 CPE Analysis of the evolution of definitions for podcasting (1990s, 2004, 2010)

Definition of a Podcast	*1990s*	*Ca 2004*	*Ca 2010*
Imaginary	1990s – Precursor Concepts	2004 – Coining of the Term & RSS-Based Audio Distribution	2010 – Emphasis on On-Demand and Mobile Media
Discourses	Whilst the term 'podcast' didn't exist in the 1990s, precursors existed, such as ***Internet Radio***, which was used to describe audio broadcasting streamed over the web, typically live. Other terms: webcasting, multicasting.	The Term 'Podcast' was coined by journalist Ben Hammersley in The Guardian in February 2004 (Hammersley, 2004). BBC podcasts highlighted by The Times article 'Will Podcasting Kill the Radio Star' Kettmann (2004). First podcast that called itself a podcast: Adam Curry's The Daily Source Code (Curry, 2004), talking about podcasting and broadcasting from Aug 2004 and making the term and podcasting popular in audio circles. Podcasts were understood as downloadable audio files or downloadable radio programmes, delivered via RSS feeds, which were believed to be an important technological feature (see Sharon, 2023, p. 326). This was fuelling the questions about the limits of the term.	Definitions evolved as smartphones became more popular, e.g. 'mp3 players' were excluded from definitions.
Definitions	'Internet radio' refers to non-interactive audio webcasts (Stockment, 2009, p. 2132).	*With the benefit of hindsight, it all seems quite obvious. MP3 players, like Apple's iPod, in many pockets, audio production software cheap or free, and weblogging an established part of the internet; all the ingredients are there for a new boom in amateur radio. But what to call it? Audioblogging? Podcasting? GuerillaMedia?* (Hammersley, 2004). The Independent writes about podcasting: *Called 'podcasting' (...), it uses open source software, MP3 players and the rambling efforts of audio webloggers ('audiobloggers') to redefine the role of radio in the mobile digital world, and offers hope to the millions who pray for the demise of inane DJs and obnoxious radio advertisements* (Goldberg, 2004). Key dictionary entries, which would have been likely first added around this time (Anon, 2021) included: *A digital audio file that can be taken from the internet and played on a computer or a device that you can carry with you.* Oxford Dictionary likely	*Media content delivered automatically to a subscriber via the Internet* (Berry, 2006, p. 144). *A means of distributing digitised audio files to subscribing audiences* (Murray, 2009, in Sharon, 2023, p.326); *a system for the automated distribution and reception of audio content* (Sellas, 2023, in Sharon, 2023, p. 326). *An Internet-based broadcast medium that relies on RSS feeds—a peer subscription service—to automatically*

(*Continued*)

Table 10.4 (Continued)

Definition of a Podcast	*1990s*	*Ca 2004*	*Ca 2010*
		added in the mid-2000s (Anon, 2005c); *A radio programme that is stored in a digital form that you can download from the internet and play on a computer or on a mobile phone.* Cambridge Dictionary (Anon, 2005b); *A program (as of music or talk) made available in digital format for automatic download over the Internet.* Merriam-Webster dictionary (Anon, 2005a).	*retrieve and upload content to a portable MP3 player* (Eckstein, 2013, p. 2).
Structural	Early adoption was due to greater broadcast freedoms when bypassing regulatory frameworks such as the FCC (US) or Ofcom (UK) licensing. From 2006 until the passing of the Webcaster Act in 2009, early ongoing controversies regarding internet radio revolved around a dispute between regulators asking for up to 100% royalties to musicians played on stations (compared to 15% satellite radio). This forced many early adopters out of business and threatened the sustainability of larger ones (AOL Radio, Yahoo! Radio) (Stockment, 2009, p. 2154).	*online radio is blooming thanks to MP3 formats, iPods, cheap audio software and weblogs* (Hammersley, 2004). Open Source movement, BloggerCON (2003 onwards) and BlogAudio.org, a website to document research in adding audio to blog posts (Doyle, 2017). Libsyn (short for liberated syndication) was launched by the end of 2004 (Son, 2025). Steve Jobs built podcast subscriptions into iTunes in 2025.	Podcast Industry takes off. Apple Podcasts launched as a standalone app in 2012, and by 2014, it was integrated into standard iOS on Apple phones. BBC iPlayer (web-based) launched in 2008 (app in 2011).

Technological	Transition from traditional to digital radio formats: Internet radio (first launched in 1993), webcasting, first digital audio services, streaming, generally not on-demand. Generally listened to through a PC, and later via smartphone apps. Most recently via dedicated devices. Streaming tech used: MP3, AAC+, Ogg, WMA, Real Audio, over TCP/UDP (Hoeg & Lauterbach, 2009, p. 26).	MP3 was introduced in 1992, perceived to improve existing formats (WMA, AAC, Vorbis, FLAC, Speex, Ogg) through better compression. Portable MP3 players became ubiquitous after a slow increase since 1995. Earliest digital audio players: AT&T (PAC music compression, later AAC); Audible for spoken word (1997); South Korean MPMan/EigerMan F10 (1998); Sony Memory Stick Walkman 1999 (ATRAC format). iPods launched in 2001 (sold until 2022) and quickly captured the market. Dave Winer and Adam Curry's work during 2004 and 2005 on RSS enclosures and podcasting tools was designed to deliver MP3 files to portable devices (Zaliva & Sova, 2004; Winer & Curry, 2004). Apple Podcatcher software (2005)	Mobile Technology takes off. Smartphones (2007 onwards). CarPlay launched in 2010, allowing podcast playing within specific models of cars.
Agency	Internet Talk Radio (1993) The US-based band 'Severe Tire Damage' was the first to live broadcast a performance in 1993, and the Everywhere Project (for Irish Diaspora) ran from 1994 to 1998. The Rolling Stones concert was a major video/audio 'cyberspace multicast concert' in 1994 (using M-Bone).	First audio blog (not yet called a podcast) to use Winer's RSS enclosures was by New York Times reporter Christopher Lydon, who in 2003 began recording interviews on politics and blogging, as part of a fellowship in Internet & Society at the Harvard Law School (Wikipedia, 2025a; Doyle, 2017). First podcast that called itself a podcast: Adam Curry's The Daily Source Code, talking about podcasting and broadcasting from Aug 2004 Curry (2004). 2004 First UK podcasts, as 'The Hitchin Hours' named itself a 'podcast' in its 2nd episode (Cridland, 2021). Steve Jobs demonstrated at MacWorld 2004 how to make a podcast with newly launched GarageBand (Son, 2025).	Advertising in podcasting begins to take hold, and various hosting and advertising platforms emerge: Blubrry launched in 2006 (founded as RawVoice in 2005 for podcast advertising) and was an early provider of podcast statistics (2007), hosting and WordPress integration (2008) (Anon, n.d.).

(*Continued*)

Table 10.4 (Continued)

Definition of a Podcast	*1990s*	*Ca 2004*	*Ca 2010*
	TuneIn Radio (2002), iHeart Radio.	George Bush, newly elected, began in 2005 to provide RSS feeds for presidential weekly radio addresses (Wikipedia, 2025c). First DIY book published in 2025, Cochrane's Podcasting (Cochrane, 2005). *This American Life* (launched 1995 on radio) began offering the show in podcast format in 2006 (Wikipedia, 2025c).	Following services came online: Podomatic 2008; Audioboom 2009; Buzzsprout 2009; Spreaker 2009; Simplecast 2013. (Sullivan, 2019, p.5). Stitcher (later included in Sirius XM) launched in 2008, supporting the shift from desktop to mobile. Podcast networks emerge Earwolf (2010), Radiotopia (2014), Gimlet Media (2014). The Podcast Wars (Spotify vs Apple) (run-up to 2015)

Table 10.5 CPE Analysis of the evolution of definitions for podcasting (2014; 2020; 2023+)

Definition of a Podcast	*2014*	*2020*	*2023+*
Imaginary	2014 – Serial and Narrative Turn	2020s – Platformisation and Video Integration	2023+ –Transmedia Ecosystem/Podcasting as a Constructed Concept
Discourses	Podcasts began being associated with narrative storytelling and journalism.	Podcasting expanded to include video, live interactions, and platform exclusivity.	Multimodality is emphasised, and increasingly the term is discussed as a cultural phenomenon, rather than a technical evolutionary point.
Definitions	*a vehicle for serialised content* (Salvati, 2015, in Sharon, 2023, p. 326). *Podcasting, for us, taps into something fundamental about oral communication, argument and even the tension between subjective and objective knowledge that has been amplified in the digital age* (Llinares et al., 2018, sec. Introduction). *a specific set of practices and cultural meanings* (Morris & Patterson, 2015, in Sharon, 2023, p. 327). Spinelli & Dann (2019, p. 1264) propose 11 characteristic features of podcasting, including '(1) complete control over the type of programme; (2) play the content whenever and wherever; (3) able to fast forward, rewind, or listen to a programme again (4) free subscriptions, seriality'. '*taps into something fundamental about oral communication*' and '*podcast can be understood within an emerging genre of personal audio narratives*' (Lindgren, 2016, p. 14)	Definitions expanded to define podcasting conceptually, not technically. Tension of audio vs video, thus included often phrases such as 'primarily audio' *podcasting can generally be understood as a delivery mechanism* (Sharon, 2023). *A podcast is a piece of episodical, downloadable or streamable, primarily spoken audio content, distributed via the internet, playable anywhere, at any time, produced by anyone who so wishes* (Rime et al., 2022, p. 1270). *The nature of podcasting is in fact its boundaries, and that its boundaries are this set of tensions, opposing forces striving for balance, representing a summation of equilibria that have characterised podcasting since its inception* (Rime et al., 2022, p. 1274). *Collaborative storytelling and canon fluidity in the adventure zone podcast. Convergence* (Wyld, 2021, pp. 343–356).	*Over the past decade, scholars and journalists have been struggling with pinning down the exact meaning of the word podcast, as it became increasingly embedded in everyday life* (Sharon, 2023, p. 324). *the nature of podcasting is in fact its boundaries, and that its boundaries are this set of tensions, opposing forces striving for balance, representing a summation of equilibria that have characterised podcasting since its inception* (Rime et al., 2022, p. 1274). 6 pairs of tension: *1. Personalisation and Automation; 2. Independent and Mainstream Production; 3. Unique and Universal Content; 4. Current Audience and Possible Demographic; 5. Immersion and Interactivity; 6. Art and Technology* (Rime et al., 2022, p. 1262ff). *hybrid cultural form between old and new media and podcasting should not be intended solely as a media object (the podcast episode) nor as a distribution technology (the .rss format, the podcast networks or the podcast streaming platforms), but as a new, hybrid, cultural form, that draws not only from radio, but also from theatre, performing arts, design, and internet culture* (Bonini, 2022, p. 19).

(*Continued*)

Table 10.5 (Continued)

Definition of a Podcast	*2014*	*2020*	*2023+*
Structural	Apple Watch started to be able to play Apple Podcasts in 2018. Amazon Echo integrates Apple podcast support in 2019. From 2014, BBC iPlayer App (Boehm, 2025b) includes 30-day access to all TV and Radio.	Apple launches optional paid subscriptions for podcast creators in 2021. Spotify starts acquiring various audio/podcasting/production companies from 2017 onwards. Spotify adds podcasts in 2018, using RSS feeds. Spotify acquired Anchor FM Inc. in 2019 and launched Spotify for Podcasters (formerly Anchor), and in 2020 acquired Megaphone (podcast advertising, monetisation). From 2021, Spotify uses private RSS feeds for paid subscriptions (Boehm, 2025c).	*Knowledge mobilization* and *Podcasts as a method involve individual or collective knowledge brokers like academics, researchers, students, community members, and organisations* (Hinic, 2025, p. 3). *Voices as data* (Hinic, 2025, p. 6), *Experiential learning that generates a multimodality which affords blurred lines and epistemological humility* (2025, pp. 5, 8); *It allows room for creativity and failure. (…) It is playful* (2025, p. 8).
Technological	By 2014, the Standard Podcast iPhone App, launched in 2012, was integrated into the standard iOS on Apple phones. In 2018, the BBC Sounds App was launched, with podcasts, some exclusive to BBC Sounds App.	The BBC Sounds aapp launched in 2018.	*Characteristics of 'podcasting culture': openness, accessibility, independence* (Bomba & Maiorano, 2025, p. 149); *like the Internet in its early days (…) desire to spread knowledge for free and independently and the culture of podcasting (…) reflects this open culture also in the minds of podcasters.* (2025, p. 150).
Agency	Podcasters start to refer to themselves as 'podcasters' to distinguish themselves from radio producers (see Berry, 2018, pp. 24–25). Content production is by 'amateurs' *who set professional standards and have a distinct set of values and beliefs characterized by entrepreneurialism, authenticity* (Sharon, 2023, p. 328). The BBC is estimated to be the 2nd largest podcaster, after US-based NPR (Anon, 2019).	Around 2019/20, Spotify started acquiring content: Gimlet Media (Reply All, Homecoming), Parcast (true crime) and Higher Ground (Obamas). Starts exclusive to Spotify podcasts. The Joe Rogan Experience, exclusive. Michelle Obama's Podcast. Archewell Audio (Prince Harry and Meghan Markle). Spotify acquired Anchor FM Inc. in 2019 and launched Spotify for Podcasters (formerly Anchor). Still allows use of RSS feeds.	*The theme of the relationship with platforms and the promotion of an independent, open, horizontal, and universally accessible podcasting model is therefore central* (Bomba & Maiorano, 2025, p. 150) *and the term horizontal communities* (2025, p. 151). *Podcasting is, after all, defined in many ways by different people at different times and is a Cultural Form that as a new, hybrid, cultural form, draws not only from radio, but also from theatre, performing arts, design, and internet culture* (Hall et al., 2025, p. 212).

Table 10.6 Broad shifts in our perception of what a podcast is

- **1990s – Precursor concepts**: Whilst the term 'podcast' didn't exist in the 1990s, precursors existed, such as 'Internet Radio', which was used to describe audio broadcasting streamed over the web, typically live.
- **2004 – Coining of the term**: The term 'Podcast' was coined in this era by journalist Ben Hammersley in The Guardian. Podcasting emerged.
- **2010 – Emphasis on on-demand and mobile media**: Definitions evolved as smartphones became more popular, e.g. 'mp3 players' were excluded from definitions.
- **Mid-2000s – RSS-based audio distribution**: Podcasts were understood as downloadable episodic audio files delivered via RSS feeds, which were believed to be an important technological feature.
- **2014 – Serial and narrative turn**: Podcasts began being associated with narrative storytelling and journalism.
- **2020s – Platformisation and video integration**: Podcasting expanded to include video, live interactions, and platform exclusivity. Definitions expanded to define podcasting conceptually, not technically. The tension of audio vs video often included phrases such as 'primarily audio'.
- **2023+ –Transmedia ecosystem/podcasting as a constructed concept**: Multimodality is emphasised and increasingly the term is discussed as a cultural phenomenon, rather than a technical evolutionary point.

omission: mainstream music in podcasts. Music podcasts often used to discuss songs without playing them, an anathema to musicians, because licensing was costly and complex. Like many, when I began podcasting in 2019, I created my own intro music via GarageBand to ensure copyright compliance. But composing full tracks was beyond my skills.

When I conceived a running podcast built around music, two barriers emerged: I couldn't compose long tracks, and mainstream music was off-limits. This changed when Spotify introduced its Music & Talk format (2020–2024), enabling playlists in podcasts. I seized the opportunity, launching *CBDB Runs*.[29] It breached my own podcast definition: it was Spotify-exclusive, lacked an RSS feed, and full songs were only for paid subscribers. My format combined 60-second to two-minute running commentaries with curated playlists, using new tools, workflows, and themed lists, as described above.

Spotify's strategy in launching Music & Talk had aimed to dominate podcasting by merging music and talk, successfully boosting ad revenue by 400% and doubling its user base. For music-centric creators, this solved the licensing dilemma, though tied to Spotify's ecosystem. *CBDB Runs* ran for 21 episodes on Spotify, with modest reach, but the driving part for me was a learning journey, motivating runs and exploring new tech. The additional feature of Music & Talk provided something that no other podcast host outside of the music sector could offer at that time. This functionality was tied to Spotify (and tied to Spotify's own contractual arrangements with labels) but made possible only by removing its RSS feed and offering streaming only. But if those caveats were acceptable, one could create a music and talk show that included, for example, 15 songs about running in windy weather, with a one-to-two-minute recorded chat in between.

And that is what I did, sounding somewhat out of breath but also sounding like a real thyroid-challenged runner who regularly runs despite an ongoing health condition. *CBDB Runs* was born, initially on Spotify. Spotify discontinued the feature in 2024, likely due to licensing complexity and revenue priorities. It may be that the licensing contracts became unmanageable on Spotify's side, which was now under more scrutiny to ensure artists are paid their fair share due to the increased focus on fair remuneration of content creators on both the European[30] and UK levels.[31] It might be that as Spotify, by that time, had hit the top spot for podcast downloads globally,[32] the added legal complexities that talk & music shows bring with them might have been perceived as simply unnecessary. Or it might be that those who used that service did so in a way that did not quite conform to what Spotify had in mind, using much more than just one or the other song, as I seem to remember that the original terms of the contract (from around 2022) stipulated a low maximum proportion of music. However, in 2025 I cannot find these terms anymore. The door to integrated music closed until Mixcloud and YouTube later secured agreements with major labels, reviving possibilities for music-based podcasting.

At the end of 2024, I moved over to Mixcloud with none of the subscriber restrictions, but also no open RSS feed. The podcast is growing steadily and, as of December 2025, has 60 different episodes, including running plans, BPM runs, walks and rows.

Conclusion

This podcast ecosystem, together with Substack, blogs, and other open RSS technologies, has a real opportunity to disrupt a broadcaster-centric model towards a user-centric on-demand model, but also with a potentially co-creative, citizen-participatory twist. In a world where co-creation and citizen participation in democratic processes are becoming more and more in demand, podcasts have a good opportunity to still grow their ecosystem for all sorts of scales, from the hyperlocal to the super-global.

These disruptions affect different sectors (entertainment, news, advertising, publishing, education, and research), but they also drive forward different innovations in these fields, in turn affecting the evolving nature of what we perceive podcasting to be. With those shifting perceptions, so do the accepted definitions change for a phenomenon that is still so very new.

The evolution of podcasting has been shaped not only by technological innovation but increasingly by legal and cultural developments. Recent advancements in music licensing – particularly the integration of music into podcast formats – are expanding the definitional boundaries of podcasting itself. As platforms such as Spotify and YouTube Music experiment with hybrid formats that combine music and spoken word, the dominance of talk-based podcasting is being challenged. These shifts suggest that podcasting may no longer be defined solely by its speech-centric origins, but rather as a flexible and multimodal form of digital expression.

Traditionally, podcasting has been understood as a technological medium, emerging from specific affordances such as RSS feeds, mobile listening capabilities, and subscription-based distribution models. These features enabled the rise of episodic, speech-based storytelling and on-demand accessibility, which became hallmarks of early podcasting. However, this medium-specific framing is increasingly insufficient to capture the complexity of contemporary podcasting practices.

As podcasting becomes more embedded in the fabric of digital and daily culture, it is more appropriately conceptualised as a cultural form – one that reflects and contributes to the dynamics of a knowledge society. Drawing on Hinic's discussion around knowledge mobilisation and podcasting, the latter can be seen as a decentralised and participatory practice that facilitates peer-to-peer learning and lifelong education. This transformation underscores the shift from podcasting as a medium to podcasting as a hybrid media practice, shaped by both technological infrastructure and socio-cultural imperatives.

The decentralisation of knowledge production, coupled with the growing demand for flexible and collaborative learning environments, positions podcasting as a key modality in contemporary digital culture. It is no longer merely a format for audio distribution, but a site of cultural negotiation, creative experimentation, educational engagement, and social innovation.

Podcasting exemplifies how social innovations in content production reshape media landscapes by decentralising authorship and amplifying participatory culture. The podcast medium thrives on its hybrid nature, blending sound, narrative, dialogue, and more recently, music in ways that transcend traditional media forms.

This hybridity fosters a democratised space where creators, often outside institutional frameworks, can produce and distribute content that reflects diverse voices, styles, and community-driven narratives. Podcasting's evolution is thus less about technological advancement and more about the reconfiguration of social practices around Culture 3.0 co-creation, content production, and consumption, enabling a reinvigoration of dialogic exchange and knowledge sharing.

To emphasise, podcasting today is not merely a technological artefact but a socially constructed phenomenon shaped by innovative modes of content production, audience engagement, and co-creation.

My podcast *CBDB Runs* exemplifies this evolving role of podcasting, set within a collective learning community focusing on health and running, and particularly supporting those individuals who experience specific health conditions. Rather than serving merely as a medium for content delivery, the podcast functions as a peer-to-peer tool for experiential learning – helping individuals acquire practical skills such as running, whilst fostering a sense of community and shared purpose. This approach situates podcasting within a broader framework of lifelong learning, where knowledge is mobilised outside formal institutions and shaped by decentralised, peer-to-peer interactions – an ethos aligned with the principles of what has been termed by me 'University 3.0'.[33]

Understanding podcasting through the lens of Culture 3.0 further illuminates its transformation into a cultural form driven by co-production, everyday creativity, and immersive engagement. In this context, podcasting is not simply a technological artefact, or a format defined by speech-based storytelling; it is a dynamic and hybrid media practice embedded in the rhythms of daily life and the aspirations of participatory knowledge cultures.

As such, podcasting should be conceptualised not as a static medium, but as a socially constructed phenomenon shaped by innovations in content production and cultural engagement. The case of *CBDB Runs* underscores how podcasting can serve as a vehicle for social innovation, enabling inclusive and decentralised learning environments that reflect the shifting contours of contemporary cultural and educational practices. With it, its definitions will change.

To conclude, I will posit my definition here. It may catch on, or it may soon be superseded by the next disruptions that provide new ways of thinking about what a podcast is. But for today,

> A Podcast is an audio-focused cultural form that is constructed by social innovation in content production.
>
> (Boehm at EPOD 2025)

Notes

1 Carola Boehm, 'Why Podcasting Needs to Lean into Culture 3.0', in *Podcasting & Education: Concepts, Communities & Case Studies*, Podcasting Through Education 1 (Routledge, 2025).
2 Robin Nelson, *Practice as Research in the Arts: Principles, Protocols, Pedagogies, Resistances*, 2013 edition (Palgrave Macmillan, 2013).
3 Nelson, *Practice as Research in the Arts*, 38–47.
4 Ngai-Ling Sum and Bob Jessop, *Towards a Cultural Political Economy: Putting Culture in Its Place in Political Economy* (Edward Elgar Publishing, 2013).
5 Carola Boehm, *Arts and Academia: The Role of the Arts in Civic Universities*, Great Debates in Higher Education (Emerald Publishing Ltd, 2022), 9–27.
6 Pier Luigi Sacco et al., 'From Culture 1.0 to Culture 3.0: Three Socio-Technical Regimes of Social and Economic Value Creation through Culture, and Their Impact on European Cohesion Policies', *Sustainability* 10, no. 11 (2018): 11, https://doi.org/10.3390/su10113923.
7 Boehm, *Arts and Academia*.
8 Carola Boehm, 'Academia in Culture 3.0: A Crime Story of Death and Rebirth (but Also of Curation, Innovation and Sector Mash-Ups)', *REPERTÓRIO: Teatro & Dança* 19, no. 27 (2016): 37–48, https://eprints.staffs.ac.uk/3185/.
9 Boehm, 'Why Podcasting Needs to Lean into Culture 3.0'.
10 Boehm, *Arts and Academia*, sec. Chapter 4: A Conceptual Framework for Revisiting Universities Futures.
11 Wikipedia, 'HealthUnlocked', in *Wikipedia*, 13 August 2024, https://en.wikipedia.org/w/index.php?title=HealthUnlocked&oldid=1240034659.
12 CBDB and Carola Boehm, *PODCAST: CBDB Runs (On Spotify) (2022-2024)*, episodes 1–23, 23 episodes of *CBDB Runs* (2022-2024), aired 2022–2024, Spotify, 40 min per show.
13 https://www.mixcloud.com/CeeBeeDeeBee/jeffing-xmas-soul-rb-retro-soul-and-my-first-mixcloud-music-and-chat-show/.
14 https://www.mixcloud.com/CeeBeeDeeBee/walk-songs-about-books-with-rich-ceebs-beatles-metallica-the-zombies-and-more/.
15 https://www.mixcloud.com/CeeBeeDeeBee/jeff-cooling-down-in-hot-weather-with-a-supercool-list-foreigner-katey-perry-elton-john/.
16 Carola Boehm, 'A New Year, a New Post-Flu Running-Recovery Plan! (Bridge to 10K, HealthUnlocked Forum)', *HealthUnlocked*, 4 January 2025, https://healthunlocked.com/bridgeto10k/posts/151597907/a-new-year-a-new-post-flu-running-recovery-plan.
17 https://www.mixcloud.com/CeeBeeDeeBee/playlists/6-weeks-to-5k/.
18 Rachel Boswell and The Runner's World Editors, 'Couch to 5K: How to Start Running in Just Six Weeks', sec. 5km, *Runner's World*, 22 November 2024, https://www.runnersworld.com/uk/training/5km/a760067/six-week-beginner-5k-schedule/.
19 https://open.spotify.com/user/21j2n6xgxchv3gsa43ofdipya/playlists.
20 Stacy Goldrick, 'Spotify Launches New Audio Experience Combining Music and Talk Content', *Spotify*, 14 October 2020, https://newsroom.spotify.com/2020-10-14/spotify-launches-new-audio-experience-combining-music-and-talk-content/.
21 Music Business Worldwide, 'Merlin Signs Multi-Year Direct Licensing Deal with Mixcloud', Music Business Worldwide, 28 November 2018, https://www.musicbusinessworldwide.com/merlin-signs-multi-year-direct-licensing-deal-with-mixcloud/; mixcloud, 'Mixcloud and Warner Music Group Announce Direct Licensing Deal', *Mixcloud Blog*, 9 October 2017, https://www.mixcloud.com/blog/2017/10/09/mixcloud-and-warner-music-group-announce-direct-licensing-deal/.
22 Wes Schlagenhauf, 'YouTube Ends Record Label Standoff, Now Has Licensing Deals with the "Big 3"', *The Hustle*, 20 December 2017, https://thehustle.co/youtube-licensing-deals-with-big-3; Geoff Weiss, 'YouTube Inks Licensing Deals With Universal And Sony Music As It Preps Paid Service (Report)', *Tubefilter*, 19 December 2017, https://www.tubefilter.com/2017/12/19/youtube-licensing-deals-universal-sony-music/.
23 Abner Li, 'YouTube Music Officially Launching Podcasts in the US on Android, iOS, and Web', *9to5Google*, 27 April 2023, https://9to5google.com/2023/04/27/youtube-music-podcasts-us/.
24 Boehm, 'Why Podcasting Needs to Lean into Culture 3.0'.
25 Tzlil Sharon, 'Peeling the Pod: Towards a Research Agenda for Podcast Studies', *Annals of the International Communication Association* 47, no. 3 (2023): 324, https://doi.org/10.1080/23808985.2023.2201593.

26 '"Just Because You Play a Guitar and Are from Nashville Doesn't Mean You Are a Country Singer": The Emergence of Medium Identities in Podcasting', in *Podcasting: New Aural Cultures and Digital Media*, ed. Dario Llinares et al. (Springer International Publishing, 2018), 26, https://doi.org/10.1007/978-3-319-90056-8_2.
27 See Boehm, 'Why Podcasting Needs to Lean into Culture 3.0', 16.
28 John L. Sullivan, *The Platforms of Podcasting: Past and Present*, 2019, 7.
29 CBDB and Boehm, *PODCAST: CBDB Runs (On Spotify) (2022-2024)*.
30 Fair MusE, *Fair MusE Releases Policy Brief on Fairness in the EU Music Ecosystem | Fair MusE Press Release* (2024), https://fairmuse.eu/press-release/fair-muse-releases-policy-brief-on--fairness-in-the-eu-music-ecosystem/; OME, 'About Open Music Europe (OpenMusE): (More Competitive, Fairer, More Sustainable, More Transparent)', 2024, https://www.openmuse.eu/about.
31 Podnews, 'Spotify Is Now #1 for Downloads', 2 May 2024, https://podnews.net/update/spotify-number-one.
32 Carola Boehm, 'Music Technology Meets University 3.0: Music Education in the Era of Co-Creation', in *Perspectives on Innovation in Music Production Education*, vol. 2, ed. Brandon Anthony et al., Perspectives on Education in Audio and Music Production (POEM) (Routledge, 2025), https://www.routledge.com/Perspectives-on-Education-in-Audio--Music-Production/book-series/POEM?srsltid=AfmBOop45q70cTv_BVI5IKjybOH_dgwKv0SoSOGWASSPhjr8HuHwhh7p.

Bibliography

Anon (n.d.). About Blubrry Podcasting. *Blubrry Podcasting*. [Online]. Available from: https://blubrry.com/about/. [Accessed: 7 September 2025].

Anon (2005a). Definition of PODCAST. *Merriam-Webster*. [Online]. Available from: https://www.merriam-webster.com/dictionary/podcast. [Accessed: 6 September 2025].

Anon (2005b). Podcast. *Cambridge Dictionary*. [Online]. Available from: https://dictionary.cambridge.org/dictionary/english/podcast. [Accessed: 6 September 2025].

Anon (2005c). Podcast Noun - Definition, Pictures, Pronunciation and Usage Notes | Oxford Dictionary. *Oxford Dictionary*. [Online]. Available from: https://www.oxfordlearnersdictionaries.com/definition/english/podcast. [Accessed: 6 September 2025].

Anon (2019). *BBC's Podcast Exclusivity Angers Listeners; Spotify Plans More*. [Online]. 11 January 2019. Available from: https://podnews.net/update/bbc-spotify-exclusivity. [Accessed: 13 September 2024].

Anon (2021). *Word Matters: What Does the Date in a Dictionary Entry Mean?* [Online]. Available from: https://www.merriam-webster.com/word-matters-podcast/episode-45-first-known-use. [Accessed: 6 September 2025].

Berry, R. (2006). Will the iPod Kill the Radio Star? Profiling Podcasting as Radio. *Convergence*. [Online]. 12 (2). pp. 143–162. Available from: https://doi.org/10.1177/1354856506066522. [Accessed: 30 August 2024].

Berry, R. (2018). 'Just Because You Play a Guitar and Are from Nashville Doesn't Mean You Are a Country Singer': The Emergence of Medium Identities in Podcasting. In: D. Llinares, N. Fox, & R. Berry (eds.). *Podcasting: New Aural Cultures and Digital Media*. [Online]. Springer International Publishing, pp. 15–33. Available from: https://doi.org/10.1007/978-3-319-90056-8_2. [Accessed: 6 September 2025].

Boehm, C. (2016). Academia in Culture 3.0: a Crime story of Death and Rebirth (but also of Curation, Innovation and Sector Mash-ups). *REPERTÓRIO: Teatro & Dança*. [Online]. 19 (27). pp. 37–48. Available from: https://portalseer.ufba.br/index.php/revteatro/article/view/20610/13262.

Boehm, C. (2022). *Arts and Academia: The Role of the Arts in Civic Universities*. Great Debates in Higher Education. Emerald Publishing Ltd.

Boehm, C. (2025a). A New Year, a New Post-Flu Running-Recovery Plan! (Bridge to 10K, HealthUnlocked Forum). *HealthUnlocked*. [Online]. Available from: https://healthunlocked.

com/bridgeto10k/posts/151597907/a-new-year-a-new-post-flu-running-recovery-plan. [Accessed: 10 August 2025].

Boehm, C. (2025b). Music Technology meets University 3.0: Music Education in the Era of Co-Creation. In: B. Anthony, P. Thompson, C. Boehm, T. Canfer, & S. Ward (eds.). *Perspectives on Innovation in Music Production Education.* Perspectives on Education in Audio and Music Production (POEM) (pp. 3–31). [Online]. Routledge. Available from: https://www.routledge.com/Perspectives-on-Education-in-Audio--Music-Production/book-series/POEM?srsltid=AfmBOop45q70cTv_BVI5IKjybOH_dgwKv0SoSOGWASSPhjr8HuHwhh7p. [Accessed: 7 September 2025].

Boehm, C. (2025c). Why Podcasting Needs to Lean into Culture 3.0. In: C. Boehm, T. Canfer, and C. Salazar (eds.). *Podcasting & Education: Concepts, Communities & Case Studies.* Podcasting Through Education. Routledge.

Bomba, M. & Maiorano, M. (2025). Educating for Podcasting: "ASSIPOD," "Casa del Podcast," and the Spreading of (Independent) Podcasting Culture in Italy. In: C. Boehm, T. Canfer, and C. Salazar (eds.). *Podcasting and Education.* Focal Press.

Bonini, T. (2022). Podcasting as a Hybrid Cultural form between Old and New Media. In: M. Lindgren and J. Loviglio (eds.). *The Routledge Companion to Radio and Podcast Studies.* Routledge.

Boswell, R. & The Runner's World Editors (2024). Couch to 5K: How to Start Running in Just Six Weeks. *Runner's World.* [Online]. Available from: https://www.runnersworld.com/uk/training/5km/a760067/six-week-beginner-5k-schedule/. [Accessed: 10 August 2025].

CBDB & Boehm, C. (2025). *PODCAST: CBDB Runs (On MixCloud) (2025).*

CBDB & Boehm, C. (2022–2024). *PODCAST: CBDB Runs (On Spotify) (2022–2024).*

CBDB, C. (2025). *CBDB Public Playlists (Spotify – Web Player).* [Online]. 2025. Spotify. Available from: https://open.spotify.com/user/21j2n6xgxchv3gsa43ofdipya/playlists. [Accessed: 7 September 2025].

Cochrane, T. (2005). *Podcasting The Do-It-Yourself Guide.* John Wiley & Sons.

Cridland, J. (2021). *The History of Podcasting in the UK.* [Online]. 20 September 2021. Available from: https://podnews.net/article/history-uk-podcasts. [Accessed: 13 September 2024].

Curry, A. (2004). *Adam Curry Daily Source Code.* [Online]. Available from: https://archive.org/details/pcs_Adam_Curry_Daily_Source_Code. [Accessed: 6 September 2025].

DCMS (2021). *Economics of Music Streaming - UK Parliamentary Inquiry (4, 10, and 23 February 2021, and 22 March 2021).* [Online]. 2021. Available from: https://committees.parliament.uk/work/646/economics-of-music-streaming/. [Accessed: 29 August 2024].

Doyle, B. (2017). *Chris Lydon - The First Podcast.* [Online]. 2017. Available from: https://www.dtvgroup.com/Chris_Lydon/. [Accessed: 6 September 2025].

Eckstein, J. (2013). Sound Reason: Radiolab and the Micropolitics of Podcasting. *Electronic Theses and Dissertations.* [Online]. Available from: https://digitalcommons.du.edu/etd/176.

Fair Mus E (2024). *Fair MusE Releases Policy Brief on Fairness in the EU Music Ecosystem | Fair MusE Press Release.* [Online]. Available from: https://fairmuse.eu/press-release/fair-muse-releases-policy-brief-on-fairness-in-the-eu-music-ecosystem/. [Accessed: 29 August 2024].

Goldberg, A. (2004). *The People's Radio. Sick of Bland DJs and Annoying Ad Breaks? A New Breed of 'Audiobloggers' Is Hoping to Give Audiences Exactly What They Want. Andy Goldberg Reports in the Independent.* [Online]. 8 December 2004. The Independent. Available from: https://www.independent.co.uk/news/science/the-people-s-radio-679858.html. [Accessed: 13 September 2024].

Goldrick, S. (2020). Spotify Launches New Audio Experience Combining Music and Talk Content. *Spotify.* [Online]. Available from: https://newsroom.spotify.com/2020-10-14/spotify-launches-new-audio-experience-combining-music-and-talk-content/. [Accessed: 7 September 2025].

Hall, M., Berry, R., McDonald, K. & Coleman, J. (2025). Podcasting and Radio Pedagogy: Rewinding Two Decades of Teaching. In: C. Boehm, T. Canfer, and C. Salazar (eds.) *Podcasting and Education.* Focal Press.

Hammersley, B. (2004). Audible revolution. *The Guardian.* [Online]. 12 February. Available from: https://www.theguardian.com/media/2004/feb/12/broadcasting.digitalmedia. [Accessed: 29 August 2024].

Hinic, M. (2025). Academic Podcast Entanglements. In: C. Boehm, T. Canfer, and C. Salazar (eds.) *Podcasting and Education*. Focal Press.

Hoeg, W. & Lauterbach, T. (2009). Google-Books-ID: T0KSa6w3qH4C.In: W. Hoeg and T. Lauterbach (eds.) *Digital Audio Broadcasting: Principles and Applications of DAB, DAB + and DMB*. John Wiley & Sons.

Kettmann, M. (2004). Tech: Will Podcasting Kill the Radio Star. *Time*. [Online]. Available from: https://content.time.com/time/subscriber/article/0,33009,1009701,00.html?utm_source=podnews.net&utm_medium=web&utm_campaign=podnews.net%3A2021-09-20. [Accessed: 13 September 2024].

Li, A. (2023). YouTube Music Officially Launching Podcasts in the US on Android, iOS, and Web. *9to5Google*. [Online]. Available from: https://9to5google.com/2023/04/27/youtube-music-podcasts-us/. [Accessed: 7 September 2025].

Lindgren, M. (2016). Personal Narrative Journalism and Podcasting. *Radio Journal: International Studies in Broadcast & Audio Media*. 14. pp. 23–41.

Llinares, D., Fox, N. & Berry, R. (2018). Introduction: Podcasting and Podcasts—Parameters of a New Aural Culture. In: D. Llinares, N. Fox, & R. Berry (eds.). *Podcasting*. [Online]. Cham: Springer International Publishing, pp. 1–13. Available from: https://link.springer.com/10.1007/978-3-319-90056-8_1. [Accessed: 5 March 2025].

mixcloud (2017). Mixcloud and Warner Music Group Announce Direct Licensing Deal. *Mixcloud Blog*. [Online]. Available from: https://www.mixcloud.com/blog/2017/10/09/mixcloud-and-warner-music-group-announce-direct-licensing-deal/. [Accessed: 7 September 2025].

Nelson, R. (2013). *Practice as Research in the Arts: Principles, Protocols, Pedagogies, Resistances*. 2013 edition. Palgrave Macmillan.

OME (2024). *About Open Music Europe (OpenMusE): (More competitive, Fairer, More sustainable, More transparent)*. [Online]. 2024. Available from: https://www.openmuse.eu/about. [Accessed: 29 August 2024].

Podnews (2024). *Spotify Is Now 1for Downloads*. [Online]. 2 May 2024. Available from: https://podnews.net/update/spotify-number-one. [Accessed: 7 September 2024].

Rime, J., Pike, C. & Collins, T. (2022). What Is a Podcast? Considering Innovations in Podcasting through the Six-Tensions Framework. *Convergence*. [Online]. 28 (5). pp. 1260–1282. Available from: https://doi.org/10.1177/13548565221104444. [Accessed: 29 January 2025].

Sacco, P.L., Ferilli, G. & Tavano Blessi, G. (2018). From Culture 1.0 to Culture 3.0: Three Socio-Technical Regimes of Social and Economic Value Creation through Culture, and Their Impact on European Cohesion Policies. *Sustainability*. [Online]. 10 (11). p.p. 3923. Available from: https://www.mdpi.com/2071-1050/10/11/3923. [Accessed: 3 November 2023].

Schlagenhauf, W. (2017). YouTube ends Record Label Standoff, Now Has Licensing Deals with the "Big 3." *The Hustle*. [Online]. Available from: https://thehustle.co/youtube-licensing-deals-with-big-3. [Accessed: 7 September 2025].

Sharon, T. (2023). Peeling the Pod: Towards a Research Agenda for Podcast Studies. *Annals of the International Communication Association*. [Online]. 47 (3). pp. 324–337. Available from: https://doi.org/10.1080/23808985.2023.2201593. [Accessed: 6 September 2025].

Son, M. (2025). *The History of Podcasts: From RSS Beginnings to 2025*. [Online]. 2025. Available from: https://www.descript.com/blog/article/history-of-podcasts. [Accessed: 6 September 2025].

Spinelli, M. & Dann, L. (2019). *Podcasting: The Audio Media Revolution*. Bloomsbury Academic USA.

Stockment, A. (2009). Internet Radio: The Case for a Technology Neutral Royalty Standard. *Virginia Law Review*. [Online]. 95 (8). pp. 2129–2179. Available from: https://www.jstor.org/stable/27759978. [Accessed: 21 August 2025].

Sullivan, J.L. (2019). *The Platforms of Podcasting: Past and Present*.

Sum, N.-L. & Jessop, B. (2013). *Towards a Cultural Political Economy: Putting Culture in its Place in Political Economy*. Edward Elgar Publishing.

Weiss, G. (2017). YouTube Inks Licensing Deals With Universal And Sony Music As It Preps Paid Service (Report). *Tubefilter*. [Online]. Available from: https://www.tubefilter.com/2017/12/19/youtube-licensing-deals-universal-sony-music/. [Accessed: 7 September 2025].

Wikipedia (2024). HealthUnlocked. *Wikipedia*. [Online]. Available from: https://en.wikipedia.org/w/index.php?title=HealthUnlocked&oldid=1240034659. [Accessed: 12 August 2025].

Wikipedia (2025a). Christopher Lydon. *Wikipedia*. [Online]. Available from: https://en.wikipedia.org/w/index.php?title=Christopher_Lydon&oldid=1279597605. [Accessed: 6 September 2025].

Wikipedia (2025b). Coverville: The Cover Music Show. *Wikipedia*. [Online]. Available from: https://en.wikipedia.org/w/index.php?title=Coverville&oldid=1276003333. [Accessed: 7 September 2025].

Wikipedia (2025c). History of Podcasting. *Wikipedia*. [Online]. Available from: https://en.wikipedia.org/w/index.php?title=History_of_podcasting&oldid=1305094636. [Accessed: 6 September 2025].

Winer, D. & Curry, A. (2004). *RSS: BitTorrent RSS Module*. [Online]. 28 November 2004. Available from: https://web.archive.org/web/20041128033108/https://www.reallysimplesyndication.com/bitTorrentRssModule. [Accessed: 6 September 2025].

Worldwide, M.B. (2018). *Merlin Signs Multi-Year Direct Licensing Deal with Mixcloud*. [Online]. 28 November 2018. Music Business Worldwide. Available from: https://www.musicbusinessworldwide.com/merlin-signs-multi-year-direct-licensing-deal-with-mixcloud/. [Accessed: 7 September 2025].

Wyld, J. (2021). Collaborative Storytelling and Canon Fluidity in The Adventure Zone Podcast. *Convergence*. [Online]. 27 (2). pp. 343–356. Available from: https://doi.org/10.1177/1354856520950555. [Accessed: 6 September 2025].

Zaliva, V. & Sova, A. (2004). *Enhanced "Enclosures" Support in RSS and ATOM Syndication*.

Index

Note: **Bold** page numbers refer to tables; *italic* page numbers refer to figures and page numbers followed by "n" denote endnotes.

For Product Safety Concerns and Information please contact our EU
representative GPSR@taylorandfrancis.com
Taylor & Francis Verlag GmbH, Kaufingerstraße 24, 80331 München, Germany

www.ingramcontent.com/pod-product-compliance
Lightning Source LLC
LaVergne TN
LVHW060159031026
849361LV00022B/303
* 9 7 8 1 0 4 1 1 5 0 1 5 2 *